JAMESTOWN 🚢 EDUCATION

Five-Star Stories

Discoveries

17 Stories of Discovery and Decision
With THEMES for Mastering Language Arts Skills

by Burton Goodman

Glencoe McGraw-Hill

New York, New York   Columbus, Ohio   Chicago, Illinois   Peoria, Illinois   Woodland Hills, California

JAMESTOWN EDUCATION

Credits

Illustrations

Hal Just: p. 166–167

John Kastner: pp. 27, 82, 182

Yoshi Miyake: pp. 8, 40–41, 107, 192–193

Don Morrison: pp. 16–17, 56, 128–129

Brock Nicol: pp. 70, 154, 209

Alan Reingold: pp. 49, 94, 144

Photographs

Harold Sund/Image Bank/Getty Images: pp. 6, 36

PhotoDisc: pp. 38, 78

Premium Stock/Corbis: pp. 80, 124

PhotoDisc: 126, 178

Glencoe/McGraw-Hill

A Division of The McGraw-Hill Companies

Send all queries to:
Glencoe/McGraw-Hill
8787 Orion Place
Columbus, OH 43240-4027

ISBN 0-07-827355-2

3 4 5 6 7 8 9 10   116/055   09 08 07 06

JAMESTOWN  EDUCATION

Five-Star Stories

Discoveries

17 Stories of Discovery and Decision
With THEMES for Mastering Language Arts Skills

by Burton Goodman

Titles in the Series

Travels	Level A
More Travels	Level A
Adventures	Level B
More Adventures	Level B
Chills	Level C
More Chills	Level C
Surprises	Level D
More Surprises	Level D
Shocks	Level E
After Shocks	Level E
Sudden Twists	Level F
More Twists	Level F
Encounters	Level G
More Encounters	Level G
Conflicts	Level H
More Conflicts	Level H
Choices	Level I
Discoveries	Level J

Contents

Unit 4 Something Unexpected

Unit 5 Searching for Answers

To the Student

Discoveries contains 17 outstanding short stories of recognized literary merit. Within these pages you will find stories by present-day writers and by time-honored authors. Many countries and cultures also are represented. The stories will capture your attention and will stimulate you to think. And, as you will see, the characters involved embark on quests that lead to *discoveries.*

The stories have been arranged in five units, each with its own particular theme. Each unit is introduced by Previewing the Unit and concludes with a Review, which consists of questions for discussion and extended writing. These questions offer opportunities to compare and contrast information and ideas in the stories and to practice writing the kinds of essays that you are likely to encounter on standardized tests.

These stories will provide you with many hours of reading pleasure, and the exercises that follow each story offer a wide variety of ways to help you improve your reading and literature skills. The exercises have been specially designed with language arts mastery in mind. Since the stories are theme oriented, the exercises employ the word **THEME:**

THINK ABOUT THE STORY will help you improve your reading comprehension skills.

HANDLE NEW VOCABULARY will help you strengthen your vocabulary skills. Often, you will be able to figure out the meaning of an unfamiliar word by using *context clues*—the words and phrases around the word. All the vocabulary words in this section appear in the stories.

EXAMINE STORY ELEMENTS will provide practice in recognizing and understanding the key elements of literature.

MASTER CRITICAL THINKING SKILLS will help you sharpen your critical thinking skills. You will have opportunities to *reason* by drawing conclusions, making inferences, and using story clues.

EXPLORE THE WRITER'S CRAFT will give you opportunities to see how stories are crafted and to learn about authors' techniques, especially their use of language.

There are four questions in each exercise. Complete all of the exercises. Then check your answers with your teacher. Use the scoring chart following each exercise to calculate your score for that exercise. Give yourself 5 points for each correct answer. Since there are four questions, you can score up to 20 points for each exercise. Use the THEME scoring chart at the end of the lesson to figure your total score. A perfect score for a lesson is 100 points. Keep track of how well you do by recording your score on the **Progress Chart** on page 224. Then plot your progress by recording your score on the **Progress Graph** on page 225.

The Questions for Writing and Discussion section offers further opportunities for thoughtful discussion and creative writing. Additional questions are provided in Questions for Discussion and Extended Writing in each Review.

On page 3 you will find **The Short Story—Literary Terms.** You may want to refer to these definitions when you answer the questions in the Examine Story Elements sections. On pages 4 and 5 you will find **The Craft of Writing—Literary Terms.** You may want to refer to these pages when you answer the questions in the Explore the Writer's Craft sections.

I feel certain that you will enjoy reading the stories in this book, and the exercises that follow will help you master a number of very important language arts skills.

Now . . . get ready for some *Discoveries!*

Burton Goodman

The Short Story— Literary Terms

Character Development: the personality traits and changes in a character revealed by a writer during the course of a story.

Characterization: the ways a writer shows what a character is like. The way a character acts, speaks, thinks, and looks *characterizes* that person.

Climax: the turning point of a story.

Conflict: a struggle or difference of opinion between characters. A character may also clash with a force of nature.

Dialogue: the exact words that a character says; usually the conversation between characters.

Foreshadowing: clues that hint at what will happen later.

Inner Conflict: a struggle that takes place in the mind of a character.

Main Character: the person the story is mostly about.

Mood: the feeling or atmosphere that the writer creates. For example, the *mood* of a story might be joyous or suspenseful.

Motive: the reason behind a character's actions.

Narrator: the person who tells the story. Usually, the narrator is the writer or a character in the story.

Plot: the series of incidents or happenings in a story. The *plot* is the outline or arrangement of events.

Purpose: the reason the author wrote the story. For example, an author's *purpose* might be to amuse or entertain, to convince, or to inform.

Setting: the time and place of the action in a story; where and when the action takes place.

Style: the way in which a writer uses language. The choice and arrangement of words and sentences help to create the writer's unique *style*.

Theme: the main, or central, idea of a story.

The Craft of Writing—Literary Terms

Alliteration: the repetition of consonant sounds at the beginnings of words. An example of *alliteration* is "Five fragrant flowers grow in the garden."

Allusion: a reference within a literary work to a famous person, place, work of literature, and so on.

Autobiography: the story of a real person's life, told by that person.

Biography: the story of a real person's life told by another person.

Connotation: a meaning or emotion associated with a word. For example, the words *thrifty* and *cheap* have a similar **denotation** (dictionary meaning), but *thrifty* has a positive *connotation*, while *cheap* has a negative connotation.

Descriptive passage: writing that tells about people, places, and things in ways that help readers picture what is being presented.

Dialect: a form of speech spoken in a particular country, region, or place.

Figurative language: language that creates vivid word pictures, especially through the use of figures of speech such as simile, metaphor, and personification.

Flashback: the interruption of the action in the plot to show an event or events that occurred at an earlier time.

Folktale: a traditional story that has been passed on from one generation to another by word of mouth.

Imagery: language that uses words and phrases that appeal to one or more of the senses—sight, taste, touch, hearing, and smell. Often *imagery* helps create a picture in the mind of the reader.

Irony: a contrast, usually between what is expected and what actually occurs. There are many kinds of *irony*. Saying "Great game!" to a player whose errors have caused his team to lose is an *ironic* remark.

Metaphor: a figure of speech in which one thing is said to be something else. Unlike a simile, a metaphor does not use the word *like* or *as*. For example, "He is an ox" is a *metaphor*, but "He is strong as an ox" is a simile.

Moral: a lesson, which is often the point of a story; what the story teaches the reader.

Onomatopoeia: the use of words whose sounds imitate their meaning. Some examples of *onomatopoeia* are *clang, pop, hiss,* and *growl*.

Personification: a figure of speech in which an animal, object, or idea is given human feelings or qualities. An example of *personification* is "The raindrops danced along the roof and skipped down the walls."

Simile: a figure of speech in which two unlike things are compared through the use of the word *like* or *as*. An example of a *simile* is "Her eyes sparkled like diamonds."

Story within a story: a story told by one character in a story to other characters in the story.

Symbol: something that has its own meaning but also stands for, or represents, something else. For example, a red heart may be a *symbol* of love; a dove *symbolizes* peace.

Friends and Enemies

"*A man cannot be too careful in the choice of his enemies.*"

–Oscar Wilde

Previewing the Unit

The great writer and wit Oscar Wilde once noted that you must exercise the greatest of care in choosing your enemies. We might have expected Wilde's sentence to end—"choosing your *friends*." Therein lies the humor of the remark. And yet, as you will see in the stories in this unit, there is not so great a distinction between enemies and friends.

THE SMUGGLER Victor Canning wrote dozens of suspenseful novels, many of which have been adapted for the movies. In his short story "The Smuggler," a local fisherman on a Mediterranean island is pitted against a tyrant who possesses unlimited power. What follows is a life-or-death situation that is charged with conflict. The conclusion revolves around a decision that relates to the matter of friends and enemies. To say more would give too much away. However, be warned: You are likely to be surprised.

INITIATION Sylvia Plath's sensitive story "Initiation" is about a high school student who is invited to join a sorority, a kind of exclusive social club for girls. Since a sorority provides that some individuals be included and others excluded, a division is created between "insiders" and "outsiders." This complicates relationships between classmates and gives rise to potential for creating enemies and friends. None of this is lost on Millicent, the main character. The initiation process, and the benefits and disadvantages of sorority membership, are issues she must confront. You may find *how* and *why* she makes her decisions as interesting as the decisions themselves.

THE STREET OF THE CAÑON One can hear echoes of *Romeo and Juliet* in Josefina Niggli's "The Street of the Cañon." In Shakespeare's great tragedy, young Romeo and Juliet are members of bitterly feuding families. Romeo and Juliet fall madly in love at first sight. Despite the fierce hostility the families feel toward each other, the lovers, determined to see each other, arrange to secretly meet. Similarly, "The Street of the Cañon" is about two feuding villages. The main characters, a young man and a young woman, are from opposing villages. You might want to guess what will happen . . . and why the story appears in a unit called "Friends and Enemies."

Notice which characters act as friends and which seem to be enemies. See whether you change your mind as you read.

They were playing a life-or-death game to determine if he was . . .

The Smuggler

by Victor Canning

The Great Man stood at the window of the Winter Palace. Across the paved courtyard, beyond the long sweep of ornamental railings and the still line of gray-uniformed guards, lay the wide bowl of the only harbor the island possessed. He raised a hand and scratched the back of his neck and the movement made the early morning April sun, reflected from the blue of the Adriatic,[1] glint on the gilt oak leaves of his epaulettes.[2]

A respectful three paces behind him the Chief of Police stirred uncomfortably and said, "That's his boat coming in now. For a year this has been going on, and until now we have never known which of the many fishermen it might be. This time our information is reliable."

---

1. **Adriatic:** the sea between Italy and Yugoslavia

2. **epaulettes:** the shoulder decorations on a military uniform

"Denunciation?"[3] The word was harsh and bitter.

"Yes."

"Anonymous?"

"Yes."

"You have suspected him?"

"He and every other fisherman on the island, but until now I would have said that he was the last man . . . "

The figure at the window turned and a pair of cold, brown eyes regarded the Chief of Police shrewdly. They were eyes which missed nothing.

"You sound almost regretful. You like him?"

"Everyone on the island likes Tasso."

The Great Man walked past the Chief of Police towards his desk and from the shadow of the curtains at the window rose the brown and black length of his great Alsatian. As his master sat down the dog dropped heavily to the floor at the side of the desk.

"Your men are waiting for him?"

"Everything is ready."

"Go down yourself and arrest him and bring him here. Do not question him. Say nothing to him. Bring him here."

The face of the Chief of Police showed his surprise. A large hand with a thick gold ring waved at him, and the ghost of a smile passed across the face of the Great Man. "Bring him here. For once I have time on my hands. I am curious to talk to a man who has found a soft corner in the heart of a Chief of Police. Such men are rare."

The Chief of Police would have spoken again but the cold, brown eyes had grown colder and the ghost of a smile had gone.

The Chief of Police saluted and left the room.

The Great Man eased his short powerful bulk back into the wide chair, and his left hand dropped to the neck of the Alsatian, the squat fingers teasing at the dog's thick fur. After a while there was the clatter of heavy boots on the wide marble stairway outside the room and then the door was opened. Tasso stood on the threshold, behind him two armed guards and behind them the Chief of Police. The Great Man eyed them in silence for a while and, in the long pause, the cries of the stall holders from the market along the quay front seeped faintly into the gilt and velvet stretches of the room.

"Let him come in alone," he said suddenly.

The doors closed behind Tasso, and the fisherman came slowly down the room. The dog by the chair side stirred, beginning to rise, but the firm fingers tapped its head gently and the animal relaxed.

Tasso stood before the polished desk. He was a short, powerful man, much like the other in build. His eyes were brown, but with a warmth in them, his face tanned and creased with years of the sea, and about the wide lips clung a subdued smile. He showed no fear, nor embarrassment, though he knew well the identity of the man before him, had seen him resplendent at ceremonial parades and known those cold, brown eyes from a thousand photographs in a thousand public places. He stood there with his shabby blue jacket swung open to show a dirty red shirt, his trousers flaked with fish scales. In the lapel of his jacket he wore a half-opened yellow rose.

"Your name?"

"Tasso Susvid."

"Age?"

---

3. denunciation: an act of informing against; an accusation against another

"Fifty-three."

"Occupation?"

"Fisherman."

"And smuggler."

"No man willingly puts his initials on a bullet."

"You have been denounced."

"The innocent as well as the guilty are often denounced."

The Great Man stirred comfortably and the ghost of a smile came back. "Let us assume that you are a smuggler for the moment."

Tasso shrugged. "Why not? I have time on my hands. My fish are caught and my wife will sell them."

"Why do you smuggle? It is against the interests of our country."

"If I do it—and we merely pass time with this game—it is to make myself more money. The better off the citizens of a country are, the better off the country."

"There are times when you smuggle out enemies of our country. A man who does that merits death."

"Why not a reward? Surely a country is healthier without its enemies?"

The lips of the Great Man tightened and for a moment his eyes narrowed. Then he laughed gently. "What do you bring in so valuable that it outweighs the risk of death?"

"Cigarettes."

"What else?"

"Whiskey."

"I prefer our own rakia."[4]

"I agree, but there are people in the capital who think differently. There are also nylons and perfumes."

"For the women in the capital?"

Tasso smiled and shook his head. "For any woman. Every goat girl on this island covets a pair of nylons, and if you tend goats you have need of perfumes."

The Great Man smiled, almost openly now, and said, "And all these things you bring from over there?" He nodded toward the sea.

"If I were a smuggler I should bring them from there, yes."

"How long would it take—in your boat?"

"Ten hours across, four hours there, and ten hours back. Twenty-four hours."

"When did you go out on this fishing trip?"

"At nine o'clock yesterday morning."

The Great Man glanced at a clock on the wall. "It is now half-past nine. It's odd—your trip lasted exactly twenty-four hours."

"I ran into bad weather last night and we had to heave-to."

"We?"

"My son works the boat with me."

"Your boat is being searched now."

"They will find nothing."

"You have a radio? Maybe someone warned you . . . "

"There's no radio. No one warned me. Remember, we are only pretending that I am a smuggler."

"It is a game not without its dangers. During the war, you were a partisan?"[5]

"Yes, I fought. Later, because I know the coast, I was a pilot for the Allied[6] naval forces."

"You like the English?"

"They understand the sea, and they keep their heads in an emergency. Both qualities I admire."

---

4. **rakia:** a strong drink made with grapes

5. **partisan:** a member of a guerrilla military group

6. **Allied:** refers to the Allies—a group of countries (especially England, the United States, and the Soviet Union) who fought together against common enemies during World War II

"Who doesn't? But even so, everything is passing from their grasp. In politics, in art, in commerce and in sport they are being swallowed up."

Tasso shrugged his shoulders. "In all these things, perhaps. But I like them still because of all these the one thing they will really care about is sport. Only being able to draw with our National football team yesterday—they will find that hard to swallow."

"You are interested in football?"

"Every man on this island is. My son is captain of the town team."

"He will be proud when you are shot for smuggling."

"The bullet has yet to be marked. Remember this is a private game between us."

"You are denounced. The game is finished."

"Denounced by whom?"

"I don't know, but I should say your wife."

"Why?"

"She is a woman. Women notice small things . . . " A large hand rubbed gently across a broad jowl for a moment and the thick gold ring caught the light from the wide windows. "Four hours over there is not long, but it is long enough for a man to forget his wife. You wear a fresh rose in your lapel. A man who lands from sea after twenty-four hours with a fresh rose in his coat gives himself away. After a ten-hour trip from over there it would be fresh. Maybe you wife has noticed it and grown jealous of the one who pins a flower to your coat before you leave. Jealousy makes all women dangerous. Yes, I think it was your wife who denounced you."

Tasso smiled and raised his hand to the rose. "I am fifty-three. At thirty-three my wife was often jealous, but those years have gone. We are still playing our game. Look—" Tasso tossed the rose on to the desk. The movement made the Alsatian rise quickly, but a broad hand went out to restrain it. The Great Man picked up the rose and saw that it was artificial, made of wax-coated silk.

Tasso said, "It was the gift of an American nurse during the war. Ask any man in this town and he will tell you that I always wear it. After six years it is still fresh."

The Great Man was silent for a moment, turning the rose over in his hand. Then he looked up and smiled.

"A man who holds my power can resent the mistakes he makes. Out of hurt vanity I might take revenge and none would question my right. A snap of my fingers and our friend here . . . " he nodded to the Alsatian, "would tear your throat out. I should let him, for you are too frank and your tongue too ready."

But the smile still played about Tasso's mouth and he slowly raised his hand to the back of his neck, saying, "If you should try—there would be two throats cut. The dog's and your own." From the back of his coat he pulled a knife and placed it on the desk. "The Chief of Police is a conscientious man, but your presence here flusters him. He was so anxious to get me up here that he made a bad job of searching me."

The Great Man picked up the knife and gently tried the edge of the blade on his thumb. Then he said reflectively, "There are a thousand men who would have liked the chance you've just thrown away."

"I am a fisherman, not an assassin."

"And also a smuggler. Some instinct told you to jettison your goods before coming in."

The Smuggler

"I am a fisherman."

"No. I may have been mistaken about your wife, but not over the smuggling. Yesterday evening you were over there."

"I was at sea—hove-to."

The Great Man went on, turning the knife in his hands as he spoke. "You left this island yesterday morning with your son. According to you, you have been twenty-four hours at sea, seeing no one and without a radio."

"That is what I said."

"And you landed here a little less than half an hour ago and were brought straight up to me without a chance to talk to anyone?"

"That is so."

"And yet you knew that our National football team had drawn with the English team? The game was played in London yesterday afternoon, after you left here. You heard the result over there when you landed. Both you and your son would be interested in the result. If you had been at sea twenty-four hours without a radio you could not have known the result. It is forbidden to go over there, but you went as you have so often gone."

Tasso's face never altered. For a moment the two men stared at one another. Then Tasso nodded slowly. "The game it seems is finished."

But the Great Man smiled and shook his head. "No, I have enjoyed the game too much to have it finish this way." He stood up. "You are free to go. What I know I shall keep to myself, and you will have no trouble with the Chief of Police."

"Why do you do this?" Tasso's face showed his surprise.

The other put his hand for a moment on Tasso's shoulder. "You made a mistake, one mistake that could have meant death. That can happen to the bravest and cleverest of men. It might happen to me one day. If it does, I shall know I have a friend on this island with a boat. A man can never have too many friends."

About the Author

Victor Canning (1911–1986) wrote more than 50 novels, most of them tales of high adventure filled with excitement and suspense. Born in Devonshire, England, Canning began writing part time in his early twenties. His first novel, published when he was 24 years old, was so successful that he began to write full time.

Canning specialized in writing mysteries and spy thrillers. His works feature gripping plots and realistic, fascinating characters that deal with the issues of good and evil. A number of Canning's books have been adapted and made into movies. "The Smuggler" is a good example of Canning's style of writing.

THINK ABOUT THE STORY. The following questions help you check your reading comprehension. Put an *x* in the box next to the correct answer.

1. What is "The Smuggler" mainly about?
   - ☐ a. the difficult life of a hard-working fisherman
   - ☐ b. how a fisherman smuggles goods onto an island
   - ☐ c. an encounter between a man of authority and a local fisherman

2. Since Tasso had not been carefully searched, what did he have in his possession?
   - ☐ a. a gun
   - ☐ b. a knife
   - ☐ c. a small radio

3. Tasso said that he had spent the previous twenty-four hours
   - ☐ a. alone at sea.
   - ☐ b. at sea with his son.
   - ☐ c. at home with his wife.

4. The Great Man knew that Tasso was lying because the fisherman
   - ☐ a. had a very guilty look on his face.
   - ☐ b. revealed information he should not have known.
   - ☐ c. had confessed earlier to the Chief of Police.

HANDLE NEW VOCABULARY WORDS. The following questions check your vocabulary skills. Put an *x* in the box next to the correct answer. Each vocabulary word appears in the story.

1. Tasso was wearing a shabby jacket, but the Great Man looked, as always, resplendent. Which of the following best defines the word *resplendent*?
   - ☐ a. sloppy or untidy
   - ☐ b. short but powerful
   - ☐ c. magnificent in appearance

2. Tasso stated, "Every goat girl on this island covets a pair of nylons." The word *covets* means
   - ☐ a. eagerly desires.
   - ☐ b. greatly deserves.
   - ☐ c. damages or ruins.

3. Because he was not an assassin, Tasso handed over his weapon. What is the meaning of the word *assassin*?
   - ☐ a. a smuggler
   - ☐ b. a murderer, especially of a public figure
   - ☐ c. a spy

4. The Great Man said that Tasso managed to jettison his goods before the ship came into port. Define the word *jettison*.
   - ☐ a. to throw overboard
   - ☐ b. to sell for a very low price
   - ☐ c. to give to friends

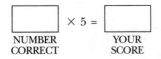

× 5 =	
NUMBER CORRECT	YOUR SCORE

× 5 =	
NUMBER CORRECT	YOUR SCORE

EXAMINE STORY ELEMENTS. The following questions check your knowledge of story elements. Put an *x* in the box next to each answer.

1. Which sentence best *characterizes* both the Great Man and Tasso?
   - ☐ a. They were extremely powerful and important political leaders.
   - ☐ b. Although they were intelligent, they lacked imagination.
   - ☐ c. They were clever and shrewd.

2. Of the following events, which happened last in the *plot* of the story?
   - ☐ a. Tasso tossed an artificial rose on the Great Man's desk.
   - ☐ b. The Great Man told Tasso he was free to go.
   - ☐ c. The Great man accused Tasso of being a smuggler.

3. The main *conflict* in "The Smuggler" is between
   - ☐ a. the Great Man and the Chief of Police.
   - ☐ b. the Great Man and Tasso.
   - ☐ c. Tasso and his wife.

4. What is the *setting* of the story?
   - ☐ a. an office in a palace
   - ☐ b. a fishing boat
   - ☐ c. a courtyard near a castle

MASTER CRITICAL THINKING. The following questions check your critical thinking skills. Put an *x* in the box next to each correct answer.

1. Evidence in the story indicates that Tasso was
   - ☐ a. hated and feared by many people on the island.
   - ☐ b. unknown to almost everyone who lived on the island.
   - ☐ c. a popular person among those on the island.

2. We may infer that the Great Man was
   - ☐ a. a dictator or a figure of very great authority.
   - ☐ b. kind to people he thought had committed a crime.
   - ☐ c. secretly fearful of Tasso.

3. The fact that the Great Man insisted on seeing and questioning Tasso alone suggests that he
   - ☐ a. did not have confidence in the Chief of Police.
   - ☐ b. had been thinking about freeing Tasso right from the start.
   - ☐ c. did not believe that Tasso was really a smuggler.

4. The ending of the story indicates that the Great Man thought that Tasso
   - ☐ a. could not be trusted.
   - ☐ b. would be useful in a situation that required a quick escape.
   - ☐ c. was not so smart after all.

	× 5 =	
NUMBER CORRECT		YOUR SCORE

	× 5 =	
NUMBER CORRECT		YOUR SCORE

14

EXPLORE THE WRITER'S CRAFT. The following questions check your knowledge of skills related to the craft of writing. Put an *x* in the box next to each correct answer. You may refer to pages 4 and 5.

1. In "The Smuggler," the Great Man remains nameless because
   ☐ a. he is a symbol of power.
   ☐ b. he does not want anyone to know who he is.
   ☐ c. the author was unable to think of a name for the character.

2. "Across the paved courtyard, beyond the long sweep of ornamental railings and the still line of gray-uniformed guards, lay the wide bowl of the only harbor the island possessed." This sentence contains imagery that appeals to the reader's sense of
   ☐ a. touch.
   ☐ b. sight.
   ☐ c. smell.

3. Tasso had found "a soft corner in the heart of a Chief of Police." This means that the Chief
   ☐ a. was nervous about Tasso.
   ☐ b. felt sympathy for Tasso.
   ☐ c. was astonished by Tasso.

4. The "firm fingers" of the Great Man gently tapped his dog's head. The words *firm fingers* are
   ☐ a. a simile.
   ☐ b. a metaphor.
   ☐ c. an example of alliteration.

	× 5 =	
NUMBER CORRECT		YOUR SCORE

Questions for Writing and Discussion

● In what ways were the Great Man and Tasso similar? How were they different?

● Tasso and the Great Man played a kind of game. It might well be called "a game of cat-and-mouse." Explain how the game was played. At the end of the story, why did Tasso say, "The game it seems is finished"?

● How did the Great Man know that Tasso had been lying and that the fisherman was, in fact, a smuggler?

● Why did the Great Man spare Tasso's life? Think of a situation in which the Great Man might need a helpful friend. Why would a man with a boat be particularly useful?

See additional questions for extended writing on pages 36 and 37.

Use the boxes below to total your scores for the exercises. Then record your scores on pages 224 and 225.

	THINK ABOUT THE STORY
+	
	HANDLE NEW VOCABULARY WORDS
+	
	EXAMINE STORY ELEMENTS
+	
	MASTER CRITICAL THINKING
+	
	EXPLORE THE WRITER'S CRAFT
▼	
	Total Score: Story 1

Tonight was the "trial by fire"—the final step in Millicent's . . .

INITIATION

by Sylvia Plath

T he basement room was dark and warm, like the inside of a sealed jar, Millicent thought, her eyes getting used to the strange dimness. The silence was soft with cobwebs, and from the small, rectangular window set high in the stone wall there sifted a faint bluish light that must be coming from the full October moon. She could see now that what she was sitting on was a woodpile next to the furnace.

Millicent brushed back a strand of hair. It was stiff and sticky from the egg that they had broken on her head as she knelt blindfolded a short while before. There had been a silence, a slight crunching sound, and then she had felt the cold, slimy egg-white flattening and spreading on her head and

sliding down her neck. She had heard someone smothering a laugh. It was all part of the ceremony.[1]

Then the girls had led her here, blindfolded still, through the corridors of Betsy Johnson's house and shut her in the cellar. It would be an hour before they came to get her, but then Court would be all over and she would say what she had to say and go home.

For tonight was the grand finale, the trial by fire. There really was no doubt now that she would get in. She could not think of anyone who had ever been invited into the high school sorority and failed to get through initiation[2] time. But even so, her case would be quite different. She would see to that. She could not exactly say what had decided her revolt, but it definitely had something to do with Tracy and something to do with the heather birds.

What girl at Lansing High would not want to be in her place now? Millicent thought, amused. What girl would not want to be one of the elect,[3] no matter if it did mean five days of initiation before and after school, ending in the climax of Court on Friday night when they made the new girls members? Even Tracy had been wistful when she heard that Millicent had been one of the five girls to receive an invitation.

"It won't be any different with us, Tracy," Millicent had told her. "We'll still go around

---

1. **the ceremony:** the initiation—in this case, a series of humiliating or embarrassing tasks that must be accomplished by one who hopes to become a member of a sorority, a social club for girls

2. **initiation:** the series of tasks that one must accomplish to become a member of the sorority

3. **the elect:** the special few; the chosen ones

Initiation

together like we always have, and next year you'll surely get in."

"I know, but even so," Tracy had said quietly, "you'll change, whether you think you will or not. Nothing ever stays the same."

And nothing does, Millicent had thought. How horrible it would be if one never changed . . . if she were condemned to be the plain, shy Millicent of a few years back for the rest of her life. Fortunately there was always the changing, the growing, the going on.

It would come to Tracy, too. She would tell Tracy the silly things the girls had said, and Tracy would change also, entering eventually into the magic circle. She would grow to know the special ritual as Millicent had started to last week.

"First of all," Betsy Johnson, the vivacious blonde secretary of the sorority, had told the five new candidates over sandwiches in the school cafeteria last Monday, "first of all, each of you has a big sister. She's the one who bosses you around, and you just do what she tells you."

"Remember the part about talking back and smiling," Louise Fullerton had put in, laughing. She was another celebrity in high school, pretty and dark and vice-president of the student council. "You can't say anything unless your big sister asks you something or tells you to talk to someone. And you can't smile, no matter how you're dying to." The girls had laughed a little nervously, and then the bell had rung for the beginning of afternoon classes.

It would be rather fun for a change, Millicent mused, getting her books out of her locker in the hall, rather exciting to be part of a closely knit group, the exclusive set

at Lansing High. Of course, it wasn't a school organization. In fact, the principal, Mr. Cranton, wanted to do away with initiation week altogether, because he thought it was undemocratic and disturbed the routine of school work. But there wasn't really anything he could do about it.

Millicent sat down at her desk in the big study hall. Tomorrow she would come to school, proudly, laughingly and then everybody would know, even the boys would know, that she was one of the elect.

A year or two ago, not many people would have guessed it. Millicent had waited a long time for acceptance, longer than most. It was as if she had been sitting for years in a pavilion outside a dance floor, looking in through the windows at the golden interior, with the lights clear and the air like honey, wistfully watching the couples waltzing to the never-ending music, laughing in pairs and groups together, no one alone.

But now at last, amid a week of fanfare and merriment, she would answer her invitation to enter the ballroom through the main entrance marked "Initiation." She would gather up her velvet skirts, her silken train, or whatever the disinherited princesses wore in the story books, and come into her rightful kingdom. . . . The bell rang to end study hall.

"Millicent, wait up!" It was Louise Fullerton behind her, Louise who had always before been very nice, very polite, friendlier than the rest, even long ago, before the invitation had come.

"Listen," Louise walked down the hall with her to Latin, their next class, "are you busy right after school today? Because I'd like to talk to you about tomorrow."

"Sure. I've got lots of time."

"Well, meet me in the hall after homeroom."

Walking beside Louise, Millicent felt a surge of pride. For all anyone could see, she and Louise were the best of friends.

"You know, I was so glad when they voted you in," Louise said.

Millicent smiled. "I was really thrilled to get the invitation," she said frankly, "but kind of sorry that Tracy didn't get in, too."

Tracy, she thought. If there is such a thing as a best friend, Tracy has been just that this last year.

"Yes, Tracy," Louise was saying, "she's a nice girl, and they put her up on the slate, but . . . well, she had three blackballs against her."

"Blackballs? What are they?"

"Well, we're not supposed to tell anybody outside the club, but seeing as you'll be in at the end of the week I don't suppose it hurts.

"You see, " Louise began explaining in a low voice, "once a year the sorority puts up all the likely girls that are suggested for membership. . . . "

Millicent listened carefully to Louise who was going on, " . . . and then there's a big meeting, and all the girls' names are read off and each girl is discussed."

"Oh?" Millicent asked mechanically, her voice sounding strange.

"Oh, I know what you're thinking," Louise laughed. "But it's really not as bad as all that. They keep it down to a minimum. They just talk over each girl and why or why not they think she'd be good for the club. And then they vote. Three blackballs eliminate a girl."

"Do you mind if I ask you what happened to Tracy?" Millicent said.

Louise laughed a little uneasily. "Well, I mean, some of them thought Tracy was just a bit *too* different. Maybe you could suggest a few things to her."

"Like what?"

"Oh, like maybe not carrying that old bookbag. I know it doesn't sound like much, but well, it's things like that which set someone apart."

"I guess so," Millicent said.

"About tomorrow," Louise went on. "You've drawn Beverly Mitchell for a big sister. I wanted to warn you that she's the toughest, but if you get through all right it'll be all the more credit for you."

"Thanks, Lou," Millicent said gratefully, thinking, this is beginning to sound serious. Worse than a loyalty test, this grilling over the coals. What's it supposed to prove anyway? That I can take orders without flinching? Or does it just make them feel good to see us run around at their beck and call?

"All you have to do really," Louise said, "is be very meek and obedient when you're with Bev and do just what she tells you. Don't laugh or talk back or try to be funny, or she'll just make it harder for you, and believe me, she's a great one for doing that. Be at her house at seven-thirty."

And she was. She rang the bell and sat down on the steps to wait for Bev. After a few minutes the front door opened and Bev was standing there, her face serious.

"Get up, gopher," Bev ordered.

There was something about her tone that annoyed Millicent. It was almost malicious. And there was an unpleasant anonymity about the label "gopher," even if that was what they always called the girls being initiated. It was degrading, like being given a number. It was a denial of individuality.

Rebellion flooded through her.

"I said get up. Are you deaf?"

Millicent got up, standing there.

"Into the house, gopher. There's a bed to be made and a room to be cleaned at the top of the stairs."

Millicent went up the stairs mutely. She found Bev's room and started making the bed. Smiling to herself, she was thinking: How absurdly funny, me taking orders from this girl like a servant.

Bev was suddenly there in the doorway. "Wipe that smile off your face," she commanded.

There seemed something about this relationship that was not all fun. In Bev's eyes, Millicent was sure of it, there was a hard, bright spark of exultation.

On the way to school, Millicent had to walk behind Bev at a distance of ten paces, carrying her books. They came up to the drugstore where there already was a crowd of boys and girls from Lansing High waiting for the show.

The other girls being initiated were there, so Millicent felt relieved. It would not be so bad now, being part of the group.

"What'll we have them do?" Betsy Johnson asked Bev. That morning Betsy had made her "gopher" carry an old colored parasol through the square and sing "I'm Always Chasing Rainbows."

"I know," Herb Dalton, the good-looking basketball captain, said.

A remarkable change came over Bev. She was all at once very soft and coquettish.[4]

"You can't tell them what to do," Bev said sweetly, "Men have nothing to say about this little deal."

"All right, all right," Herb laughed, stepping back and pretending to fend off a blow.

"It's getting late," Louise had come up. "Almost eight-thirty. We'd better get them marching on to school."

The "gophers" had to do a Charleston[5] step all the way to school, and each one had her own song to sing, trying to drown out the other four. During school, of course, you couldn't fool around, but even then, there was a rule that you mustn't talk to boys outside of class or at lunchtime . . . or any time at all after school. So the sorority girls would get the most popular boys to go up to the "gophers" and ask them out, or try to start them talking, and sometimes a "gopher" was taken by surprise and began to say something before she could catch herself. And then the boy reported her and she got a black mark.

Herb Dalton approached Millicent as she was getting an ice cream at the lunch counter that noon. She saw him coming before he spoke to her, and looked down quickly, thinking: He is too princely, too dark and smiling. And I am much too vulnerable. Why must he be the one I have to be careful of?

---

4. **coquettish:** acting in a flirting manner

5. **Charleston:** a lively dance, especially popular during the 1920s

I won't say anything, she thought, I'll just smile very sweetly.

She smiled up at Herb very sweetly and mutely. His return grin was rather miraculous. It was surely more than was called for in the line of duty.

"I know you can't talk to me," he said, very low. "But you're doing fine, the girls say."

Bev was coming toward them, then, her red mouth set in a bright, calculating smile. She ignored Millicent and sailed up to Herb.

"Why waste your time with gophers?" she caroled gaily. "Their tongues are tied, but completely."

Herb managed a parting shot. "But that one keeps *such* an attractive silence."

Millicent smiled as she ate her sundae at the counter with Tracy. Generally, the girls who were outsiders now, as Millicent had been, scoffed at the initiation antics as childish and absurd to hide their secret envy. But Tracy was understanding, as ever.

"Tonight's the worst, I guess, Tracy," Millicent told her. "I hear that the girls are taking us on a bus over to Lewiston and going to have us performing in the square."

"Just keep a poker face[6] outside," Tracy advised. "But keep laughing like mad inside."

Millicent and Bev took a bus ahead of the rest of the girls; they had to stand up on the way to Lewiston Square. Bev seemed very cross about something. Finally she said, "You were talking with Herb Dalton at lunch today."

"No," said Millicent honestly.

"Well, I *saw* you smile at him. That's

practically as bad as talking. Remember not to do it again."

Millicent kept silent.

"It's fifteen minutes before the bus gets into town," Bev was saying then. "I want you to go up and down the bus asking people what they eat for breakfast. Remember, you can't tell them you're being initiated."

Millicent looked down the aisle of the crowded bus and felt suddenly quite sick. She thought: How will I ever do it, going up to all those stony-faced people who are staring coldly out of the window. . . ?

"You heard me, gopher."

"Excuse me, madam," Millicent said politely to the lady in the first seat of the bus, "but I'm taking a survey. Could you please tell me what you eat for breakfast?"

"Why . . . er . . . just orange juice, toast, and coffee," she said.

"Thank you very much." Millicent went on to the next person, a young business man. He ate eggs sunny side up, toast and coffee.

By the time Millicent got to the back of the bus, most of the people were smiling at her. They obviously know, she thought, that I'm being initiated into something.

Finally, there was only one man left in the corner of the back seat. He was small and jolly, with a ruddy, wrinkled face that spread into a beaming smile as Millicent approached. In his brown suit with the forest-green tie he looked something like a gnome or a cheerful leprechaun.

"Excuse me, sir," Millicent smiled, "but I'm taking a survey. What do you eat for breakfast?"

"Heather birds' eyebrows on toast," the little man rattled off.

6. poker face: a face that shows no expression

Initiation

"*What?*" Millicent exclaimed.

"Heather birds' eyebrows," the little man explained. "Heather birds live on the mythological moors and fly about all day long, singing wild and sweet in the sun. They're bright purple and have *very* tasty eyebrows."

Millicent broke out into spontaneous laughter. Why, this was wonderful, the way she felt a sudden comradeship with a stranger.

"Are you mythological, too?"

"Not exactly," he replied, "but I certainly hope to be someday. Being mythological does wonders for one's ego."

The bus was swinging into the station now; Millicent hated to leave the little man. She wanted to ask him more about the birds.

And from that time on, initiations didn't bother Millicent at all. She went gaily about Lewiston Square from store to store asking for broken crackers and mangoes, and she just laughed inside when people stared and then brightened, answering her crazy questions as if she were quite serious and really a person of consequence. So many people were shut up tight inside themselves like boxes, yet they would open up, unfolding quite wonderfully, if only you were interested in them. And really, you didn't have to belong to a club to feel related to other human beings.

One afternoon Millicent had started talking with Liane Morris, another of the girls being initiated, about what it would be like when they were finally in the sorority.

"Oh, I know pretty much what it'll be like," Liane had said. "My sister belonged before she graduated from high school two years ago."

"Well, just what *do* they do as a club?" Millicent wanted to know.

"Why, they have a meeting once a week . . . each girl takes turns entertaining at her house. . . ."

"You mean it's just a sort of exclusive social group. . . ."

"I guess so . . . though that's a funny way of putting it. But it sure gives a girl prestige value."

No, it wasn't bad, Millicent had thought, lying in bed on the morning of Court and listening to the sparrows chirping in the gutters. She thought of Herb. Would he ever have been so friendly if she were without the sorority label? Would he ask her out (if he ever did) just for herself, no strings attached?

Then there was another thing that bothered her. Leaving Tracy on the outskirts. Because that is the way it would be; Millicent had seen it happen before.

Outside, the sparrows were still chirping, and as she lay in bed Millicent visualized them, pale gray-brown birds in a flock, one like the other, all exactly alike.

And then, for some reason, Millicent thought of the heather birds. Swooping carefree over the moors, they would go singing and crying out across the great spaces of air, dipping and darting, strong and proud in their freedom and their sometime loneliness. It was then that she made her decision.

Seated now on the woodpile in Betsy Johnson's cellar, Millicent knew that she had come triumphant through the trial of fire, the searing period of the ego which could end in two kinds of victory for her. The easiest of which would be her coronation, labeling her conclusively as one of the select flock.

The other victory would be much harder, but she knew that it was what she wanted. It was not that she was being noble or anything. It was just that she had learned there were other ways of getting into the great hall, blazing with lights, of people and of life.

It would be hard to explain to the girls tonight, of course, but she could tell Louise later just how it was. How she had proved something to herself by going through everything, even Court, and then deciding not to join the sorority after all. And how she could still be friends with everybody. Sisters with everybody. Tracy, too.

The door behind her opened and a ray of light sliced across the soft gloom of the basement room.

"Hey Millicent, come on out now. This is it." There were some of the girls outside.

"I'm coming," she said, getting up and moving out of the soft darkness into the glare of light, thinking: This is it, all right. The worst part, the hardest part, the part of initiation that I figured out myself.

But just then, from somewhere far off, Millicent was sure of it, there came a melodic fluting, quite wild and sweet, and she knew that it must be the song of the heather birds as they went wheeling and gliding against wide blue horizons through vast spaces of air, their wings flashing quick and purple in the bright sun.

Within Millicent another melody soared, strong and exuberant, a triumphant answer to the music of the darting birds that sang so clear and lilting over the far lands. And she knew that her own private initiation had just begun.

About the Author

Sylvia Plath (1921–1963) lived a short but highly productive life. Born in Boston, Massachusetts, Plath was a gifted student who graduated with honors from Smith College. She subsequently went to Cambridge University in England, where she met and later married English poet Ted Hughes. While still in her teens, Plath won many awards, and her stories and poems appeared in national magazines. In fact, "Initiation" was published in *Seventeen* magazine when Plath was 20 years old. Although Plath wrote fiction, she was primarily a poet. Her poetry is highly autobiographical and reflects a life filled with anguish and powerful emotions. Plath's most famous works are her only published novel, *The Bell Jar,* and a volume of poetry, *The Colossus.* In 1982, almost 20 years after her death, Plath's work was awarded the Pulitzer Prize for poetry.

THINK ABOUT THE STORY. The following questions help you check your reading comprehension. Put an *x* in the box next to the correct answer.

1. Which sentence best expresses the main idea of the story?
   - ☐ a. All sororities are bad and should be abolished.
   - ☐ b. A young woman makes a difficult decision about joining a sorority.
   - ☐ c. Students sometimes act unkindly toward each other.

2. When Bev gave Millicent orders, Millicent was expected to
   - ☐ a. obey without questioning.
   - ☐ b. laugh and talk back.
   - ☐ c. make a joke or try to be funny.

3. As part of her initiation, Millicent had to ask the people on a bus
   - ☐ a. where they were going.
   - ☐ b. what kind of work they did.
   - ☐ c. what they ate for breakfast.

4. At the end of the story, the last thing that Millicent heard was
   - ☐ a. some girls laughing.
   - ☐ b. the song of the heather birds.
   - ☐ c. the sound of Tracy's voice.

HANDLE NEW VOCABULARY WORDS. The following questions check your vocabulary skills. Put an *x* in the box next to the correct answer. Each vocabulary word appears in the story.

1. Millicent mused about the events that had taken place. The word *mused* means
   - ☐ a. thought.
   - ☐ b. wrote.
   - ☐ c. forgot.

2. Millicent felt vulnerable because she could not defend her rights. What is the meaning of the word *vulnerable*?
   - ☐ a. sorrowful or sad
   - ☐ b. ridiculous or foolish
   - ☐ c. open to attack

3. Millicent was so amused by what the man said that she "broke out into spontaneous laughter." Which of the following best defines the word *spontaneous*?
   - ☐ a. piercing or shrill
   - ☐ b. sudden or unplanned
   - ☐ c. soft or subdued

4. Liane suggested that belonging to an exclusive club gave the members prestige. The word *prestige* means
   - ☐ a. power to command the respect or admiration of others.
   - ☐ b. the ability to acquire great wealth.
   - ☐ c. remarkable knowledge and skills.

☐ × 5 = ☐

NUMBER
CORRECT

YOUR
SCORE

☐ × 5 = ☐

NUMBER
CORRECT

YOUR
SCORE

EXAMINE STORY ELEMENTS. The following questions check your knowledge of story elements. Put an *x* in the box next to each correct answer.

1. Who is the *main character* in "Initiation"?
   □ a. Louise Fullerton
   □ b. Beverly Mitchell
   □ c. Millicent

2. Which of the following statements best presents a character's *inner conflict*?
   □ a. Tracy advised Millicent to do what she was told but to "keep laughing like mad inside."
   □ b. Millicent wanted to be a member of the sorority but also had strong reservations about joining.
   □ c. Millicent felt a surge of pride when she and Louise walked together.

3. Of the following events, which happened last in the *plot* of the story?
   □ a. A man told Millicent that he ate heather birds' eyebrows for breakfast.
   □ b. Millicent rose to leave the basement room, her mind made up.
   □ c. Louise explained why Tracy had not been invited to join the sorority.

4. What is the story's *theme*?
   □ a. It is not necessary to belong to an exclusive club to feel special.
   □ b. Young people desire, above all, to be respected and admired.
   □ c. Some people will do just about anything to join a popular organization.

□ ×5 = □

NUMBER CORRECT · YOUR SCORE

MASTER CRITICAL THINKING. The following questions check your critical thinking skills. Put an *x* in the box next to each correct answer.

1. We may infer that Millicent decided
   □ a. to accept sorority membership.
   □ b. to join the sorority but only if Tracy were accepted too.
   □ c. not to join the sorority after all.

2. Based on what occurs in the story, the reader may conclude that Millicent
   □ a. proved something to herself— something valuable and enduring.
   □ b. acted unwisely and wasted her time.
   □ c. would never again be friendly with any of the girls at her school.

3. Which sentence is most closely related to the story's theme?
   □ a. "Nothing ever stays the same."
   □ b. "You didn't have to belong to a club to feel related to other human beings."
   □ c. "Millicent had waited a long time for acceptance."

4. At the end of the story, the author implies that the most difficult test that Millicent will have to face is
   □ a. remaining friends with Tracy.
   □ b. attempting to join the sorority in the future.
   □ c. explaining why she has decided not to join the sorority and accepting the consequences of her decision.

□ ×5 = □

NUMBER CORRECT · YOUR SCORE

EXPLORE THE **W**RITER'S **C**RAFT. The following questions check your knowledge of skills related to the craft of writing. Put an *x* in the box next to each correct answer. You may refer to pages 4 and 5.

1. "The basement room was dark and warm, like the inside of a sealed jar." This sentence contains
   ☐ a. a metaphor.
   ☐ b. a simile.
   ☐ c. an example of personification.

2. Heather birds seem to have strongly influenced Millicent. What do the heather birds symbolize?
   ☐ a. personal freedom
   ☐ b. the need for caution
   ☐ c. the beauty of nature

3. As opposed to swooping, singing heather birds, sparrows were "pale gray-brown birds in a flock, one like the other, all exactly alike." This comparison inspired Millicent to
   ☐ a. join the sorority and be like the other members.
   ☐ b. ask others for assistance.
   ☐ c. think and act as an individual.

4. Millicent "learned there were other ways of getting into the great hall, blazing with lights, of people and of life." Here, the author is referring to various ways of
   ☐ a. doing well at school.
   ☐ b. guarding against danger.
   ☐ c. participating in activities and relating to others.

	× 5 =	
NUMBER CORRECT		YOUR SCORE

Questions for Writing and Discussion

- What were some of the "tests" Millicent had to face during her initiation? How did she handle them? How do you feel about those "tests"?
- Explain why Millicent made the decision she did. Show how the incident with the man on the bus influenced her actions.
- The heather birds are mentioned several times during the story. Briefly explain the significance of the birds.
- Read the last sentence of the story again. Tell what you think it means.

See additional questions for extended writing on pages 36 and 37.

Use the boxes below to total your scores for the exercises. Then record your scores on pages 224 and 225.

☐	**T**HINK ABOUT THE STORY
+	
☐	**H**ANDLE NEW VOCABULARY WORDS
+	
☐	**E**XAMINE STORY ELEMENTS
+	
☐	**M**ASTER CRITICAL THINKING
+	
☐	**E**XPLORE THE WRITER'S CRAFT
▼	
☐	**Total Score:** Story 2

The Street of the Cañon

by Josefina Niggli

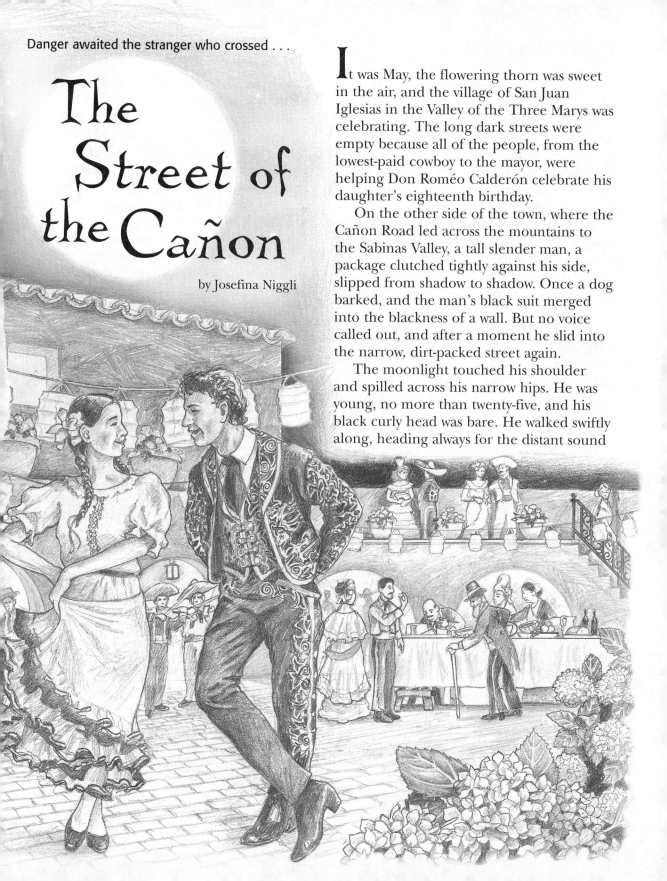

It was May, the flowering thorn was sweet in the air, and the village of San Juan Iglesias in the Valley of the Three Marys was celebrating. The long dark streets were empty because all of the people, from the lowest-paid cowboy to the mayor, were helping Don Roméo Calderón celebrate his daughter's eighteenth birthday.

On the other side of the town, where the Cañon Road led across the mountains to the Sabinas Valley, a tall slender man, a package clutched tightly against his side, slipped from shadow to shadow. Once a dog barked, and the man's black suit merged into the blackness of a wall. But no voice called out, and after a moment he slid into the narrow, dirt-packed street again.

The moonlight touched his shoulder and spilled across his narrow hips. He was young, no more than twenty-five, and his black curly head was bare. He walked swiftly along, heading always for the distant sound

The Street of the Cañon

of guitar and flute. If he met anyone now, who could say from which direction he had come? He might be a trader from Monterrey, or a buyer of cow's milk from farther north in the Valley of the Three Marys. Who would guess that an Hidalgo[1] man dared to walk alone in the moonlit streets of San Juan Iglesias?

Carefully adjusting his flat package so that it was not too prominent, he squared his shoulders and walked jauntily across the street to the laughter-filled house. Little boys packed in the doorway made way for him, smiling and nodding to him. The long, narrow room with the orchestra at one end was filled with whirling dancers. Rigid-backed chaperones were gossiping together, seated in their straight chairs against the plaster walls. Over the scene was the yellow glow of kerosene lanterns, and the air was hot with the too-sweet perfume of gardenias and the pungent scent of close-packed humanity.

The man in the doorway, while trying to appear at ease, was carefully examining every smiling face. If just one person recognized him, the room would turn on him like a den of snarling mountain cats, but so far all the laughter-dancing eyes were friendly.

Suddenly a plump, officious little man, his round cheeks glistening with perspiration, pushed his way through the crowd. His voice, many times too large for his small body, boomed at the man in the doorway. "Welcome, stranger, welcome to our house." Thrusting his arm through the stranger's, and almost dislodging the package, he started to lead the way through the maze of dancers. "Come and drink a

1. **Hidalgo:** a nearby village whose people are enemies of the people of San Juan Iglesias.

toast to my daughter—to my beautiful Sarita. She is eighteen this night."

In the square patio the gentle breeze ruffled the pink and white oleander bushes. A long table set up on sawhorses held loaves of flaky crusted French bread, stacks of thin, delicate tortillas, plates of barbecued beef, and long red rolls of spicy sausages. But most of all there were cheeses, for the Three Marys was a cheese-eating valley. There were yellow cheese and white cheese and curded cheese from cow's milk. There was even a flat white cake of goat cheese from distant Linares, a delicacy too expensive for any but feast days.

To set off this feast, a table was covered with bottles of wine. Don Roméo Calderón thrust a glass into the stranger's hand. "Drink, friend, to the prettiest girl in San Juan. On her wedding day she takes to her man, and may she find him soon, the best fighter in my flock. Drink deep, friend. Even the rivers flow with wine." The Hidalgo man laughed and raised his glass high.

Someone called to Don Roméo that more guests were arriving, and with a final delighted pat on the stranger's shoulder, the little man scurried away. As the young fellow smiled after his retreating host, his eyes caught and held another pair of eyes— laughing black eyes set in a young girl's face. The last time he had seen that face it had been white and tense with rage, and the lips clenched tight to prevent an outgushing stream of angry words. That had been in February, and she had worn a white lace shawl over her hair. Now it was May, and a gardenia was a splash of white in the glossy dark braids. The moonlight had mottled his face that February night, and he knew that she did not recognize him. He grinned impudently back at her, and her eyes widened, then slid sideways to one of the chaperones. The fan in her small hand snapped shut. She tapped its parchment tip against her mouth and slipped away to join the dancing couples in the front room. The gestures of a fan translate into a coded language on the frontier. The stranger raised one eyebrow as he interpreted the signal.

But he did not move toward her at once. Instead, he inched slowly back against the table. No one was behind him, and his hands quickly unfastened the package he had been guarding so long. Then he nonchalantly walked into the front room.

The girl was sitting close to a chaperone. As he came up to her he swerved slightly toward the bushy-browed old lady.

"Your servant, señora. I kiss your hands and feet."

The chaperone stared at him in astonishment. Such fine manners were not common to the town of San Juan Iglesias.

"Eh, you're a stranger," she said. "I thought so."

"But a stranger no longer, señora, now that I have met you." He bent over her, so close she could smell the faint fragrance of talcum on his freshly shaven cheek.

"Will you dance the *parada* with me?"

This request startled her eyes into popping open beneath the heavy brows. "So, my young rooster, would you flirt with me, and I old enough to be your grandmother?"

"Can you show me a prettier woman to flirt with in the Valley of the Three Marys?" he asked audaciously.

She grinned at him and turned toward the girl at her side. "This young fool wants to meet you, my child."

The girl blushed to the roots of her hair and shyly lowered her white lids. The old woman laughed aloud.

"Go out and dance, the two of you."

The next moment they had joined the circle of dancers and Sarita was trying to control her laughter.

"She is the worst dragon in San Juan. And how easily you won her!"

"What is a dragon," he asked imperiously, "when I longed to dance with you?"

"Ay," she retorted, "you have a quick tongue. I think you are a dangerous man."

In answer he drew her closer to him, and turned her toward the orchestra. As he reached the chief violinist he called out, "Play 'The Shy Young Maiden.'"

The violinist's mouth opened in soundless surprise. The girl in his arms said sharply, "You heard him, play 'Farewell, My Darling.'"

With a relieved grin, the violinist tapped his music stand with his bow, and the music swung into the sad farewell of a man to his sweetheart:

Farewell, my darling,
I must go to the capital
To serve the master
Who makes me weep for my return.

The stranger frowned down at her. "Is this a joke, señorita?" he asked coldly.

"No," she whispered, looking about her quickly to see if the incident had been observed. "But 'The Shy Young Maiden' is the favorite song of Hidalgo, a village on the other side of the mountains in the next valley. The people of Hidalgo and San Juan Iglesias do not speak."

"That is a stupid thing," said the man from Hidalgo as he swung her around in a large turn. "Is not music free as air? Why should one town own the rights to a song?"

The girl shuddered slightly. "Those people from Hidalgo—they are wicked monsters. Can you guess what they did not six months since?"

The man started to point out that the space of time from February to May was three months, but he thought it better not to appear too wise. "Did these Hidalgo monsters frighten you, señorita? If they did, I personally will fight them all."

She moved closer against him and tilted her face until her mouth was close to his ear. "They attempted to steal the bones of Don Rómolo Balderas."

"Is it possible?" He made his eyes grow round and his lips purse up in disdain. "Surely not that! Why, all the world knows that Don Rómolo Balderas was the greatest historian in the entire Republic. Every school child reads his books. Wise men from Quintana Roo to the Rio Bravo bow their heads in admiration to his name. What a wicked thing to do!" He hoped his virtuous tone was not too virtuous for plausibility, but she did not seem to notice.

"It is true! In the night they came. Three. The blacksmith surprised them. He raised such a shout that all of San Juan rushed to his aid, for they were fighting, I can tell you. Especially one of them—their leader."

"And who was he?"

"You have heard of him doubtless. A wild one named Pepe Gonzalez."

"And what happened to them?"

"They had horses and got away, but one, I think, was hurt."

The Hidalgo man twisted his mouth remembering how Rubén the candymaker had ridden across the whitewashed line high on the cañon trail that marked the division between the Three Marys' and the Sabinas' sides of the mountains, and then had fallen in a faint from his saddle because his left arm was broken. There was no candy in Hidalgo for six weeks, and the entire Sabinas Valley resented that broken arm as fiercely as did Rubén.

The stranger tightened his arm in reflexed anger about Sarita's waist as she said, "All the world knows that the men of Hidalgo are sons of the mountain witches."

"But even devils are shy of disturbing the honored dead," he said gravely.

"'Don Rómolo was born in our village,' Hidalgo says. 'His bones belong to us.' Well, anyone in the valley can tell you he died in San Juan Iglesias, and here his bones will stay! Is it not proper? Is that not right?"

To keep from answering, he guided her through an intricate dance pattern that led them past the patio door. Over her head he could see two men and a woman staring with amazement at the open package on the table.

His eyes on the patio, he asked blandly, "You say the leader was one Pepe Gonzalez? The name seems to have a familiar sound."

"But naturally. He has a talent." She tossed her head and stepped away from him as the music stopped. It was a dance of two *paradas*. He slipped his hand through her arm and guided her into place in the large oval of parading couples. Twice around the room and the orchestra would play again.

"A talent?" he prompted.

"For doing the impossible. When all the world says a thing cannot be done, he does it to prove the world wrong. Why, he climbed to the top of the Prow, and not even the long vanished Joaquín Castillo had ever climbed that mountain before. And this same Pepe caught a mountain lion with nothing to aid him but a rope and his two bare hands."

"He doesn't sound such a bad friend," protested the stranger, slipping his arm around her waist as the music began to play the merry song of the soap bubbles:

Pretty bubbles of a thousand colors
That ride on the wind
And break as swiftly
As a lover's heart.

The events in the patio were claiming his attention. Little by little he edged her closer to the door. The group at the table had considerably enlarged. There was a low murmur of excitement from the crowd.

"What has happened?" asked Sarita, attracted by the noise.

"There seems to be something wrong at the table," he answered, while trying to peer over the heads of the people in front of him. Realizing that this might be the last moment of peace he would have that evening, he bent toward her.

"If I come back on Sunday, will you walk around the plaza with me?"

She was startled into exclaiming, "Ay, no!"

"Please. Just once around."

"And you think I'd walk more than once with you, señor, even if you were no stranger? In San Juan Iglesias, to walk around the plaza with a girl means a wedding."

"Ha, and you think that is common to San Juan alone? Even the devils of Hidalgo respect that law." He added hastily at her puzzled upward glance. "And so they do in all the villages." To cover his lapse he said softly, "I don't even know your name."

A mischievous grin crinkled the corners of her eyes. "Nor do I know yours, señor. Strangers do not often walk the streets of San Juan."

Before he could answer, the chattering in the patio swelled to louder proportions. Don Roméo's voice lay on top, like thick cream on milk. "I tell you it is a jewel of a cheese. Such flavor, such texture, such whiteness. It is a jewel of a cheese."

"What has happened?" Sarita asked of a woman at her elbow.

"A fine goat's cheese appeared as if by magic on the table. No one knows where it came from."

"Probably an extra one from Linares," snorted a fat bald man on the right.

"Linares never made such a cheese as this," said the woman decisively.

"Silence!" roared Don Roméo. "Old Tío Daniel would speak a word to us."

A great hand of silence closed down over the mouths of the people. The girl was standing on tiptoe trying vainly to see what was happening. She was hardly aware of the stranger's whispering voice although she remembered the words that he said. "Sunday night—once around the plaza."

She did not realize that he had moved away, leaving a gap that was quickly filled by the blacksmith.

Old Tío Daniel's voice was a shrill squeak, and his thin, stringy neck jutted forth from his body like a turtle's from its shell. "This is no cheese from Linares," he said with authority, his mouth sucking in over his toothless gums between his sentences. "Years ago, when the great Don Rómolo Balderas was still alive, we had such cheese as this—ay, in those days we had it.

But after he died and was buried. . . ."

"Yes, yes," muttered voices in the crowd. He glared at the interruption. As soon as there was silence again, he continued:

"After he died, we had it no more. Shall I tell you why?"

"Tell us, Tío Daniel," said the voices humbly.

"Because it is made in Hidalgo!"

The sound of a waterfall, the sound of a wind in a narrow cañon, and the sound of an angry crowd are much the same. There were no distinct words, but the sound was enough.

"Are you certain, Tío?" boomed Don Roméo.

"As certain as I am that a donkey has long ears. The people of Hidalgo have been famous for generations for making cheese like this—especially that wicked one, that owner of a cheese factory, Timotéo Gonzalez, father to Pepe, the wild one, whom we have good cause to remember."

"We do, we do," came the sigh of assurance.

"But on the whole northern frontier there are no vats like his to produce so fine a product. Ask the people of Chihuahua, of Sonora. Ask the man on the bridge at Laredo, or the man in his boat at Tampico, '*Hola,* friend, who makes the finest goat cheese?' And the answer will always be the same, 'Don Timotéo of Hidalgo.'"

It was the blacksmith who asked the question. "Then where did that cheese come from, and we haters of Hidalgo these ten long years?"

No voice said, "The stranger," but with one fluid movement every head in the patio turned toward the girl in the doorway. She also turned, her eyes wide with something that she realized to her own amazement was more apprehension than anger.

But the stranger was not in the room. When the angry, muttering men pushed through to the street, the stranger was not on the plaza. He was not anywhere in sight. "Who was he?" one voice asked another. But Sarita, who was meekly listening to a lecture from Don Roméo on the propriety of dancing with strangers, did not have to ask. She had a strong suspicion that she had danced that night within the circling arm of Pepe Gonzalez.

About the Author

Josefina Niggli (1910–1983) was born in Mexico and came to the United States with her family when she was three years old. The family settled in San Antonio, Texas. While still in her teens, Niggli's stories were published in magazines such as *Colliers, Mexican Life,* and *Ladies Home Journal.* Later, Niggli wrote many plays, as well as poetry, movie scripts, and novels. Niggli is probably best known for *Mexican Village,* a collection of stories from which "The Street of the Cañon" is taken. Like much of Niggli's work, the story is set in Mexico and reflects the author's knowledge and concern with Mexican culture, history, and traditions.

THINK ABOUT THE STORY. The following questions help you check your reading comprehension. Put an *x* in the box next to the correct answer.

1. What is "The Street of the Cañon" mainly about?
   - □ a. the difficulties involved in bringing peace to two feuding villages
   - □ b. what occurs when an uninvited, and possibly unwelcome, stranger suddenly appears at a birthday party
   - □ c. the great pride that Don Roméo Calderón displayed for his daughter

2. When a stranger appeared at the party, Don Roméo
   - □ a. greeted him warmly.
   - □ b. asked him who he was.
   - □ c. suggested that he leave.

3. How did Sarita feel about the people from Hidalgo?
   - □ a. She thought that they were friendly but misunderstood.
   - □ b. She believed that they were honorable and brave.
   - □ c. She was convinced that they were wicked monsters.

4. At the end of the story, Sarita suspected that she
   - □ a. had probably met a trader or merchant from a nearby village.
   - □ b. had seen the stranger before but had forgotten his name.
   - □ c. had been dancing with Pepe Gonzalez.

	× 5 =	
NUMBER CORRECT		YOUR SCORE

HANDLE NEW VOCABULARY WORDS. The following questions check your vocabulary skills. Put an *x* in the box next to the correct answer. Each vocabulary word appears in the story.

1. The air was filled with "the pungent scent of close-packed humanity." As used here, the word *pungent* means
   - □ a. having a strong smell.
   - □ b. active or busy.
   - □ c. delightful.

2. The stranger calmly took his time; then he nonchalantly walked toward the young woman. What is the meaning of the word *nonchalantly*?
   - □ a. urgently
   - □ b. foolishly
   - □ c. casually

3. The picture of self-confidence, the stranger audaciously flirted with an older woman in order to meet Sarita. Define the word *audaciously*.
   - □ a. sorrowfully
   - □ b. boldly
   - □ c. hesitantly

4. Sarita received a lecture from her father "on the propriety of dancing with strangers." Which of the following best defines the word *propriety*?
   - □ a. serious danger
   - □ b. proper behavior
   - □ c. pleasant experience

	× 5 =	
NUMBER CORRECT		YOUR SCORE

EXAMINE STORY ELEMENTS. The following questions check your knowledge of story elements. Put an *x* in the box next to each correct answer.

1. The *setting* of "The Street of the Cañon" is
   - ☐ a. a village in California.
   - ☐ b. the village of Hidalgo.
   - ☐ c. the village of San Juan Iglesias.

2. Of the following events, which happened first in the *plot* of the story?
   - ☐ a. Don Roméo asked the stranger to drink a toast to Sarita.
   - ☐ b. A man slipped from shadow to shadow toward a laughter-filled house.
   - ☐ c. The villagers discovered a very fine goat's cheese on the table.

3. Which of the following statements best *characterizes* the stranger?
   - ☐ a. He was cautious, calculating, and unwilling to take risks.
   - ☐ b. He was tall, slender, and daring.
   - ☐ c. Although he was handsome, he was timid and shy.

4. Who is the *narrator* of the story?
   - ☐ a. the stranger
   - ☐ b. Sarita
   - ☐ c. the author

MASTER CRITICAL THINKING. The following questions check your critical thinking skills. Put an *x* in the box next to each correct answer.

1. We may infer that the stranger was
   - ☐ a. someone who happened to be passing by.
   - ☐ b. a friend of a guest who was at the party.
   - ☐ c. Pepe Gonzalez, the villagers' enemy.

2. Evidence in the story suggests that the stranger came to the party
   - ☐ a. to meet Sarita.
   - ☐ b. to defend the reputation of the people of Hidalgo.
   - ☐ c. to start a fight with Don Roméo.

3. The stranger probably departed when he did because
   - ☐ a. he realized that Sarita did not like him.
   - ☐ b. to stay longer would have been dangerous.
   - ☐ c. he was far from home, and it was already dark.

4. It is reasonable to conclude that the stranger left the fine cheese
   - ☐ a. by accident.
   - ☐ b. to make fun of the villagers.
   - ☐ c. as a peace offering and gift.

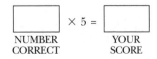

NUMBER CORRECT × 5 = YOUR SCORE

NUMBER CORRECT × 5 = YOUR SCORE

EXPLORE THE WRITER'S CRAFT. The following questions check your knowledge of skills related to the craft of writing. Put an *x* in the box next to each correct answer. You may refer to pages 4 and 5.

1. The stranger knew that if he were recognized, the villagers "would turn on him like a den of snarling mountain cats." This sentence contains an example of
   ☐ a. dialect.
   ☐ b. alliteration.
   ☐ c. a simile.

2. When the author refers to the "dancing eyes" of the townfolk, she is using a figure of speech known as
   ☐ a. a metaphor.
   ☐ b. a simile.
   ☐ c. personification.

3. According to the chaperone, the stranger was a "young rooster." This sentence contains
   ☐ a. a metaphor.
   ☐ b. an example of onomatopoeia.
   ☐ c. an illustration of inner conflict.

4. Identify the sentence that contains a simile.
   ☐ a. "The moonlight touched his shoulder."
   ☐ b. "His thin, stringy neck jutted forth from his body like a turtle's from its shell."
   ☐ c. "The long, narrow room . . . was filled with whirling dancers."

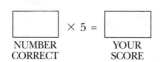

NUMBER CORRECT   × 5 =   YOUR SCORE

Questions for Writing and Discussion

- Find the earliest indication in the story that hostility existed between the residents of Hidalgo and the people of San Juan Iglesias.
- Describe the latest incident that further inflamed the feud between the two villages.
- Explain why the stranger had knowledge of the incident you described above and how that knowledge provided clues to the stranger's identity.
- By the end of the evening, might Sarita have changed her opinion of the people of Hidalgo? Give reasons. Is it likely that the two young people will meet again? Why?

See additional questions for extended writing on pages 36 and 37.

Use the boxes below to total your scores for the exercises. Then record your scores on pages 224 and 225.

     THINK ABOUT THE STORY

+

     HANDLE NEW VOCABULARY WORDS

+

     EXAMINE STORY ELEMENTS

+

     MASTER CRITICAL THINKING

+

     EXPLORE THE WRITER'S CRAFT

▼

     Total Score: Story 3

Friends and Enemies

Questions for Discussion and Extended Writing

The following questions provide opportunities to express your thoughts and feelings about the selections in this unit. Your teacher may assign selected questions. When you write your responses, remember to state your point of view clearly and to support your position by presenting specific details—examples, illustrations, and references drawn from the story and, in some cases, from your life. Organize your writing carefully and check your work for correct spelling, capitalization, punctuation, and grammar.

1. The theme of this unit is "Friends and Enemies." Show how each story in the unit is related to the theme.

2. A proverb states, "Do you have fifty friends? It is not enough. Do you have one enemy? It is too much." To which character in the unit do you think this proverb most directly applies? Support your opinion.

3. In which two selections in the unit does the setting of the story play the most important role? Give titles and authors, and present reasons for your answers.

4. Of the characters in the unit, Millicent in "Initiation" is called upon to make the most difficult decision. Do you agree with this statement? Support your opinion by referring to the stories.

5. In which story do you think conflict played the most significant role? Identify the conflict or conflicts in the story you selected.

6. Compare and contrast the Great Man in "The Smuggler" and Pepe Gonzalez in "The Street of the Cañon." In what ways are they similar? How are they different?

7. At some time following the conclusion of each selection, one or more characters may embark on a "personal journey" or an adventure. Select two characters in the unit and discuss what you think the future holds for each. Give titles and authors.

8. Draw upon material found in "The Street of the Cañon" to write a descriptive essay about the setting or the characters in the story.

9. If every story were predictable, few stories would prove interesting. Often the actions of a character surprise the reader. Select one story from the unit and indicate how a character's actions were different from what you anticipated. State what you expected and what eventually occurred.

10. This unit is titled "Friends and Enemies." Often issues of friendship and ill will are related to disputes that are (or are *not*) settled to the satisfaction of the individuals involved. Write an essay about an argument, a disagreement, or a dispute. Explain what the main issue was and whether the problem was resolved. Your essay should have an introduction, a body, and a conclusion. Be sure to include a title for your essay.

Achievements

*"All good things are
difficult to achieve."*

—Morarji Desai,
former Prime Minister of India

Previewing the Unit

Achievements come in various sizes and shapes. What is most important to remember is that "All good things are difficult to achieve." The characters in this unit are varied, but all of them have at least one thing in common: Each can take credit for an important achievement.

THE HORSE OF THE SWORD Filipino writer Manuel Buaken has written a captivating tale about a strong-willed young man who sets out to tame a wild, defiant, and unmanageable horse. Maning, the main character, ignores the warnings he has received about the horse. He is determined to achieve, and perhaps even surpass, the goal he has set for himself. As you might expect, since the selection is about a horse, the story includes a thrilling horse race. You can almost hear the sound of pounding hooves as the story thunders to its close.

GERALDINE MOORE THE POET In Toni Cade Bambara's moving story "Geraldine Moore the Poet," the main character discovers that she has been evicted from her home. Forced to move in with her neighbor, Miss Gladys, Geraldine must confront the realities of life. Ultimately Geraldine makes a stunning achievement. How she deals with the challenges she faces and what impact she has on others (particularly her English teacher, Miss Scott) form the basis for this touching story.

CHEE'S DAUGHTER Set against the sprawling landscape of America's Southwest, "Chee's Daughter" features characterization and conflict in a duel in which age-old tradition plays a powerful role. Chee, a young Navaho, is intent on regaining the daughter he has lost. But it is not at all clear that he can achieve that result, since customs die hard and his opponents are stubborn. This extraordinary story is rich with detail, and it resounds with the clear ring of truth.

TOM EDISON'S SHAGGY DOG Kurt Vonnegut's humorous tale provides an amusing change of pace from the other selections in this unit. How does a stranger deal with an annoying intruder? "Revenge is sweet," according to an old saying. But will the stranger achieve revenge? And just what is a "shaggy-dog story"? You will be able to answer these questions when you have completed the story.

As you read, think about the things you have already accomplished in your life and what you still hope to achieve.

No one had succeeded before, but the boy was confident he could tame . . .

The Horse of the Sword

by Manuel Buaken

"**B**oy, get rid of that horse," said one of the wise old men from Abra where the racing horses thrive on the good Bermuda grass of Luzon[1] uplands. "That's a bandit's horse. See that Sign of Evil on him. Something tragic will happen to you if you keep him."

But another one of the old horse traders who had gathered at that auction declared: "That's a good omen. The Sword he bears on his shoulder means leadership and power. He's a true mount for a chieftain. He's a free man's fighting horse."

As for me, I knew this gray colt was a wonder horse the moment I saw him. These other people were blind. They only saw that this gray, shaggy horse bore the marks of many whips, that his ribs almost stuck through his mangy hide, that his great eyes rolled in defiance and fear as the

---

1. **Luzon:** chief island in the Philippines

40

auctioneer approached him. They couldn't
see the meaning of that Sword he bore—a
marking not in the color, which was a
uniform gray, but in the way that the hair
had arranged itself permanently: it was
parted to form an outline of a sword that
was broad on his neck and tapered to a fine
point on his shoulder.

Father, too, was blind against this horse.
He argued with me and scolded: "Maning,
when I promised you a pony as a reward for
good work in high school English, I
thought you'd use good judgment in
choosing. It is true, this horse has good
blood, for he came from the Santiago
stables—they have raised many fine racers,
but this colt has always been worthless. He
is bad-tempered, would never allow himself
to be bathed and curried, and no one has

ever been able to ride him. Now, that black
over there is well trained—"

"Father, you promised I could choose for
myself," I insisted. "I choose this horse.
None of them can tame him, but I can. He's
wild because his mouth is very tender—see
how it is bled. That's his terrible secret."

My father always kept his promises, so he
paid the few *pesos* they asked for this outlaw
colt and made arrangements to have the
animal driven, herded, up to our summer
home in the hills.

"I used to play, but now I have work to
do," I told Father. "I'll show you and
everybody else what a mistake you made
about my horse."

Father agreed with me solemnly, and
smiled over my head at Mother, but she
wasn't agreeing at all. "Don't you go near

41

that bad horse your father foolishly let you buy. You know he has kicked so many people."

It hurt me to disobey Mother, and I consoled myself with the thought she'd change her mind when I had tamed my Horse of the Sword.

But could I win where all others, smart grown men, had failed? I could, if I was right. So early in the morning I slipped off to the meadow. The Horse of the Sword was cropping the grass industriously, but defiantly, alert for any whips. He snorted a warning at me, and backed away skittishly as I approached. "What a body you have," I said, talking to accustom him to my voice and to assure him of my peaceful intentions. "Wide between the shoulders—that's for strength and endurance. Long legs for speed, and a proud arched neck, that's some Arabian aristocracy you have in you, Sword Horse."

I kept walking slowly toward him and talking softly, until he stopped backing away. He neighed defiance at me, and his eyes rolled angrily, those big eyes that were so human in their dare and their appeal. He didn't move now as I inched closer, but I could see his muscles twitch. Very softly and gently I put my hand on his shoulder. He jumped away. I spoke softly and again put my hand on the Sword of his shoulder. This time he stood. I kept my hand on his shaggy shoulder. Then slowly I slipped it up to his head, then down again to his shoulder, down his legs to his fetlocks.[2] It was a major victory.

That very day I began grooming him, currying his coat, getting out the collection of insects that had burrowed into his skin.

He sometimes jumped away, but he never kicked at me. And next day I was able to lead my gray horse across the meadow to the spring, with my hand on his mane as his only guide—this "untamable outlaw" responded to my light touch. It was the simple truth—his mouth was too tender for a jerking bridle bit. The pain just drove him wild; that's all that had made him an outlaw. Gentle handling, no loud shouts, no jerks on his tender mouth, good food and a cleaned skin—these spelled health and contentment. Kindness had conquered. In a few days the gaunt hollows filled out with firm flesh to give the gray horse beauty. Reckless spirit he always had.

Every morning I slipped off to the meadow—Mother was anxious to have the house quiet so Father could write his pamphlet on the language and Christianization of the Tinggians, so I had a free hand. It didn't take more than a month to change my find from a raging outlaw to a miracle of glossy horseflesh. But was his taming complete? Could I ride him? Was he an outlaw at heart?

In the cool of a late afternoon, I mounted to his back. If he threw me I should be alone in my defeat and my fall would be cushioned by the grass. He trembled a little as I leaped to his back. But he stood quiet. He turned his head, his big eyes questioning me. Then, obedient to my "*Kiph*"—"Go"—he trotted slowly away.

I knew a thrill then, the thrill of mastery and of fleet motion on the back of this steed whose stride was so smooth, so much like flying. He ran about the meadow eagerly, and I turned him into the mountain lane. "I know how a butterfly

---

2. **fetlock:** the lower part of a horse's leg, near the hoof

feels as he skims along," I crowed delightedly. Down the lane where the trees made dappled shade around our high-roofed bungalow we flew along. Mother stood beside her cherished flame tree, watching sister Dominga as she pounded the rice.

The Horse of the Sword pranced into the yard. Mother gasped in amazement. "Mother, I disobeyed you," I blurted out quickly. "I'm sorry, but I had to show you, and you were wrong, everybody was wrong about this horse."

Mother tried to be severe with me, but soon her smile warmed me, and she said, "Yes, I was wrong, Maning. What have you named your new horse?"

"A new name for a new horse, that's a good idea. Mother, you must name him."

Mother's imagination was always alive. It gave her the name at once. "Glory, that's his name. *MoroGlorioso*. Gray Glory." So MoroGlory it was.

Too soon, vacation was over and I had to go back to school. But MoroGlory went with me. "You take better care of that horse than you do of yourself," Father complained. "If you don't stop neglecting your lessons, I'll have the horse taken up to the mountain pasture again."

"Oh, no, Father, you can't do that," I exclaimed. "MoroGlory must be here for his lessons too. Every day I teach him and give him practice so that next spring, at the Feria, he is going to show his heels to all those fine horses they boast about so much."

Father knew what I meant. Those boasts had been mosquito bites in his mind too; for our barrio was known to be horse-crazy.

For instance, it was almost a scandal the way the Priest, Father Anastacio, petted his horse Tango. Tango ate food that was better than the priest's, they said. He was a beauty, nobody denied that, but the good Father's boasts were a little hard to take, especially for the Presidente.

The Presidente had said in public, "My Bandirado Boyo is a horse whose blood lines are known back to an Arabian stallion imported by the Conquistadores—these others are mere plow animals."

But the horse that really set the tongues wagging in Santa Lucia and in Candon was Allahsan, a gleaming sorrel who belonged to Bishop Aglipay and was said to share the Bishop's magic power. There were magic wings on his hooves, it was said, that let him carry the Bishop from Manila to Candon in one flying night.

Another boaster was the Municipal Treasurer—the Tesero, who had recently acquired a silver-white horse, Purao, the horse with the speed and power of the foam-capped waves.

The Chief of Police hung his head in shame now. His Castano had once been the pride of Santa Lucia, had beaten Katarman—the black satin horse from the near-by barrio of Katarman who had so often humbled Santa Lucia's pride. Much as the horses of Santa Lucia set their owners to boasting against one another, all united against Katarman. Katarman, so the tale went, was so enraged if another horse challenged him that he ran until the muscles of his broad withers parted and blood spattered from him upon his rider, but he never faltered till his race was won.

These were the boasts and boasters I had set out to dust with defeat.

The Horse of the Sword

Winter was soon gone, the rice harvested and the sugar cane milled. Graduation from high school approached. At last came the Feria day, and people gathered, the ladies in sheer flowing gowns of many colors, the men in loose flowing shirts over cool white trousers. Excitement was a wild thing in the wind at the Feria, for the news of the challenge of the wonder horse MoroGlory had spread. I could hear many people shouting "*Caballo a Bintuangin*—The Horse of the Sword." These people were glad to see the once despised outlaw colt turn by magic change into the barrio's pride. They were cheering for my horse, but the riders of the other horses weren't cheering. I was a boy, riding an untried and yet feared horse. They didn't want me there, so they raised the entrance fee. But Father had fighting blood also, and he borrowed the money for the extra fee.

As we paraded past the laughing, shouting crowds in the Plaza, the peddlers who shouted "Sinuman—Delicious Cascarones" stopped selling these coconut sweets and began to shout the praises of their favorite. I heard them calling: "Allahsan for me. Allahsan has magic hooves." The people of Katarman's village were very loud. They cried out: "Katarman will win. Katarman has the muscles of the carabao.[3] Katarman has the speed of the deer."

The race was to be a long-distance trial of speed and endurance—run on the Provincial Road for a racetrack. A mile down to the river, then back to the Judge's stand in the Plaza.

MoroGlory looked them over, all the big-name horses. I think he measured his speed against them and knew they didn't have

enough. I looked them over too. I was so excited, yet I knew I must be on guard as the man who walks where the big snakes hide. These riders were experienced; so were their horses. MoroGlory had my teaching only. I had run him this same course many times. MoroGlory must not spend his strength on the first mile; he must save his speed for a sprint. In the high school, I had made the track team. An American coach had taught me, and I held this teaching in my head now.

The starter gave his signal and the race began. Allahsan led out at a furious pace; the other horses set themselves to overtake him. It hurt my pride to eat the dust of all the others—all the way out the first mile. I knew it must be done. "Oomh, Easy," I commanded, and MoroGlory obeyed me as always. We were last, but MoroGlory ran that mile feather-light on his feet.

At the river's bank all the horses turned quickly to begin the fateful last mile. The Flagman said, "Too late, Boy," but I knew MoroGlory.

I loosened the grip I held and he spurted ahead in flying leaps. In a few space-eating strides he overtook the tiring Allahsan. The pacesetter was breathing in great gasps. "Where are your magic wings?" I jeered as we passed.

"Kiph," I urged MoroGlory. I had no whip. I spoke to my horse and knew he would do his best. I saw the other riders lashing their mounts. Only MoroGlory ran as he willed.

Oh, it was a thrill, the way MoroGlory sped along, flew along, his hooves hardly seeming to touch the ground. The wind whipped at my face and I yelled just for pleasure. MoroGlory thought I was commanding more speed and he gave it.

---

3. **carabao:** water buffalo

He flattened himself closer to the ground as his long legs reached forward for more and more. Up, and up. Past the strong horses from Abra, past the bright Tango. Bandirado Boyo was next in line. "How the Presidente's daughter will cry to see her Bandirado Boyo come trailing home, his banner tail in the dust," I said to myself as MoroGlory surged past him. The Tesero's Purao yielded his place without a struggle.

Now there was only Katarman, the black thunder horse ahead, but several lengths ahead. Could MoroGlory make up this handicap in this short distance, for we were at the Big Mango tree—this was the final quarter.

"Here it is, MoroGlory. This is the big test." I shouted. "Show Katarman how your Sword conquers him."

Oh, yes, MoroGlory could do it. And he did. He ran shoulder to shoulder with Katarman.

I saw that Katarman's rider was swinging his whip wide. I saw it came near to MoroGlory's head. I shouted to the man and the wind brought his answering curse at me. I must decide now—decide between MoroGlory's danger and the winning of the race. That whip might blind him. I knew no winning was worth that. I pulled against him, giving up the race.

MoroGlory had always obeyed me. He always responded to my lightest touch. But this time my sharp pull at his bridle brought no response. He had the bit between his teeth. Whip or no whip, he would not break his stride. And so he pulled ahead of Katarman.

"MoroGlory—The Horse of the Sword," the crowd cheered as the gray horse swept past the judges, a winner by two lengths.

I leaped from his back and caught his head. Blood streamed down the side of his head, but his eyes were unharmed. The Sword on this shoulder was touched with a few drops of his own blood.

Men also leaped at Katarman, dragged his rider off and punished him before the Judges could interfere. The winner's wreath and bright ribbon went to MoroGlory, and we paraded in great glory. I was so proud. The Horse of the Sword had run free, without a whip, without spurs. He had proved his leadership and power. He had proved himself a "true mount for a chieftain, a free man's fighting horse," as the old Wise Man had said.

Golden days followed for MoroGlorioso. Again and again we raced,—in Vigan, in Abra, and always MoroGlory won.

Then came the day when my Father said, "The time has come for you, my son, to prove your Sword, as MoroGlory proved his. You must learn to be a leader," Father said.

And so I sailed away to America, to let the world know my will. As MoroGlory had proved himself, so must I.

About the Author

Manuel Buaken is a Filipino writer who was educated in American universities. According to a number of accounts, this story is based on an incident that occurred during Buaken's youth.

THINK ABOUT THE STORY. The following questions help you check your reading comprehension. Put an *x* in the box next to the correct answer.

1. "The Horse of the Sword" is mainly about
   - ☐ a. how a boy turns a bad-tempered, shaggy horse into a champion.
   - ☐ b. the dangers that rider and horse face during a close race.
   - ☐ c. why a boy decides to disobey his parents.

2. The most important thing Maning noticed about the "worthless" colt was that
   - ☐ a. it was so thin that its ribs almost stuck through its hide.
   - ☐ b. its body had whip marks on it.
   - ☐ c. its mouth was very tender and bled easily.

3. When he raced MoroGlory, Maning
   - ☐ a. whipped the horse to urge it to run faster.
   - ☐ b. never said a word to the horse.
   - ☐ c. spoke to the horse and did not use a whip or spurs.

4. At the end of the story, Maning was willing to lose the race
   - ☐ a. because he realized that the other horse ran faster.
   - ☐ b. to protect the eyesight of his horse.
   - ☐ c. because he thought that MoroGlory was not trying hard enough to win.

HANDLE NEW VOCABULARY WORDS. The following questions check your vocabulary skills. Put an *x* in the box next to the correct answer. Each vocabulary word appears in the story.

1. Few people were interested in an uncombed, untidy colt with a mangy hide. What is the meaning of the word *mangy*?
   - ☐ a. sensitive or thin
   - ☐ b. uncontrollable or wild
   - ☐ c. dirty and shabby

2. When Maning approached the horse, it snorted and "backed away skittishly." The word *skittishly* means
   - ☐ a. in a fascinated way.
   - ☐ b. nervously.
   - ☐ c. contentedly.

3. The horse's "proud arched neck" suggested that it came from aristocracy. As used here, the word *aristocracy* means
   - ☐ a. a country in Asia.
   - ☐ b. poverty or being poor.
   - ☐ c. a noble background.

4. The trees made "dappled shade" around the bungalow. Which of the following best defines the word *dappled*?
   - ☐ a. marked with spots
   - ☐ b. brilliant or very bright
   - ☐ c. astounding or beyond belief

	× 5 =	
NUMBER CORRECT		YOUR SCORE

	× 5 =	
NUMBER CORRECT		YOUR SCORE

EXAMINE STORY ELEMENTS. The following questions check your knowledge of story elements. Put an *x* in the box next to each correct answer.

1. Which statement best *characterizes* Maning?
   - ☐ a. He demonstrated poor judgment in selecting a horse.
   - ☐ b. He had a keen eye for horses and was strong-minded and determined.
   - ☐ c. Generally, he was rebellious toward his parents and often defied them.

2. The story's main *conflict* occurs when
   - ☐ a. Maning's father says he will set the horse free if Maning doesn't stop neglecting his lessons.
   - ☐ b. Maning's mother learns that her son has disobeyed her.
   - ☐ c. MoroGlory races against Katarman.

3. Of the following events, which happened last in the *plot* of the story?
   - ☐ a. MoroGlory disregarded Maning and charged ahead to victory.
   - ☐ b. A wise old man warned Maning to get rid of the horse.
   - ☐ c. Maning carefully brushed and cleaned MoroGlory's coat.

4. What is the story's *theme*?
   - ☐ a. Kindness and hard work help produce a champion.
   - ☐ b. Many veteran horse traders do not know a good horse when they see it.
   - ☐ c. It is almost impossible to tame a high-spirited "outlaw" horse.

MASTER CRITICAL THINKING. The following questions check your critical thinking skills. Put an *x* in the box next to each correct answer.

1. At first MoroGlory hardly looked impressive, but the horse proved to be outstanding. This suggests that
   - ☐ a. first impressions are usually correct.
   - ☐ b. it is foolish to rely on the advice of others.
   - ☐ c. appearances can be deceiving.

2. We may infer that Maning's father paid just a few pesos for the colt because
   - ☐ a. he was too poor to pay more.
   - ☐ b. the horse was considered almost worthless.
   - ☐ c. he was friendly with the sellers, so they gave him a good price.

3. Probably one reason MoroGlory developed into such a fine racehorse was that
   - ☐ a. the horse was thin, so it was able to run very fast.
   - ☐ b. the horse had "good blood" and came from fine stables.
   - ☐ c. no one had raced the horse before, so it was eager and enthusiastic.

4. Judging by what occurred in the story, it is reasonable to predict that Maning
   - ☐ a. will be successful in America.
   - ☐ b. will become conceited and will make many enemies.
   - ☐ c. will soon train many other "untamable" horses.

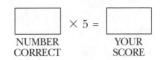

	× 5 =	
NUMBER CORRECT		YOUR SCORE

EXPLORE THE WRITER'S CRAFT. The following questions check your knowledge of skills related to the craft of writing. Put an *x* in the box next to each correct answer. You may refer to pages 4 and 5.

1. On the basis of the outcome of the story, the mark of the sword on MoroGlory is a symbol that represents
   ☐ a. something evil.
   ☐ b. a warning to stay away.
   ☐ c. leadership and power.

2. To Father, the boasts of the others "had been mosquito bites in his mind." This sentence contains
   ☐ a. a simile that compares Father to a mosquito.
   ☐ b. a metaphor that compares stinging words to insect bites.
   ☐ c. personification in which a mosquito has the power to speak.

3. Since MoroGlory ran the first mile slowly, Maning had "to eat the dust of all the others." What is true of this sentence?
   ☐ a. It contains figurative language.
   ☐ b. It provides an allusion.
   ☐ c. It illustrates onomatopoeia.

4. "These were the boasts and boasters I had set out to dust with defeat." This sentence contains
   ☐ a. irony.
   ☐ b. a moral.
   ☐ c. alliteration.

☐ × 5 = ☐
NUMBER   YOUR
CORRECT   SCORE

Questions for Writing and Discussion

- Maning stated, "I'll show you and everybody else what a mistake you made about my horse." What "mistake" did Maning mean? How did Maning prove everyone wrong?
- Why had MoroGlory been an "untamable outlaw"? Explain how Maning tamed the colt.
- Maning did not race MoroGlory the usual, or traditional, way. Support this statement by providing examples.
- Offer examples from the story to illustrate traits that Maning and MoroGlory had in common.
- Why did Maning leave for America after he had achieved such success?

See additional questions for extended writing on pages 78 and 79.

Use the boxes below to total your scores for the exercises. Then record your scores on pages 224 and 225.

☐ **T**HINK ABOUT THE STORY
   +
☐ **H**ANDLE NEW VOCABULARY WORDS
   +
☐ **E**XAMINE STORY ELEMENTS
   +
☐ **M**ASTER CRITICAL THINKING
   +
☐ **E**XPLORE THE WRITER'S CRAFT
   ▼
☐ **Total Score:** Story 4

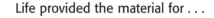

Life provided the material for . . .

Geraldine Moore the Poet

by Toni Cade Bambara

Geraldine paused at the corner to pull up her knee socks. The rubber bands she was using to hold them up made her legs itch. She dropped her books on the sidewalk while she gave a good scratch. But when she pulled the socks up again, two fingers poked right through the top of her left one.

"That stupid dog," she muttered to herself, grabbing her books and crossing against traffic. "First he chews up my gym suit and gets me into trouble, and now my socks."

Geraldine shifted her books to the other hand and kept muttering angrily to herself about Mrs. Watson's dog, which she minded two days a week for a dollar. She passed the hot-dog man on the corner and waved. He shrugged as if to say business was very bad.

Must be, she thought to herself. *Three guys before you had to pack up and forget it. Nobody's got hot-dog money around here.*

Geraldine turned down her street, wondering what her sister Anita would have for her lunch. She was glad she didn't have to eat the free lunches in high school any more. She was sick of the funny-looking tomato soup and the dried-out cheese sandwiches and those oranges that were more green than orange.

When Geraldine's mother first took sick and went away, Geraldine had been on her own except when Miss Gladys next door came in on Thursdays and cleaned the apartment and made a meat loaf so Geraldine could have dinner. But in those days Geraldine never quite managed to get breakfast for herself. So she'd sit through social studies class, scraping her feet to cover up the noise of her stomach growling.

Now Anita, Geraldine's older sister, was living at home waiting for her husband to get out of the Army. She usually had something good for lunch—chicken and dumplings if she managed to get up in time, or baked ham from the night before and sweet-potato bread. But even if there was only a hot dog and some baked beans— sometimes just a TV dinner if those soap operas kept Anita glued to the TV set— anything was better than the noisy school lunchroom where monitors kept pushing you into a straight line or rushing you to the tables. Anything was better than that.

Geraldine was almost home when she stopped dead. Right outside her building was a pile of furniture and some boxes. That wasn't anything new. She had seen people get put out in the street before, but this time the ironing board looked familiar.

And she recognized the big, ugly sofa standing on its arm, its underbelly showing the hole where Mrs. Watson's dog had gotten to it.

Miss Gladys was sitting on the stoop, and she looked up and took off her glasses. "Well, Gerry," she said slowly, wiping her glasses on the hem of her dress, "looks like you'll be staying with me for a while." She looked at the men carrying out a big box with an old doll sticking up over the edge. "Anita's upstairs. Go on up and get your lunch."

Geraldine stepped past the old woman and almost bumped into the superintendent. He took off his cap to wipe away the sweat.

"Darn shame," he said to no one in particular. "Poor people sure got a hard row to hoe."

"That's the truth," said Miss Gladys, standing up with her hands on her hips to watch the men set things on the sidewalk.

Upstairs, Geraldine went into the apartment and found Anita in the kitchen.

"I dunno, Gerry," Anita said. "I just don't know what we're going to do. But everything's going to be all right soon as Ma gets well." Anita's voice cracked as she set a bowl of soup before Geraldine.

"What's this?" Geraldine said.

"It's tomato soup, Gerry."

Geraldine was about to say something. But when she looked up at her big sister, she saw how Anita's face was getting all twisted as she began to cry.

That afternoon, Mr. Stern, the geometry teacher, started drawing cubes and cylinders on the board. Geraldine sat at her desk adding up a column of figures in her notebook—the rent, the light and gas bills, a new gym suit, some socks. Maybe they would move somewhere else, and she could have her own room. Geraldine turned the squares and triangles into little houses in the country.

"For your homework," Mr. Stern was saying with his back to the class, "set up your problems this way." He wrote GIVEN: in large letters, and then gave the formula for the first problem. Then he wrote TO FIND: and listed three items they were to include in their answers.

Geraldine started to raise her hand to ask what all these squares and angles had to do with solving real problems, like the ones she had. *Better not,* she warned herself, and sat on her hands. *Your big mouth got you in trouble last term.*

In hygiene class, Mrs. Potter kept saying that the body was a wonderful machine. Every time Geraldine looked up from her notebook, she would hear the same thing. "Right now your body is manufacturing all the proteins and tissues and energy you will need to get through tomorrow."

And Geraldine kept wondering, *How? How does my body know what it will need, when I don't even know what I'll need to get through tomorrow?*

As she headed down the hall to her next class, Geraldine remembered that she hadn't done the homework for English. Mrs. Scott had said to write a poem, and Geraldine had meant to do it at lunchtime. After all, there was nothing to it—a flower here, a raindrop there, moon, June, rose, nose. But the men carrying off the furniture had made her forget.

"And now put away your books," Mrs. Scott was saying as Geraldine tried to scribble a poem quickly. "Today we can give King Arthur's knights a rest. Let's talk about poetry."

Mrs. Scott moved up and down the aisles, talking about her favorite poems and reciting a line now and then. She got very excited whenever she passed a desk and could pick up the homework from a student who had remembered to do the assignment.

"A poem is your own special way of saying what you feel and what you see," Mrs. Scott went on, her lips moist. It was her favorite subject.

"Some poets write about the light that . . . that . . . makes the world sunny," she said, passing Geraldine's desk. "Sometimes an idea takes the form of a picture—an image."

For almost half an hour, Mrs. Scott stood at the front of the room, reading poems and talking about the lives of the great poets. Geraldine drew more houses, and designs for curtains.

"So for those who haven't done their homework, try it now," Mrs. Scott said. "Try expressing what it is like to be . . . to be alive in this . . . this glorious world."

"Oh, brother," Geraldine muttered to herself as Mrs. Scott moved up and down the aisles again, waving her hands and leaning over the students' shoulders and saying, "That's nice," or "Keep trying." Finally she came to Geraldine's desk and stopped, looking down at her.

"I can't write a poem," Geraldine said flatly, before she even realized she was going to speak at all. She said it very loudly, and the whole class looked up.

"And why not?" Mrs. Scott asked, looking hurt.

"I can't write a poem, Mrs. Scott, because nothing lovely's been happening in my life. I haven't seen a flower since Mother's Day, and the sun don't even shine on my side of the street. No robins come sing on my window sill."

Geraldine swallowed hard. She thought about saying that her father doesn't even come to visit any more, but changed her mind. "Just the rain comes," she went on, "and the bills come, and the men to move out our furniture. I'm sorry, but I can't write no pretty poem."

Teddy Johnson leaned over and was about to giggle and crack the whole class up, but Mrs. Scott looked so serious that he changed his mind.

"You have just said the most . . . the most poetic thing, Geraldine Moore," said Mrs. Scott. Her hands flew up to touch the silk scarf around her neck. "'Nothing lovely's been happening in my life.'" She repeated it so quietly that everyone had to lean forward to hear.

"Class," Mrs. Scott said very sadly, clearing her throat, "you have just heard the best poem you will ever hear." She went to the board and stood there for a long time staring at the chalk in her hand.

"I'd like you to copy it down," she said. She wrote it just as Geraldine had said it, bad grammar and all.

Nothing lovely's been happening in my life.
I haven't seen a flower since Mother's Day,
And the sun don't even shine on my side of
 the street.
No robins come sing on my window sill.
Just the rain comes, and the bills come,
And the men to move out our furniture.
I'm sorry, but I can't write no pretty poem.

Mrs. Scott stopped writing, but she kept her back to the class for a long time—long after Geraldine had closed her notebook.

And even when the bell rang, and everyone came over to smile at Geraldine or to tap her on the shoulder or to kid her about being the school poet, Geraldine waited for Mrs. Scott to put the chalk down and turn around. Finally Geraldine stacked up her books and started to leave. Then she thought she heard a whimper—the way Mrs. Watson's dog whimpered sometimes—and she saw Mrs. Scott's shoulders shake a little.

About the Author

Toni Cade Bambara (1939–1995) had a distinguished career as an author and as a professor of English and of African American studies. She was born Toni Cade in New York City, the setting of many of her stories. She added "Bambara" to her name after she found the word on a sketchbook in her great-grandmother's trunk.

Bambara directed educational and social programs and taught every level of school, from kindergarten through college. She edited the anthologies *The Black Woman* and *Tales and Stories for Black Folks.* Among Bambara's best-known works are *The Salt Eaters,* a novel, and *Gorilla, My Love,* a collection of short stories.

THINK ABOUT THE STORY. The following
questions help you check your reading
comprehension. Put an *x* in the box
next to the correct answer.

1. This story is mainly about
   - □ a. a typical day at an unidentified high
     school.
   - □ b. how a high school student creates
     a poem by expressing her strong
     feelings.
   - □ c. an English lesson about poetry and
     the lives of great poets.

2. After her mother became ill, Geraldine
   - □ a. asked her sister, Anita, for money.
   - □ b. went to live with her grandparents.
   - □ c. lived alone for a while.

3. According to Mrs. Scott, poetry is about
   - □ a. making up rhymes that use words
     like *June* and *moon.*
   - □ b. telling a story that is very beautiful.
   - □ c. the special way that a person says
     what she or he feels.

4. After the bell rang, Mrs. Scott
   - □ a. kept her back to the class and did
     not turn around.
   - □ b. tapped Geraldine on the shoulder.
   - □ c. kidded Geraldine about being the
     class poet.

HANDLE NEW VOCABULARY WORDS. The
following questions check your vocabulary
skills. Put an *x* in the box next to the
correct answer. Each vocabulary word
appears in the story.

1. She saw a hole in the underbelly of the
   sofa. As used here, *underbelly* means
   - □ a. soft fabric.
   - □ b. lowest part.
   - □ c. pillow.

2. The body continually manufactures all
   the proteins one needs. Which best
   defines *proteins*?
   - □ a. certain substances essential to the
     growth and repair of human tissue
   - □ b. thoughts and ideas that an individ-
     ual needs to communicate
   - □ c. the emotions that determine the
     way someone feels

3. In geometry, the class used a formula to
   solve a problem. Here, *formula* means
   - □ a. the chemical ingredients that make
     up a compound
   - □ b. a mathematical statement used for
     figuring out answers
   - □ c. a recipe or prescription

4. "Sometimes an idea takes the form of a
   picture—an image." As used here, the
   word *image* means
   - □ a. art underserving of its fame.
   - □ b. something false or untrue.
   - □ c. a description, comparison, or figure
     of speech.

☐ × 5 = ☐

NUMBER
CORRECT

YOUR
SCORE

☐ × 5 = ☐

NUMBER
CORRECT

YOUR
SCORE

EXAMINE STORY ELEMENTS. The following questions check your knowledge of story elements. Put an *x* in the box next to each correct answer.

1. Of the following events, which happened first in the *plot* of the story?
   - ☐ a. Geraldine recognized the furniture in the street outside her building.
   - ☐ b. Mrs. Scott wrote Geraldine's poem on the board.
   - ☐ c. Geraldine started to raise her hand in geometry class.

2. The *setting* in which most of the story takes place is
   - ☐ a. a house.
   - ☐ b. a street.
   - ☐ c. a school.

3. "I can't write a poem." Who uttered this line of *dialogue* and why?
   - ☐ a. Mrs. Scott, because she believed that only great poets were capable of writing poetry
   - ☐ b. Geraldine Moore, because nothing lovely had happened in her life lately
   - ☐ c. Anita, because she was too busy doing various chores

4. The *narrator* of the story is
   - ☐ a. Geraldine Moore.
   - ☐ b. the author.
   - ☐ c. Mrs. Scott.

MASTER CRITICAL THINKING. The following questions check your critical thinking skills. Put an *x* in the box next to each correct answer.

1. When Geraldine saw familiar furniture in the street, she probably felt
   - ☐ a. troubled and sad.
   - ☐ b. curious about why the furniture was there.
   - ☐ c. pleased that someone had removed the old worn items.

2. The fact that Geraldine "turned the squares and triangles into little houses in the country" in geometry class suggests that she
   - ☐ a. was planning to become an artist or an illustrator.
   - ☐ b. was seriously considering a career as an architect.
   - ☐ c. hoped to have a house of her own one day.

3. Evidence in the story indicates that after Mrs. Scott wrote Geraldine's poem on the board, the other students
   - ☐ a. ignored Geraldine.
   - ☐ b. congratulated Geraldine.
   - ☐ c. felt jealous of Geraldine.

4. We may infer from the last paragraph that Mrs. Scott was
   - ☐ a. not concerned about her students.
   - ☐ b. moved, upset, and emotional.
   - ☐ c. thinking about the next class she was going to teach.

☐ × 5 = ☐
NUMBER CORRECT   YOUR SCORE

☐ × 5 = ☐
NUMBER CORRECT   YOUR SCORE

EXPLORE THE WRITER'S CRAFT. The following questions check your knowledge of skills related to the craft of writing. Put an *x* in the box next to each correct answer. You may refer to pages 4 and 5.

1. Some programs "kept Anita glued to the TV set." This sentence contains figurative language that means
   - ☐ a. whenever Anita was stuck at home, she enjoyed watching TV.
   - ☐ b. when Anita sat down to watch TV, it was difficult for her to get up.
   - ☐ c. Anita couldn't take her eyes away from some TV programs.

2. Mrs. Potter said that "the body was a wonderful machine." This sentence contains
   - ☐ a. a metaphor.
   - ☐ b. a simile.
   - ☐ c. alliteration.

3. Which of the following illustrates irony?
   - ☐ a. asking a group of students to try writing a poem
   - ☐ b. complaining about a dog that chews up clothing
   - ☐ c. telling a dejected girl that she lives in a "glorious world"

4. Geraldine wrote that the sun didn't "even shine on [her] side of the street." This can be viewed as
   - ☐ a. a symbol that things will improve.
   - ☐ b. figurative language that expresses unhappiness.
   - ☐ c. an example of onomatopoeia.

```
┌──────┐        ┌──────┐
│      │  × 5 = │      │
└──────┘        └──────┘
NUMBER           YOUR
CORRECT          SCORE
```

Questions for Writing and Discussion

- Why had Geraldine forgotten to do her homework for English?
- Mrs. Scott told the students that they had just heard the best poem that they will ever hear. How can the reader tell that she was sincere?
- As Geraldine was about to leave, "she heard a whimper," and then "she saw Mrs. Scott's shoulders shake a little." What has happened?
- Find the exact words that Mrs. Scott used to define a poem. How effectively does Geraldine's poem satisfy that definition?

See additional questions for extended writing on pages 78 and 79.

Use the boxes below to total your scores for the exercises. Then record your scores on pages 224 and 225.

```
┌──────┐
│      │  THINK ABOUT THE STORY
└──────┘
  +
┌──────┐
│      │  HANDLE NEW VOCABULARY WORDS
└──────┘
  +
┌──────┐
│      │  EXAMINE STORY ELEMENTS
└──────┘
  +
┌──────┐
│      │  MASTER CRITICAL THINKING
└──────┘
  +
┌──────┐
│      │  EXPLORE THE WRITER'S CRAFT
└──────┘
  ▼
┌──────┐
│      │  Total Score: Story 5
└──────┘
```

Customs, tradition, and a stubborn man stand between Chee and . . .

Chee's Daughter

by Juanita Platero and Siyowin Miller

The hat told the story, the big black drooping Stetson.[1] It was not at the proper angle, the proper rakish angle for so young a Navaho.[2] There was no song, and that was not in keeping either. There should have been at least a humming, a faint, all-to-himself "he he he heya," for it was a good horse he was riding, a slender-legged, high-stepping buckskin that would race the wind with light knee urging. This was a day for singing, a warm winter day, when the touch of the sun upon the back belied the snow high on distant mountains.

Wind warmed by the sun touched his high-boned cheeks like flicker feathers, and still he rode on silently, deeper into Little Canyon, until the red rock walls rose straight upward from the stream bed and only a narrow piece of blue sky hung above. Abruptly the sky widened where the canyon walls were pushed back to make a wide place, as though in ancient times an angry stream had tried to go all ways at once.

This was home—this wide place in the canyon—levels of jagged rock and levels of rich red earth. This was home to Chee, the rider of the buckskin, as it had been to many generations before him.

He stopped his horse at the stream and sat looking across the narrow ribbon of water to the bare-branched peach trees. He was seeing them each springtime with their age-gnarled limbs transfigured beneath veils of blossom pink; he was seeing them in autumn laden with their yellow fruit, small

and sweet. Then his eyes searched out the indistinct furrows of the fields beside the stream, where each year the corn and beans and squash drank thirstily of the overflow from summer rains. Chee was trying to outweigh today's bitter betrayal of hope by gathering to himself these reminders of the integrity of the land. Land did not cheat! His mind lingered deliberately on all the days spent here in the sun caring for the young plants, his songs to the earth and to the life springing from it—"In the middle of the wide field . . . Yellow Corn Boy . . . He has started both ways . . ."—then the harvest and repayment in full measure. Here was the old feeling of wholeness and of oneness with the sun and earth and growing things.

Chee urged the buckskin toward the family compound where, secure in a recess of overhanging rock, was his mother's dome-shaped hogan,[3] red rock and red adobe like the ground on which it nestled. Not far from the hogan was the half circle of brush like a dark shadow against the canyon wall—corral for sheep and goats. Farther from the hogan, in full circle, stood the horse corral made of heavy cedar branches sternly interlocked. Chee's long, thin lips curved into a smile as he passed his daughter's tiny hogan squatted like a round Pueblo[4] oven beside the corral. He remembered the summer day when together they sat back on their heels and plastered wet adobe all about the circling wall of rock and the woven dome of pinyon[5] twigs.

---

1. **Stetson:** a hat, usually with a wide brim and a high crown

2. **Navaho:** a member of the Navaho tribe; the largest Indian tribe in the United States, living in the Southwest

3. **hogan:** a Navaho house; often made with logs and adobe, a claylike earth

4. **Pueblo:** in the style of certain Indian tribes in the Southwest; an oven made of adobe

5. **pinyon:** a shrublike pine tree that grows in the Southwest

How his family laughed when the Little One herded the bewildered chickens into her tiny hogan as the first snow fell.

Then the smile faded from Chee's lips, and his eyes darkened as he tied his horse to the corral post and turned to the strangely empty compound. "Someone has told them," he thought, "and they are inside weeping." He passed his mother's deserted loom on the south side of the hogan and pulled the rude wooden door toward him, bowing his head, hunching his shoulders to get inside.

His mother sat sideways by the center fire, her feet drawn up under her full skirts. Her hands were busy kneading dough in the chipped white basin. With her head down, her voice was muffled when she said, "The meal will soon be ready, Son."

Chee passed his father sitting against the wall, hat over his eyes as though asleep. He passed his older sister, who sat turning mutton ribs on a crude wire grill over the coals, noticed tears dropping on her hands. "She cared more for my wife than I realized," he thought.

Then, because something must be said sometime, he tossed the black Stetson upon a bulging sack of wool and said, "You have heard, then." He could not shut from his mind how confidently he had set the handsome new hat on his head that very morning, slanting the wide brim over one eye: he was going to see his wife and today he would ask the doctors about bringing her home; last week she had looked so much better.

His sister nodded but did not speak. His mother sniffled and passed her velveteen sleeve beneath her nose. Chee sat down, leaning against the wall. "I suppose I was a fool for hoping all the time. I should have

expected this. Few of our people get well from the coughing sickness.[6] But *she* seemed to be getting better."

His mother was crying aloud now and blowing her nose noisily on her skirt. His father sat up, speaking gently to her.

Chee shifted his position and started a cigarette. His mind turned back to the Little One. At least she was too small to understand what had happened, the Little One who had been born three years before in the sanitarium where his wife was being treated for the coughing sickness, the Little One he had brought home to his mother's hogan to be nursed by his sister whose baby was a few months older. As she grew fat cheeked and sturdy legged, she followed him about like a shadow; somehow her baby mind had grasped that of all those at the hogan who cared for her and played with her, he—Chee—belonged most to her. She sat cross-legged at his elbow when he worked silver at the forge; she rode before him in the saddle when he drove the horses to water; often she lay wakeful on her sheep pelts until he stretched out for the night in the darkened hogan and she could snuggle warm against him.

Chee blew smoke slowly, and some of the sadness left his dark eyes as he said, "It is not as bad as it might be. It is not as though we are left with nothing."

Chee's sister arose, sobs catching in her throat, and rushed past him out the doorway. Chee sat upright, a terrible fear possessing him. For a moment his mouth could make no sound. Then: "The Little One! Mother, where is she?"

---

6. **the coughing sickness:** tuberculosis, a disease that affects the lungs

His mother turned her stricken face to him. "Your wife's people came after her this morning. They heard yesterday of their daughter's death through the trader at Red Sands."

Chee started to protest, but his mother shook her head slowly. "I didn't expect they would want the Little One either. But there is nothing you can do. She is a girl child and belongs to her mother's people; it is custom."

Frowning, Chee got to his feet, grinding his cigarette into the dirt floor. "Custom! When did my wife's parents begin thinking about custom? Why, the hogan where they live doesn't even face the East!" He started toward the door. "Perhaps I can overtake them. Perhaps they don't realize how much we want her here with us. I'll ask them to give my daughter back to me. Surely, they won't refuse."

His mother stopped him gently with her outstretched hand. "You couldn't overtake them now. They were in the trader's car. Eat and rest, and think more about this."

"Have you forgotten how things have always been between you and your wife's people?" his father said.

That night, Chee's thoughts were troubled—half-forgotten incidents became disturbingly vivid—but early the next morning he saddled the buckskin and set out for the settlement of Red Sands. Even though his father-in-law, Old Man Fat, might laugh, Chee knew that he must talk to him. There were some things to which Old Man Fat might listen.

Chee rode the first part of the fifteen miles to Red Sands expectantly. The sight of sandstone buttes[7] near Cottonwood Spring reddening in the morning sun brought a song almost to his lips. He twirled his reins in salute to the small boy herding sheep toward many-colored Butterfly Mountain, watched with pleasure the feathers of smoke rising against tree-darkened western mesas from the hogans sheltered there. But as he approached the familiar settlement sprawled in mushroom growth along the highway, he began to feel as though a scene from a bad dream was becoming real.

Several cars were parked around the trading store, which was built like two log hogans side by side, with red gas pumps in front and a sign across the tarpaper roofs: *Red Sands Trading Post—Groceries Gasoline Cold Drinks Sandwiches Indian Curios.* Back of the trading post an unpainted frame house and outbuildings squatted on the drab, treeless land. Chee and the Little One's mother had lived there when they stayed with his wife's people. That was according to custom—living with one's wife's people—but Chee had never been convinced that it was custom alone which prompted Old Man Fat and his wife to insist that their daughter bring her husband to live at the trading post.

Beside the Post was a large hogan of logs, with brightly painted pseudo-Navaho[8] designs on the roof—a hogan with smoke-smudged windows and a garish[9] blue door, which faced north to the highway. Old Man Fat had offered Chee a hogan like this one. The trader would build it if he and his wife

---

7. **butte:** (by$\overline{oo}$t) a steep hill that has a flat top and stands alone

8. **pseudo-Navaho:** imitation Navaho

9. **garish:** loud and flashy; showy

would live there and Chee would work at his forge making silver jewelry where tourists could watch him. But Chee had asked instead for a piece of land for a cornfield and help in building a hogan far back from the highway and a corral for the sheep he had brought to this marriage.

A cold wind blowing down from the mountains began to whistle about Chee's ears. It flapped the gaudy Navaho rugs which were hung in one long, bright line to attract tourists. It swayed the sign *Navaho Weaver at Work* beside the loom where Old Man Fat's Wife sat hunched in her striped blanket, patting the colored thread of a design into place with a wooden comb. Tourists stood watching the weaver. More tourists stood in a knot before the hogan where the sign said: *See Inside a Real Navaho Home 25¢.*

Then the knot seemed to unravel as a few people returned to their cars; some had cameras; and there against the blue door Chee saw the Little One standing uncertainly. The wind was plucking at her new purple blouse and wide green skirt; it freed truant strands of soft, dark hair from the meager queue[10] into which it had been tied with white yarn.

"Isn't she cunning!" one of the women tourists was saying as she turned away.

Chee's lips tightened as he began to look around for Old Man Fat. Finally he saw him passing among the tourists, collecting coins.

Then the Little One saw Chee. The uncertainty left her face, and she darted through the crowd as her father swung down from his horse. Chee lifted her in his arms, hugging her tight. While he listened to her breathless chatter, he watched Old Man Fat bearing down on them, scowling.

As his father-in-law walked heavily across the graveled lot, Chee was reminded of a statement his mother sometimes made: "When you see a fat Navaho, you see one who hasn't worked for what he has."

Old Man Fat was fattest in the middle. There was indolence in his walk even though he seemed to hurry, indolence in his cheeks so plump they made his eyes squint, eyes now smoldering with anger.

Some of the tourists were getting into their cars and driving away. The old man said belligerently to Chee, "Why do you come here? To spoil our business? To drive people away?"

"I came to talk with you," Chee answered, trying to keep his voice steady as he faced the old man.

"We have nothing to talk about," Old Man Fat blustered and did not offer to touch Chee's extended hand.

"It's about the Little One." Chee settled his daughter more comfortably against his hip as he weighed carefully all the words he had planned to say. "We are going to miss her very much. It wouldn't be so bad if we knew that *part* of each year she could be with us. That might help you too. You and your wife are no longer young people, and you have no young ones here to depend upon." Chee chose his next words remembering the thriftlessness of his wife's parents, and their greed. "Perhaps we could share the care of this little one. Things are good with us. So much snow this year will make lots of grass for the sheep. We have good land for corn and melons."

---

10. **queue:** (kyū) a braid of hair hanging down from the back of the head

Chee's words did not have the expected effect. Old Man Fat was enraged. "Farmers all of you! Long-haired farmers! Do you think everyone must bend his back over the short-handled hoe in order to have food to eat?" His tone changed as he began to brag a little. "We not only have all the things from cans at the trader's, but when the Pueblos come past here on their way to town we buy their salty jerked mutton,[11] young corn for roasting, dried sweet peaches."

Chee's dark eyes surveyed the land along the highway as the old man continued to brag about being "progressive." *He* no longer was tied to the land. He and his wife made money easily and could *buy* all the things they wanted. Chee realized too late that he had stumbled into the old argument between himself and his wife's parents. They had never understood his feeling about the land—that a man took care of his land and it in turn took care of him. Old Man Fat and his wife scoffed at him, called him a Pueblo farmer, all during that summer when he planted and weeded and harvested. Yet they ate the green corn in their mutton stews, and the chili paste from the fresh ripe chilies, and the tortillas from the cornmeal his wife ground. None of this working and sweating in the sun for Old Man Fat, who talked proudly of his easy way of living—collecting money from the trader who rented his strip of land beside the highway, collecting money from the tourists.

Yet Chee had once won that argument. His wife had shared his belief in the integrity of the earth, that jobs and people might fail one but the earth never would. After that first year she had turned from her own people and gone with Chee to Little Canyon.

Old Man Fat was reaching for the Little One. "Don't be coming here with plans for my daughter's daughter," he warned. "If you try to make trouble, I'll take the case to the government man in town."

The impulse was strong in Chee to turn and ride off while he still had the Little One in his arms. But he knew his time of victory would be short. His own family would uphold the old custom of children, especially girl children, belonging to the mother's people. He would have to give his daughter up if the case were brought before the Headman of Little Canyon, and certainly he would have no better chance before a strange white man in town.

He handed the bewildered Little One to her grandfather, who stood watching every movement suspiciously. Chee asked, "If I brought you a few things for the Little One, would that be making trouble? Some velvet for a blouse, or some of the jerky she likes so well . . . this summer's melon?"

Old Man Fat backed away from him. "Well," he hesitated, as some of the anger disappeared from his face and beads of greed shone in his eyes. "Well," he repeated. Then as the Little One began to squirm in his arms and cry, he said, "No! No! Stay away from here, you and all your family."

The sense of his failure deepened as Chee rode back to Little Canyon. But it was not until he sat with his family that evening in the hogan, while the familiar bustle of

---

11. **jerked mutton:** strips of lamb, dried and preserved; often called "jerky"

meal preparing went on about him, that he began to doubt the wisdom of the things he'd always believed. He smelled the coffee boiling and the oily fragrance of chili powder dusted into the bubbling pot of stew; he watched his mother turning round, crusty fried bread in the small black skillet. All around him was plenty—a half of mutton hanging near the door, bright strings of chili drying, corn hanging by the braided husks, cloth bags of dried peaches. Yet in his heart was nothing.

He heard the familiar sounds of the sheep outside the hogan, the splash of water as his father filled the long drinking trough from the water barrel. When his father came in, Chee could not bring himself to tell a second time of the day's happenings. He watched his wiry, soft-spoken father while his mother told the story, saw his father's queue of graying hair quiver as he nodded his head with sympathetic exclamations.

Chee's doubting, acrid thoughts kept forming: Was it wisdom his father had passed on to him, or was his inheritance only the stubbornness of a long-haired Navaho resisting change? Take care of the land and it will take care of you. True, the land had always given him food, but now food was not enough. Perhaps if he had gone to school he would have learned a different kind of wisdom, something to help him now. A schoolboy might even be able to speak convincingly to this government man whom Old Man Fat threatened to call, instead of sitting here like a clod of earth itself—Pueblo farmer indeed. What had the land to give that would restore his daughter?

In the days that followed, Chee herded sheep. He got up in the half light, drank the hot coffee his mother had ready, then started the flock moving. It was necessary to drive the sheep a long way from the hogan to find good winter forage.[12] Sometimes Chee met friends or relatives who were on their way to town or the road camp where they hoped to get work; then there was friendly banter and an exchange of news. But most of the days seemed endless; he could not walk far enough or fast enough from his memories of the Little One or from his bitter thoughts. Sometimes it seemed his daughter trudged beside him, so real he could almost hear her footsteps— the muffled pad-pad of little feet clad in deer hide. In the glare of a snow bank he would see her vivid face, brown eyes sparkling. Mingling with the tinkle of sheep bells he heard her laughter.

When, weary of following the small, sharp hoof marks that crossed and re-crossed in the snow, he sat down in the shelter of a rock, it was only to be reminded that in his thoughts he had forsaken his brotherhood with the earth and sun and growing things. If he remembered times when he had flung himself against the earth to rest, to lie there in the sun until he could no longer feel where he left off and the earth began, it was to remember also that now he sat like an alien against the same earth; the belonging together was gone. The earth was one thing and he was another.

It was during the days when he herded sheep that Chee decided he must leave Little Canyon. Perhaps he would take a job silversmithing for one of the traders in town. Perhaps even though he spoke little

12. **forage:** food or provision; to forage is "to search for food"

English, he could get a job at the road camp with cousins; he would ask them about it.

Springtime transformed the mesas. The peach trees in the canyon were shedding fragrance and pink blossoms on the gentled wind. The sheep no longer foraged for the yellow seeds of chamiso[13] but ranged near the hogan with the long-legged new lambs, eating tender young grass.

Chee was near the hogan on the day his cousins rode up with the message for which he waited. He had been watching with mixed emotions while his father and his sister's husband cleared the fields beside the stream.

"The boss at the camp says he needs an extra hand, but he wants to know if you'll be willing to go with the camp when they move it to the other side of the town?" The tall cousin shifted his weight in the saddle.

The other cousin took up the explanation. "The work near here will last only until the new cut-off beyond Red Sands is finished. After that, the work will be too far away for you to get back here often."

That was what Chee had wanted—to get away from Little Canyon—yet he found himself not so interested in the job beyond town as in this new cut-off which was almost finished. He pulled a blade of grass, split it thoughtfully down the center as he asked questions of his cousins. Finally he said: "I need to think more about this. If I decide on this job, I'll ride over."

Before his cousins were out of sight down the canyon, Chee was walking toward the

fields, a bold plan shaping in his mind. As the plan began to flourish, wild and hardy as young tumbleweed, Chee added his own voice softly to the song his father was singing: " . . . In the middle of the wide field . . . Yellow Corn Boy . . . I wish to put in."

Chee walked slowly around the field, the rich red earth yielding to his footsteps. His plan depended upon this land and upon the things he remembered most about his wife's people.

Through planting time Chee worked zealously and tirelessly. He spoke little of the large, new field he was planting because he felt so strongly that just now this was something between himself and the land. The first days he was ever stooping, piercing the ground with the pointed stick, placing the corn kernels there, walking around the field and through it singing, " . . . His track leads into the ground . . . Yellow Corn Boy . . . his track leads into the ground." After that, each day Chee walked through his field watching for the tips of green to break through; first a few spikes in the center and then more and more until the corn in all parts of the field was above ground. Surely, Chee thought, if he sang the proper songs, if he cared for this land faithfully, it would not forsake him now, even though through the lonely days of winter he had betrayed the goodness of the earth in his thoughts.

Through the summer Chee worked long days, the sun hot upon his back, pulling weeds from around young corn plants; he planted squash and pumpkin; he terraced a small piece of land near his mother's hogan and planted carrots and onions and the moisture-loving chili. He was increasingly restless. Finally he told his family what he hoped the harvest from this land would

---

13. **chamiso:** a desert shrub

bring him. Then the whole family waited with him, watching the corn: the slender, graceful plants that waved green arms and bent to embrace each other as young winds wandered through the field, the maturing plants flaunting their pollen-laden tassels in the sun, the tall and sturdy parent corn with new-formed ears and a froth of purple, red and yellow corn beards against the dusty emerald of broad leaves.

Summer was almost over when Chee slung the bulging packs across two pack ponies. His mother helped him tie the heavy rolled pack behind the saddle of the buckskin. Chee knotted the new yellow kerchief about his neck a little tighter, gave the broad black hat brim an extra tug, but these were only gestures of assurance and he knew it. The land had not failed him. That part was done. But this he was riding into? Who could tell?

When Chee arrived at Red Sands, it was as he had expected to find it—no cars on the highway. His cousins had told him that even the Pueblo farmers were using the new cut-off to town. The barren gravel around the Red Sands Trading Post was deserted. A sign banged against the dismantled gas pumps, *Closed Until Further Notice.*

Old Man Fat came from the crude summer shelter built beside the log hogan from a few branches of scrub cedar and the sides of wooden crates. He seemed almost friendly when he saw Chee.

"Get down, my son," he said, eyeing the bulging packs. There was no bluster in his voice today and his face sagged, looking somewhat saddened; perhaps because his cheeks were no longer quite full enough to push his eyes upward at the corners. "You are going on a journey?"

Chee shook his head. "Our fields gave us so much this year, I thought to sell or trade this to the trader. I didn't know he was no longer here."

Old Man Fat sighed, his voice dropping to an injured tone. "He says he and his wife are going to rest this winter; then after that he'll build a place up on the new highway."

Chee moved as though to be traveling on, then jerked his head toward the pack ponies. "Anything you need?"

"I'll ask my wife," Old Man Fat said as he led the way to the shelter. "Maybe she has a little money. Things have not been too good with us since the trader closed. Only a few tourists come this way." He shrugged his shoulders. "And with the trader gone—no credit."

Chee was not deceived by his father-in-law's unexpected confidences. He recognized them as a hopeful bid for sympathy and, if possible, something for nothing. Chee made no answer. He was thinking that so far he had been right about his wife's parents: their thriftlessness had left them with no resources to last until Old Man Fat found another easy way of making a living.

Old Man Fat's Wife was in the shelter working at her loom. She turned rather wearily when her husband asked with noticeable deference if she would give him money to buy supplies. Chee surmised that the only income here was from his mother-in-law's weaving.

She peered around the corner of the shelter at the laden ponies, and then she looked at Chee. "What do you have there, my son?"

Chee smiled to himself as he turned to pull the pack from one of the ponies, dragged it to the shelter where he untied the ropes. Pumpkins and hard-shelled squash tumbled out, and the ears of corn—pale yellow husks fitting firmly over plump, ripe kernels, blue corn, red corn, yellow corn, many-colored corn, ears and ears of it—tumbled into every corner of the shelter.

"Yoooooh," Old Man Fat's Wife exclaimed as she took some of the ears in her hands. Then she glanced up at her son-in-law. "But we have no money for all this. We have sold almost everything we own—even the brass bed that stood in the hogan."

Old Man Fat's brass bed. Chee concealed his amusement as he started back for another pack. That must have been a hard parting. Then he stopped, for coming from the cool darkness of the hogan was the Little One, rubbing her eyes as though she had been asleep. She stood for a moment in the doorway, and Chee saw that she was dirty, barefoot, her hair uncombed, her little blouse shorn of all its silver buttons. Then she ran toward Chee, her arms outstretched. Heedless of Old Man Fat and his wife, her father caught her in his arms, her hair falling in a dark cloud across his face, the sweetness of her laughter warm against his shoulder.

It was the haste within him to get this slow waiting game played through to the finish that made Chee speak unwisely. It was the desire to swing her before him in the saddle and ride fast to Little Canyon that prompted his words. "The money doesn't matter. You still have something . . . "

Chee knew immediately that he had overspoken. The old woman looked from him to the corn spread before her. Unfriendliness began to harden in his father-in-law's face. All the old arguments between

himself and his wife's people came pushing and crowding in between them now.

Old Man Fat began kicking the ears of corn back onto the canvas as he eyed Chee angrily. "And you rode all the way over here thinking that for a little food we would give up our daughter's daughter?"

Chee did not wait for the old man to reach for the Little One. He walked dazedly to the shelter, rubbing his cheek against her soft dark hair and put her gently into her grandmother's lap. Then he turned back to the horses. He had failed. By his own haste he had failed. He swung into the saddle, his hand touching the roll behind it. Should he ride on into town?

Then he dismounted, scarcely glancing at Old Man Fat, who stood uncertainly at the corner of the shelter, listening to his wife. "Give me a hand with this other pack of corn, Grandfather," Chee said, carefully keeping the small bit of hope from his voice.

Puzzled but willing, Old Man Fat helped carry the other pack to the shelter, opening it to find more corn as well as carrots and round pale yellow onions. Chee went back for the roll behind the buckskin's saddle and carried it to the entrance of the shelter, where he cut the ropes and gave the canvas a nudge with his toe. Tins of coffee rolled out, small, plump cloth bags; jerked meat from several butcherings spilled from a flour sack, and bright red chilies splashed like flames against the dust.

"I will leave all this anyhow," Chee told them. "I would not want my daughter nor even you old people to go hungry."

Old Man Fat picked up a shiny tin of coffee, then put it down. With trembling hands he began to untie one of the cloth bags—dried sweet peaches.

The Little One had wriggled from her grandmother's lap and was on her knees, digging her hands into the jerked meat.

"There is almost enough food here to last all winter." Old Man Fat's Wife sought the eyes of her husband.

Chee said, "I meant it to be enough. But that was when I thought you might send the Little One back with me." He looked down at this daughter noisily sucking jerky. Her mouth, both fists were full of it. "I am sorry that you feel you cannot bear to part with her."

Old Man Fat's Wife brushed a straggly wisp of gray hair from her forehead as she turned to look at the Little One. Old Man Fat was looking too. And it was not a thing to see. For in that moment the Little One ceased to be their daughter's daughter and became just another mouth to feed.

"And why not?" the old woman asked wearily.

Chee was settled in the saddle, the barefooted Little One before him. He urged the buckskin faster, and his daughter clutched his shirtfront. The purpling mesas flung back the echo: " . . . My corn embrace each other. On the middle of the wide field . . . Yellow Corn Boy, embrace each other."

About the Author

Juanita Platero and Siyowin Miller worked together to create "Chee's Daughter." The collaboration of Platero, a Navaho Indian, and Miller began in 1929 and has produced short stories as well as the novel *The Winds Erase Your Footprints.* Many of Platero and Miller's short stories explore the conflicts resulting from the coming together of different worlds—the traditional life of the Navaho people and the ways of the modern world.

THINK ABOUT THE STORY. The following questions help you check your reading comprehension. Put an *x* in the box next to the correct answer.

1. This story is mainly about
   - ☐ a. how a man plants and harvests a large field.
   - ☐ b. how the death of his wife brings a man great sorrow.
   - ☐ c. how a young Navaho succeeds in regaining his daughter.

2. Old Man Fat and his wife could claim the Little One because
   - ☐ a. they loved the girl more than Chee did.
   - ☐ b. the custom was that a girl was sent to the mother's people.
   - ☐ c. they were wealthier than Chee.

3. At the beginning of the story, Old Man Fat did very well by
   - ☐ a. collecting money from the trader and from tourists.
   - ☐ b. working on the land.
   - ☐ c. making silver jewelry.

4. At the end of the story, what did Chee give his in-laws?
   - ☐ a. packs filled with food
   - ☐ b. enough money to last the winter
   - ☐ c. brightly colored clothing

HANDLE NEW VOCABULARY WORDS. The following questions check your vocabulary skills. Put an *x* in the box next to the correct answer. Each vocabulary word appears in the story.

1. Chee exchanged news and friendly banter with relatives and friends. The word *banter* means
   - ☐ a. a sum of money.
   - ☐ b. good-natured teasing or joking.
   - ☐ c. valuable gifts.

2. He "worked zealously and tirelessly" day after day. What is the meaning of the word *zealously*?
   - ☐ a. eagerly or enthusiastically
   - ☐ b. unwillingly or reluctantly
   - ☐ c. very sorrowfully

3. Old Man Fat asked his wife "with noticeable deference if she would give him money to buy supplies." Which of the following best defines the word *deference*?
   - ☐ a. defiance
   - ☐ b. contentment
   - ☐ c. respectfulness for the opinion or wishes of another

4. The Trading Post was deserted, so Chee surmised that the family was being supported by his mother-in-law's income. The word *surmised* means
   - ☐ a. hoped.
   - ☐ b. guessed.
   - ☐ c. worried.

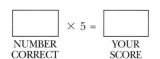

	× 5 =	
NUMBER CORRECT		YOUR SCORE

	× 5 =	
NUMBER CORRECT		YOUR SCORE

EXAMINE STORY ELEMENTS. The following questions check your knowledge of story elements. Put an *x* in the box next to each correct answer.

1. Who is the *main character* in the story?
   - ☐ a. Chee
   - ☐ b. Old Man Fat
   - ☐ c. the Little One

2. Of the following events, which happened last in the *plot* of "Chee's Daughter"?
   - ☐ a. Chee rode home, the Little One clutching his shirt.
   - ☐ b. Old Man Fat told Chee, "Stay away from here."
   - ☐ c. Chee returned home and discovered that his daughter was gone.

3. Which of the following *foreshadows* the fact that business will decline at the trading post?
   - ☐ a. The Navaho rugs at the trading post were gaudy—too bright and showy to be in good taste.
   - ☐ b. The weather seemed to be unusually warm, discouraging tourists.
   - ☐ c. A new cut-off to town was being constructed.

4. "Chee's Story" is *set*
   - ☐ a. in a big city in the East.
   - ☐ b. somewhere in the southwestern part of the United States.
   - ☐ c. in a town in Florida.

MASTER CRITICAL THINKING. The following questions check your critical thinking skills. Put an *x* in the box next to each correct answer.

1. Clues in the story suggest that Old Man Fat and his wife claimed Chee's daughter
   - ☐ a. because they wanted her to have the best possible life.
   - ☐ b. for spiteful reasons, since there had been a history of disagreements with Chee.
   - ☐ c. to make their lives less lonely.

2. The name Old Man Fat suggests that the character
   - ☐ a. worked hard all his life to get what he has.
   - ☐ b. is wealthy and generous.
   - ☐ c. is lazy or overweight.

3. "Take care of the land and it will take care of you." This principle
   - ☐ a. proved false in the story.
   - ☐ b. does not apply to the story.
   - ☐ c. proved true; the land's yield helped Chee win back his daughter.

4. Probably one reason that Old Man Fat and his wife were willing to return the Little One was that
   - ☐ a. they both loved Chee and were eager to see him happy.
   - ☐ b. the child would have been an expense.
   - ☐ c. Chee promised to bring them food and supplies for as long as necessary.

[ ] × 5 = [ ]

NUMBER CORRECT   YOUR SCORE

[ ] × 5 = [ ]

NUMBER CORRECT   YOUR SCORE

EXPLORE THE WRITER'S CRAFT. The following questions check your knowledge of skills related to the craft of writing. Put an *x* in the box next to each correct answer. You may refer to pages 4 and 5.

1. "He rode on silently . . . until the red rock walls rose straight upward from the stream bed and only a narrow piece of blue sky hung above." This provides
   ☐ a. an example of imagery.
   ☐ b. an example of a flashback.
   ☐ c. an example of symbolism.

2. "Each year, the corn and beans and squash drank thirstily." This sentence illustrates
   ☐ a. onomatopoeia.
   ☐ b. personification.
   ☐ c. irony.

3. Which sentence does not contain a simile?
   ☐ a. The child "followed him about like a shadow."
   ☐ b. Chee did not like the idea of working in front of tourists.
   ☐ c. He sat silently "like a clod of earth."

4. Which sentence illustrates descriptive language?
   ☐ a. "That night, Chee's thoughts were troubled."
   ☐ b. "If you try to make trouble, I'll take the case to the government man in town."
   ☐ c. Chee "sat looking across the narrow ribbon of water to the bare-branched peach trees."

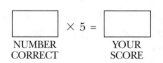

NUMBER CORRECT × 5 = YOUR SCORE

Questions for Writing and Discussion

- Identify basic differences between the views of Old Man Fat and Chee. Show how these opposing points of view led to different lifestyles and to conflicts.
- What was Chee's first offer to Old Man Fat? Why was it rejected?
- Explain Chee's plan for regaining his daughter. What had to occur for the plan to succeed?
- The story would have ended differently if Old Man Fat and his wife had been thrifty or had remained prosperous. Do you agree with this statement? Explain.
- What morals does the story teach?

See additional questions for extended writing on pages 78 and 79.

Use the boxes below to total your scores for the exercises. Then record your scores on pages 224 and 225.

☐ **T**HINK ABOUT THE STORY
+
☐ **H**ANDLE NEW VOCABULARY WORDS
+
☐ **E**XAMINE STORY ELEMENTS
+
☐ **M**ASTER CRITICAL THINKING
+
☐ **E**XPLORE THE WRITER'S CRAFT
▼
☐ **Total Score:** Story 6

Tom Edison's Shaggy Dog

by Kurt Vonnegut Jr.

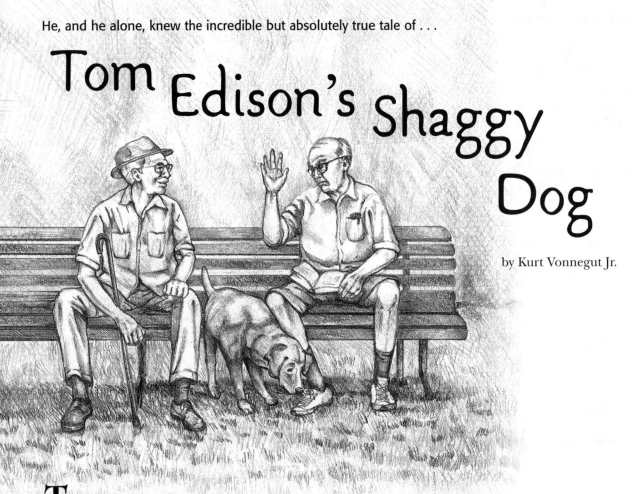

Two old men sat on a park bench one morning in the sunshine of Tampa, Florida—one trying doggedly to read a book he was plainly enjoying while the other, Harold K. Bullard, told him the story of his life in the full, round tones of a public address system. At their feet lay Bullard's Labrador retriever,[1] who further tormented the aged listener by probing his ankles with a large, wet nose.

Bullard, who had been, before he retired, successful in many fields, enjoyed reviewing his important past. But he faced

the problem that complicates the lives of cannibals—namely: that a single victim cannot be used over and over. Anyone who had passed the time of day with him and his dog refused to share a bench with them again.

So Bullard and his dog set out through the park each day in quest of new faces. They had had good luck this morning, for they had found this stranger right away, clearly a new arrival in Florida, with nothing better to do than read.

"Yes," said Bullard, rounding out the first hour of his lecture, "made and lost five fortunes in my time."

---

1. **Labrador retriever**: a breed of dog

"So you said," said the stranger, whose name Bullard had neglected to ask. "Easy, boy. No, no, no, boy," he said to the dog, who was growing more aggressive toward his ankles.

"Oh? Already told you that, did I?" said Bullard.

"Twice."

"Two in real estate, one in scrap iron, and one in oil and one in trucking."

"So you said."

"I did? Yes, guess I did. Two in real estate, one in scrap iron, one in oil, and one in trucking. Wouldn't take back a day of it."

"No, I suppose not," said the stranger. "Pardon me, but do you suppose you could move your dog somewhere else? He keeps—"

"Him?" said Bullard, heartily. "Friendliest dog in the world. Don't need to be afraid of him."

"I'm not afraid of him. It's just that he drives me crazy, sniffing at my ankles."

"Plastic," said Bullard, chuckling.

"What?"

"Plastic. Must be something plastic on your sneakers. I'll bet it's those laces. Sure as we're sitting here, the ends of your laces must be plastic. That dog is nuts about plastic. Don't know why that is, but he'll sniff it out and find it if there's a speck around. Must be a deficiency in his diet, though he eats better than I do. Once he chewed up a whole plastic laundry basket. Can you beat it? *That's* the business I'd go into now, by glory, if the pill rollers hadn't told me to let up, to give the old ticker a rest."

"You could tie the dog to that tree over there," said the stranger.

"I get so sore at all the youngsters these days!" said Bullard. "All of 'em moaning about no frontiers any more. There never have been so many frontiers as there are today. You know what Horace Greeley[2] would say today?"

"His nose is wet," said the stranger, and he pulled his ankles away, but the dog moved forward in steady pursuit. "Stop it, boy!"

"His wet nose shows he's healthy," said Bullard. "'Go plastic, young man!' That's what Greeley'd say. 'Go atom, young man!'"

The dog had definitely located the plastic laces on the stranger's sneakers and was moving his head one way and another, thinking out ways of bringing his teeth to bear on those delicacies.

"Scat!" said the stranger.

"'Go electronic, young man!'" said Bullard. "Don't talk to me about no opportunity any more. Opportunity's knocking down every door in the country, trying to get in. When I was young, a man had to go out and find opportunity and drag it home by the ears. Nowadays—"

"Sorry," said the stranger, evenly. He slammed his book shut, stood and jerked his ankle away from the dog. "I've got to be on my way. So good day, sir."

He stalked across the park, found another bench, sat down with a sigh and began to read. His respiration had just returned to normal, when he felt the wet sponge of the dog's nose on his ankles again.

"Oh—it's you!" said Bullard, sitting down beside him. "He was tracking you. He was on the scent of something, and I just let him have his head. What'd I tell you about plastic?" He looked about contentedly.

---

2. **Horace Greeley:** an American newspaper editor whose famous words of advice were "Go West, young man."

"Don't blame you for moving on. It was stuffy back there. No shade to speak of and not a sign of a breeze."

"Would the dog go away if I bought him a plastic laundry basket?" said the stranger.

"Pretty good joke, pretty good joke," said Bullard, amiably. Suddenly he clapped the stranger on his knee. "Sa-ay, you aren't in plastics are you? Here I've been blowing off about plastics, and for all I know that's your line."

"My line?" said the stranger crisply, laying down his book. "Sorry—I've never had a line. I've been a drifter since the age of nine, since Edison set up his laboratory next to my home, and showed me the intelligence analyzer."

"Edison?" said Bullard. "Thomas Edison, the inventor?"

"If you want to call him that, go ahead," said the stranger.

"If I *want* to call him that?"—Bullard guffawed—"I guess I just will! Father of the light bulb and I don't know what all."

"If you want to think he invented the light bulb, go ahead. No harm in it." The stranger resumed his reading.

"Say, what is this?" said Bullard, suspiciously. "You pulling my leg? What's this about an intelligence analyzer? I never heard of that."

"Of course you haven't," said the stranger. "Mr. Edison and I promised to keep it a secret. I've never told anyone. Mr. Edison broke his promise and told Henry Ford, but Ford made him promise not to tell anybody else—for the good of humanity."

Bullard was entranced. "Uh, this intelligence analyzer," he said, "it analyzed intelligence, did it?"

"It was an electric butter churn," said the stranger.

"Seriously now," Bullard coaxed.

"Maybe it *would* be better to talk it over with someone," said the stranger. "It's a terrible thing to keep bottled up inside me, year in and year out. But how can I be sure that it won't go any further?"

"My word as a gentleman," Bullard assured him.

"I don't suppose I could find a stronger guarantee than that, could I?" said the stranger, judiciously.

"There is no stronger guarantee," said Bullard, proudly.

"Very well." The stranger leaned back and closed his eyes, seeming to travel backward through time. He was silent for a full minute, during which Bullard watched with respect.

"It was way back," said the stranger at last, softly. "Back in the village of Menlo Park, New Jersey. I was a boy. A young man we all thought was a wizard had set up a laboratory next door to my home, and there were flashes and crashes inside, and all sorts of scary goings on. The neighborhood children were warned to keep away, not to make any noise that would bother the wizard.

"I didn't get to know Edison right off, but his dog Sparky and I got to be steady pals. A dog a whole lot like yours, Sparky was, and we used to wrestle all over the neighborhood. Yes, sir, your dog is the image of Sparky."

"Is that so?" said Bullard, flattered.

"Absolute truth," replied the stranger. "Well, one day Sparky and I were wrestling around, and we wrestled right up to the door of Edison's laboratory. The next thing

I knew, Sparky had pushed me in through the door, and bam! I was sitting on the laboratory floor, looking up at Mr. Edison himself."

"Bet he was sore," said Bullard, delighted.

"You can bet I was scared," said the stranger. "Edison had wires hooked to his ears and they ran down to a little black box in his lap! I started to scoot, but he caught me by my collar and made me sit down.

"'Boy,' said Edison, 'it's always darkest before the dawn. I want you to remember that.'

"'Yes, sir,' I said.

"'For over a year, my boy,' Edison said to me, 'I've been trying to find a filament that will last in an incandescent lamp. Hair, string, splinters—nothing works. So while I was trying to think of something else to try, I started tinkering with another idea of mine, just letting off steam. I put this together,' he said, showing me the little black box. 'I thought maybe intelligence was just a certain kind of electricity, so I made this intelligence analyzer here. It works! You're the first one to know about it, my boy. But I don't know why you shouldn't be. It will be your generation that will grow up in the glorious new era when people will be as easily graded as oranges.'"

"I don't believe it!" said Bullard.

"May I be struck by lightning this very instant!" said the stranger. "And it did work, too. Edison had tried out the analyzer on the men in his shop, without telling them what he was up to. The smarter a man was, by gosh, the farther the needle on the indicator in the little black box swung to the right. I let him try it on me, and the needle just lay where it was and trembled. But dumb as I was, then is when I made my

one and only contribution to the world. As I say, I haven't lifted a finger since."

"Whadja do?" said Bullard, eagerly.

"I said, 'Mr. Edison, sir, let's try it on the *dog*.' And I wish you could have seen the show that dog put on when I said it! Old Sparky barked and howled and scratched to get out. When he saw we meant business, that he wasn't going to get out, he made a beeline right for the intelligence analyzer and knocked it out of Edison's hands. But we cornered him, and Edison held him down while I touched the wires to his ears. And would you believe it, that needle sailed clear across the dial, way past a little red pencil mark on the dial of the face!"

"The dog busted it," said Bullard.

"'Mr. Edison, sir,' I said, 'what's that red mark mean?'

"'My boy,' said Edison, 'it means that the instrument is broken, because that red mark is me.'"

"I'll say it was broken," said Bullard.

The stranger said gravely, "But it wasn't broken. No, sir. Edison checked the whole thing, and it was in apple-pie order. When Edison told me that, it was then that Sparky, crazy to get out, gave himself away."

"How?" said Bullard, suspiciously.

"We really had him locked in, see? There were three locks on the door—a hook and eye, a bolt, and a regular knob and latch. That dog stood up, unhooked the hook, pushed the bolt back and had the knob in his teeth when Edison stopped him."

"No!" said Bullard.

"Yes!" said the stranger, his eyes shining. "And that is when Edison showed me what a great scientist he was. He was willing to face the truth, no matter how unpleasant it might be.

"'So!' said Edison to Sparky, 'Man's best friend, huh? Dumb animal, huh?'

"That Sparky was a caution. He pretended not to hear. He scratched himself and bit fleas and went around growling at ratholes—anything to get out of looking Edison in the eye.

"'Pretty soft, isn't it, Sparky?' said Edison. 'Let somebody else worry about getting food, building shelters and keeping warm, while you sleep in front of a fire or go chasing after the girls or run around with the other dogs. No mortgages, no politics, no war, no work, no worry. Just wag the old tail or lick a hand, and you're all taken care of.'

"'Mr. Edison,' I said, 'do you mean to tell me that dogs are smarter than people?'

"'Smarter?' said Edison. 'I'll tell the world! And what have I been doing for the past year? Slaving to work out a light bulb so dogs can play at night!'

"'Look, Mr. Edison,' said Sparky, 'why not—'"

"Hold on!" roared Bullard.

"Silence!" shouted the stranger, triumphantly. "'Look, Mr. Edison,' said Sparky, 'why not keep quiet about this? It's been working out to everybody's satisfaction for hundreds of thousands of years. Let sleeping dogs lie. You forget all about it, destroy the intelligence analyzer, and I'll tell you what to use for a lamp filament.'"

"Hogwash!" said Bullard, his face purple.

The stranger stood. "You have my solemn word as a gentleman. That dog rewarded *me* for my silence with a stock-market tip that made me independently wealthy for the rest of my days. And the last words that Sparky ever spoke were to Thomas Edison. 'Try a piece of carbonized cotton thread,' he said. Later, he was torn to bits by a pack of dogs that had gathered outside the door, listening."

The stranger removed a lace from one of his sneakers and handed it to Bullard's dog. "A small token of esteem, sir, for an ancestor of yours who talked himself to death. Good day." He tucked his book under his arm and walked away.

About the Author

Kurt Vonnegut Jr. (1922–) is one of America's leading authors. Born in Indianapolis, Indiana, Vonnegut attended Cornell University and the University of Chicago. Many of Vonnegut's works deal with serious issues such as human values, war and peace, and the future of society. Although some of Vonnegut's themes may seem grim, he has the ability to treat them with his own special brand of charm, irony, and humor.

These qualities may be seen in "Tom Edison's Shaggy Dog," which is taken from *Welcome to the Monkey House,* a collection of Vonnegut's short fiction. Vonnegut has written novels, short stories, essays, and plays. Among his best-known novels are *Cat's Cradle* and *Slaughterhouse Five,* which have been translated into several languages and have been enjoyed by readers all over the world.

THINK ABOUT THE STORY. The following questions help you check your reading comprehension. Put an *x* in the box next to the correct answer.

1. "Tom Edison's Shaggy Dog" is mainly about
   - ☐ a. the life of Thomas Edison, the great inventor.
   - ☐ b. a man who is unaware that his dog bothers other people.
   - ☐ c. an incredible tale told to silence an annoying individual.

2. Bullard said that his dog was attracted to
   - ☐ a. strangers.
   - ☐ b. plastic.
   - ☐ c. places that have shade.

3. If the stranger is to be believed, he became independently wealthy
   - ☐ a. by making a fortune in real estate.
   - ☐ b. by starting businesses in scrap iron, oil, and trucking.
   - ☐ c. through a stock market tip given to him by Sparky.

4. According to the story, dogs are
   - ☐ a. wonderful pets who can do no wrong.
   - ☐ b. not as smart as people believe they are.
   - ☐ c. capable of talking and more intelligent than human beings.

HANDLE NEW VOCABULARY WORDS. The following questions check your vocabulary skills. Put an *x* in the box next to the correct answer. Each vocabulary word appears in the story.

1. Although he was continually interrupted, the stranger tried "doggedly to read a book." The word *doggedly* means
   - ☐ a. cheerfully.
   - ☐ b. stubbornly.
   - ☐ c. lazily.

2. The dog ate a great deal, but there still seemed to be a deficiency in his diet. Which of the following best defines the word *deficiency*?
   - ☐ a. a large quantity
   - ☐ b. a steady improvement
   - ☐ c. a lack of something

3. When Bullard offered his "word as a gentleman," the stranger judiciously accepted the man's guarantee. When you do something *judiciously*, you
   - ☐ a. show good judgment.
   - ☐ b. express serious doubts.
   - ☐ c. laugh uproariously.

4. Bullard's dog received a lace from the stranger as "a small token of esteem." The word *esteem* means
   - ☐ a. anger.
   - ☐ b. favorable opinion.
   - ☐ c. huge fortune.

☐ × 5 = ☐
NUMBER CORRECT   YOUR SCORE

☐ × 5 = ☐
NUMBER CORRECT   YOUR SCORE

EXAMINE STORY ELEMENTS. The following questions check your knowledge of story elements. Put an *x* in the box next to each correct answer.

1. Which of the following best illustrates *character development*?
   - ☐ a. At the beginning of the story, the stranger was a "victim," but later he managed to "victimize" his tormentor.
   - ☐ b. Bullard was not sensitive to the feelings of people he engaged in conversation.
   - ☐ c. Although Edison was a genius, he did not immediately solve some problems he encountered.

2. The stranger's *motive* for telling Bullard the story about Thomas Edison was
   - ☐ a. to correct a mistaken impression.
   - ☐ b. to repay a kindness.
   - ☐ c. to gain revenge, or get even.

3. The *mood* of "Tom Edison's Shaggy Dog" is best described as
   - ☐ a. humorous.
   - ☐ b. mysterious.
   - ☐ c. serious.

4. What was the author's *purpose* in writing the story?
   - ☐ a. to convince or persuade
   - ☐ b. to amuse or entertain
   - ☐ c. to teach or instruct

☐ × 5 = ☐
NUMBER   YOUR
CORRECT   SCORE

MASTER CRITICAL THINKING. The following questions check your critical thinking skills. Put an *x* in the box next to each correct answer.

1. A "shaggy-dog story" is a specific kind of story. Judging by this selection, it may be defined as
   - ☐ a. a joke that has been expanded into a comical tale.
   - ☐ b. a legend about a famous inventor.
   - ☐ c. a folktale that is told to a stranger.

2. In his shaggy-dog story, the stranger suggests that
   - ☐ a. Edison was not really a great inventor.
   - ☐ b. the "intelligence analyzer" did not work.
   - ☐ c. a dog named Sparky helped Edison invent the light bulb.

3. Probably the reason that Sparky "was torn to bits by a pack of dogs" was that
   - ☐ a. they were jealous of him because Sparky knew Thomas Edison.
   - ☐ b. they mistook, or confused, him for a dog they hated.
   - ☐ c. Sparky was responsible for revealing their great secret.

4. It is reasonable to infer that the stranger
   - ☐ a. will eventually become friendly with Bullard.
   - ☐ b. will no longer be bothered by Bullard.
   - ☐ c. will never return to the park where he met Bullard.

☐ × 5 = ☐
NUMBER   YOUR
CORRECT   SCORE

EXPLORE THE WRITER'S CRAFT. The following questions check your knowledge of skills related to the craft of writing. Put an *x* in the box next to each correct answer. You may refer to pages 4 and 5.

1. References to people such as Henry Ford and Horace Greeley are examples of
   ☐ a. poetic language.
   ☐ b. metaphor.
   ☐ c. allusion.

2. "Sparky had pushed me in through the door, and bam! I was sitting on the laboratory floor." The word *bam* is an example of
   ☐ a. onomatopoeia.
   ☐ b. personification.
   ☐ c. alliteration.

3. The stranger gives Bullard's dog a gift as well as his "solemn word as a gentleman." Neither is given with sincerity, so these are examples of
   ☐ a. inner conflict.
   ☐ b. irony.
   ☐ c. imagery.

4. "Tom Edison's Shaggy Dog" is an example of what is known as "a story within a story" because
   ☐ a. the story appears in a book that contains other stories.
   ☐ b. the story is one selection in a unit.
   ☐ c. a character in the story tells a story to another character in the story.

```
┌──────┐        ┌──────┐
│      │ × 5 =  │      │
└──────┘        └──────┘
NUMBER          YOUR
CORRECT         SCORE
```

Questions for Writing and Discussion

- Why did the stranger find Harold K. Bullard and his dog so annoying?
- The stranger told Bullard a "shaggy-dog story" in which the dog that is punished is "the image of" Bullard's dog. Why was the stranger's shaggy-dog story particularly appropriate to the situation?
- When do you think the stranger first decided to tell Bullard the story? When did Bullard become aware that the stranger was deceiving him?
- Explain why the title is a pun—a play on words in which words have more than one meaning—and why "the *pun*ishment fits the crime."

See additional questions for extended writing on pages 78 and 79.

Use the boxes below to total your scores for the exercises. Then record your scores on pages 224 and 225.

```
┌──────┐
│      │  THINK ABOUT THE STORY
└──────┘
  +
┌──────┐
│      │  HANDLE NEW VOCABULARY WORDS
└──────┘
  +
┌──────┐
│      │  EXAMINE STORY ELEMENTS
└──────┘
  +
┌──────┐
│      │  MASTER CRITICAL THINKING
└──────┘
  +
┌──────┐
│      │  EXPLORE THE WRITER'S CRAFT
└──────┘
  ▼
┌──────┐
│      │  Total Score: Story 7
└──────┘
```

Achievements

Questions for Discussion and Extended Writing

The following questions provide you with opportunities to express your thoughts and feelings about the selections in this unit. Your teacher may assign selected questions. When you write your responses, remember to state your point of view clearly and to support your position by presenting specific details—examples, illustrations, and references drawn from the story and, in some cases, from your life. Organize your writing carefully and check your work for correct spelling, capitalization, punctuation, and grammar.

1. The theme of this unit is "Achievements." Show how each story in the unit is related to the theme.

2. According to a line by the famed playwright and poet William Shakespeare, "Some are born great, some achieve greatness, and some have greatness thrust upon them." Of the characters in this unit, which one do you think attained the greatest achievement? Support your opinion by referring to the story.

3. In which story do you think that conflict played the most important role? Identify the conflict or conflicts in the story you chose.

4. Which character in the unit did you most care about or admire? Explain why.

5. In which two stories in the unit does the setting of the story play the most significant role? Give titles and authors, and present reasons for your answer.

6. In many ways, "Tom Edison's Shaggy Dog" is different from the other stories in this unit. Do you agree or disagree with this statement? Support your position by referring to the selections.

7. Select two characters in the unit and demonstrate that the characters you chose had to overcome serious obstacles. Identify the obstacles the characters faced. Give titles and authors.

8. Draw upon material found in one of the selections to write a descriptive essay. Specify which story you chose. Give your essay a title.

9. Young people are the main characters in two of the stories in the unit; adults are the main characters in the other two stories. Which one of the four stories appealed to you most? Did the main character's age influence your decision? Discuss.

10. "Hitch your wagon to a star," advised Ralph Waldo Emerson. Use Emerson's words as the theme of a carefully developed essay. Explain what Emerson's statement means and how it relates to your plans for the future. Whenever possible, refer to *achievements*. The essay should have an introduction, a body, and a conclusion. Title the essay "Hitching Your Wagon to a Star."

Masters of Mystery

"*The human heart is a strange mystery.*"

–Alexandre Dumas

Previewing the Unit

This unit contains selections by "Masters of Mystery." What do the authors have in common—aside from the fact that the stories they wrote deal with crime and detection? We can easily clear up *that* mystery. All the authors are English, and each one is not only famous but is also a legend.

THE INSPIRATION OF MR. BUDD

Dorothy L. Sayers's works are so well constructed that almost every sentence she writes adds to characterization or helps advance the plot of the story. This can be seen in "The Inspiration of Mr. Budd," the charming tale of a timid barber who comes face to face with a ruthless hardened criminal. The way Mr. Budd reacts to this intriguing confrontation, and Budd's "great inspiration," are the heart of the story.

THE CASE OF THE PERFECT MAID

Agatha Christie is probably the most widely read mystery writer of all time. One of Christie's most famous creations is Miss Jane Marple, an amateur detective whom you will meet in "The Case of the Perfect Maid." In this story, Miss Marple is called upon to assist when her maid's cousin, Gladys, is fired by Miss Lavinia, "a tall, gaunt, bony female of fifty." Subsequent events arouse Miss Marple's suspicion, and she is not surprised when a daring crime is committed. All the clues to its solution are there for you to find— if you can—and Miss Marple does!

THE RED-HEADED LEAGUE

Sherlock Holmes and Dr. Watson, his devoted companion, are among the most beloved characters in the history of the detective story. Sherlock Holmes clubs exist all over the world, and countless fans of Holmes believe that he actually lived. When Sir Arthur Conan Doyle had Holmes killed in a story many years ago, the public clamor was so great that the author was forced, in another tale, to "bring him back to life." Conan Doyle truly created an immortal character! "The Red-Headed League" is one of the author's most brilliant stories. It starts when a red-headed man wins a highly prized job—*copying the encyclopedia!* And it ends when . . . but you'll have to find that out for yourself.

Clues abound in all of the stories. Look for them as you read to help you figure out the endings to the stories.

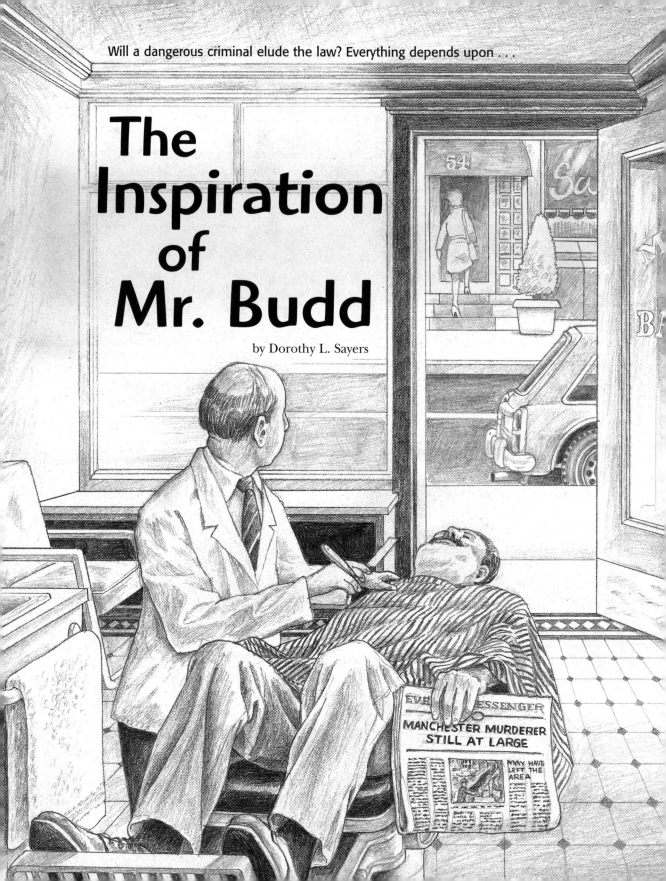

Will a dangerous criminal elude the law? Everything depends upon . . .

The Inspiration of Mr. Budd

by Dorothy L. Sayers

£500[1] Reward

The *Evening Messenger,* ever anxious to further the ends of justice, has decided to offer the above reward to any person who shall give information leading to the arrest of the man, William Strickland, alias Bolton, who is wanted by the police in connection with the murder of the late Emma Strickland at 59 Acacia Crescent, Manchester.

Description of the Wanted Man

The following is the official description of William Strickland: Age 43; height 6 ft. 1 or 2; hair silver-gray and abundant, may dye[2] same; full gray mustache and beard, may now be clean-shaven; eyes light gray, rather close-set; hawk nose; teeth strong and white, displays them somewhat prominently when laughing, left upper eye-tooth filled with gold; left thumbnail disfigured by a recent blow.

Speaks in rather loud voice; quick, decisive manner.

May be dressed in a gray or dark blue suit and soft gray hat.

May have left, or will endeavor to leave, the country.

Mr. Budd read the description carefully once again and sighed. It was in the highest degree unlikely that William Strickland should choose his small and unsuccessful shop, out of all the barbers' shops in London, for a haircut or a shave, still less for "dyeing same"; even if he was in London, which Mr. Budd saw no reason to suppose.

Three weeks had gone by since the murder, and the odds were a hundred to one that William Strickland had already left the country. Nevertheless, Mr. Budd committed the description, as well as he could, to memory. Any headline with money in it could attract Mr. Budd's fascinated eye in these difficult days, whether it offered a choice between fifty thousand pounds or merely a modest hundred or so.

Had not the hairdresser across the street lately bought out the grocer next door, and engaged a staff of exquisitely coiffed[3] assistants to adorn his *new* "Ladies' Hair-dressing Department" with its purple and orange curtains, its two rows of gleaming marble basins, and an apparatus like a Victorian chandelier for permanent waving?

Had the man not installed a large electric sign surrounded by a scarlet border that ran round and round perpetually, like a kitten chasing its own tail? And was there not at this moment an endless stream of young ladies hastening into those heavily perfumed parlors in the desperate hope of somehow getting a shampoo and a wave "squeezed in" before closing time?

If the reception clerk there shook a regretful head, they did not think of crossing the road to Mr. Budd's dimly lighted window. They made an appointment for days ahead and waited patiently, anxiously fingering the bristly growth at the back of the neck and the straggly bits behind the ears that so soon got out of hand.

---

1. **£500:** five hundred pounds; a pound is a unit of money in the United Kingdom

2. **dye:** to color (hair in this case); the chemical used for dying, or coloring, hair

3. **coiffed:** with stylishly arranged hair

The Inspiration of Mr. Budd

Day after day Mr. Budd watched them flit in and out of the rival establishment, willing, praying even, in a vague manner, that some of them would come over to him; but they never did.

And yet Mr. Budd knew himself to be the finer artist. He could cut hair long or short, beautifully tapered in the most fashionable manner. And he did his work for half the price!

Then there was the "tinting"—his own pet subject, which he had studied so carefully and lovingly—if only those wealthy customers would come to him! He would gently dissuade them from that dreadful mahogany dye that made them look like metallic robots—he would warn them against that widely advertised preparation which was so awful in its effects; he would use the cunning skill which long experience had matured in him—tint them with the infinitely delicate art which conceals itself.

Yet nobody came to Mr. Budd but some young laborers and people who just dropped by.

And why could not Mr. Budd also have burst out into marble and electricity and swum to fortune on the rising tide?

The reason is very distressing, and, as it fortunately has no bearing on the story, shall be told with merciful brevity.

Mr. Budd had a younger brother, Richard, whom he had promised his mother to look after. In happier days Mr. Budd had owned a flourishing business in their native town of Northampton, and Richard had been a bank clerk. Richard had got into a bad way. Richard had tried to take money from the bank. You need to be very much more skillful than Richard to juggle successfully with bank ledgers.

The bank manager was a hard man of the old school: he prosecuted. Mr. Budd paid the bank while Richard was in prison, and when Richard came out, Mr. Budd gave him some money to start life over.

But it took all the profits of the hairdressing business, and he couldn't face all the people in Northampton any more, who had known him all his life. So he had run to vast London, the refuge of all who shrink from the eyes of their neighbors, and bought this little shop, which had done fairly well, until the new hairdresser across the street opened his fancy shop.

That is why Mr. Budd's eye was so painfully fascinated by headlines with money in them.

He put the newspaper down, and as he did so, caught sight of his own reflection in the mirror and smiled, for he was not without a sense of humor. He did not look quite the man to catch a brutal murderer single-handed. He was well on into middle age—a trifle paunchy, with fluffy pale hair, getting a trifle thin on top (partly hereditary, partly worry, that was), five feet six at most, and soft-handed, as a hairdresser must be.

Even razor in hand, he would hardly be a match for William Strickland, height six feet one or two, who had so ferociously battered his old aunt to death. Shaking his head dubiously, Mr. Budd advanced to the door, to cast a forlorn eye at the busy establishment across the way, and nearly ran into a bulky customer who dived in rather suddenly.

"I beg your pardon, sir," murmured Mr. Budd, fearful of alienating a customer; "just stepping out for a breath of fresh air, sir. Shave, sir?"

The large man tore off his overcoat without waiting for Mr. Budd's obsequious hands.

"Are you prepared to die?" he demanded abruptly.

The question chimed in so alarmingly with Mr. Budd's thoughts about murder that for a moment it quite threw him off his professional balance.

"I beg your pardon, sir," he stammered, and in the same moment decided that the man must be a preacher of some kind. He looked rather like it, with his odd, light eyes, his fiery hair and short beard.

"Do you do dyeing?" said the man impatiently.

"Oh!" said Mr. Budd, relieved, "yes, sir, certainly, sir."

A stroke of luck, this. Dyeing meant quite a big sum. He could charge well for the job.

"Good," said the man, sitting down and allowing Mr. Budd to put an apron about his neck. (He was safely gathered in now—he could hardly dart away down the street with a couple of yards of white cotton flapping from his shoulders.)

"Fact is," said the man, "my young lady doesn't like red hair. She says it's conspicuous. The other young ladies in the firm make jokes about it. So, as she's a good bit younger than I am, you see, I like to oblige her, and I was thinking perhaps it could be changed into something quieter, eh? Dark brown, now—that's the color she has a fancy for. What do you say?"

It occurred to Mr. Budd that the young ladies might consider this abrupt change even funnier than the original color, but in the interests of business he agreed that dark brown would be very becoming and a

great deal less noticeable than red. Besides, very likely there was no young lady. A woman, he knew, will say frankly that she wants different colored hair for a change, or just to try, or because she fancies it would suit her, but if a man is going to do a silly thing he prefers, if possible, to shuffle the responsibility on to someone else.

"Very well, then," said the customer, "go ahead. And I'm afraid the beard will have to go. My young lady doesn't like beards."

"A great many young ladies don't, sir," said Mr. Budd. "They're not so fashionable nowadays as they used to be. You can stand a clean shave very well, sir. You have just the chin for it."

"Do you think so?" said the man, examining himself a little anxiously. "I'm glad to hear it."

"Will you have the mustache off as well, sir?"

"Well, no—no, I think I'll stick to that as long as I'm allowed to." He laughed loudly, and Mr. Budd approvingly noted shiny teeth and a gold filling. The customer was obviously ready to spend money on his personal appearance.

In fancy, Mr. Budd saw this well-off and gentlemanly customer advising all his friends to visit "his man"—"wonderful fellow—wonderful—round at the back of Victoria Station—you'd never find it by yourself—only a little place, but he knows what he's about—I'll write it down for you." It was imperative that there should be no fiasco. Hair-dyes were awkward things. He must do the job very well.

"I see you have been using a dye before, sir," said Mr. Budd with respect. "Could you tell me—?"

"Eh?" said the man. "Oh, yes—well, fact is, as I said, my fiancée's a good bit younger than I am. As I expect you can see I began to go gray early—my father was just the same—all our family—so I had it touched up—streaky bits restored, you see. But she doesn't take to the color, so I thought, if I have to dye it at all, why not a color she does fancy while we're about it, eh?"

Mr. Budd subjected his customer's locks to the scrutiny of trained eye and fingers. Never—never in the process of Nature could hair of that texture and quality have been red. It was naturally black hair, prematurely turned, as some black hair will turn, to a silvery gray. However that was none of his business. He elicited the information he really needed—the name of the dye formerly used, and noted that he would have to be careful. Some dyes do not mix kindly with other dyes.

Chatting pleasantly, Mr. Budd lathered his customer, removed the offending beard, and executed a vigorous shampoo, preliminary to the dyeing process. As he wielded the drier, he discussed sports and politics and passed naturally on to the subject of the Manchester murder.

"The police seem to have given it up in despair," said the man.

"Perhaps the reward will liven things up a bit," said Mr. Budd, the thought being naturally uppermost in his mind.

"Oh, there's a reward, is there? I hadn't seen that."

"It's in tonight's paper, sir. Maybe you'd like to have a look at it."

"Thanks, I should."

Mr. Budd left the drier to blow the fiery head of hair at its own wild will for a moment, while he fetched the *Evening Messenger*. The stranger read the paragraph carefully and Mr. Budd, watching him in the mirror, saw him suddenly draw back his left hand, which was resting carelessly on the arm of the chair, and thrust it under the apron.

But not before Mr. Budd had seen it. Not before he had taken conscious note of the misshapen thumbnail. Many people had such an ugly mark, Mr. Budd told himself hurriedly—there was his friend, Bert Webber, who had sliced the top of his thumb right off in a motorcycle accident— his nail looked very much like that. Mr. Budd thought and thought.

The man glanced up, and the eyes of his reflection became fixed on Mr. Budd's face with a penetrating scrutiny—a horrid warning that the real eyes were steadfastly interrogating the reflection of Mr. Budd.

"Well," said Mr. Budd, "the man is safely out of the country, I reckon. They've waited too long."

The man laughed in a pleasant, conversational way.

"I reckon they have," he said. Mr. Budd wondered whether many men with smashed left thumbs had a gold left upper eyetooth. Probably there were hundreds of people like that going about the country. Likewise with silver-gray hair ("may dye same") and aged about forty-three. Undoubtedly.

Mr. Budd turned off the drier and took up a comb and drew it through the hair that Nature had never, never made such as fiery red.

There came back to him, with an accuracy which quite unnerved him, the exact number and extent of the brutal wounds inflicted upon the Manchester victim. Glaring through the door, Mr. Budd noticed that his rival over the way had closed. The streets were full of people. How easy it would be—

"Be as quick as you can, won't you?" said the man, a little impatiently, but pleasantly enough. "It's getting late. I'm afraid it will keep you overtime."

"Not at all, sir," said Mr. Budd. "It's of no consequence—not the least."

No—if he tried to rush out of the door, his terrible customer would leap upon him, drag him back, throttle his cries, and then with one frightful blow like the one he had smashed in his aunt's skull with—

Yet surely Mr. Budd was in a position of advantage. A determined man would do it. He would be out in the street before the customer could disentangle himself from the chair. Mr. Budd began to edge round towards the door.

"What's the matter?" said the customer.

"Just stepping out to look at the time, sir," said Mr. Budd, meekly pausing. (Yet he might have done it then, if he only had the courage to make the first swift step.)

"It's five-and-twenty past eight," said the man, "I'll pay extra for the overtime."

"Not on any account," said Mr. Budd. Too late now, he couldn't make another effort. He vividly saw himself tripping on the threshold—falling—the terrible fist lifted to smash him into a pulp. Or, perhaps, under the familiar white apron, the disfigured hand was actually clutching a pistol.

Mr. Budd retreated to the back of the shop, collecting his materials. If only he had been quicker—more like a detective in a book—he would have observed that thumbnail, that tooth, put two and two together, and run out to give the alarm

while the man's beard was wet and soapy and his face buried in the towel. Or he could have dabbed lather in his eyes— nobody could possibly commit a murder or even run away down the street with his eyes full of soap.

Even now—Mr. Budd took down a bottle, shook his head and put it back on the shelf—even now, was it really too late? Why could he not take a bold course? He had only to open a razor, go quietly up behind the unsuspecting man and say in a firm, loud, convincing voice: "William Strickland, put up your hands. Your life is at my mercy. Stand up till I take your gun away. Now walk straight out to the nearest policeman." Surely, in his position, that was what Sherlock Holmes would do.

But as Mr. Budd returned with a little tray of requirements, he realized that he was not of the stuff of which great detectives are made. For he could not seriously see that attempt "coming off." Because if he held the razor to the man's throat and said: "Put up your hands," the man would probably merely catch him by the wrists and take the razor away. And greatly as Mr. Budd feared his customer unarmed, he felt it would be madness to put a razor in his hands.

Or supposing he said, "Put up your hands," and the man just said, "I won't." What was he to do next? They could not remain there, fixed in one position, till the boy came to do out the shop in the morning.

Perhaps the policeman would notice the light on and the door unfastened and come in? Then he would say, "I congratulate you, Mr. Budd, on having captured a very dangerous criminal." But supposing the policeman didn't happen to notice—and Mr. Budd would have to stand all the time, and he would get exhausted and his attention would relax and then—

After all, Mr. Budd wasn't called upon to arrest the man himself. "Information leading to arrest"—those were the words. He would be able to tell them the wanted man had been there, that he would now have dark brown hair and mustache and no beard. He might even follow him when he left—he might—

It was at this moment that the great Inspiration came to Mr. Budd.

As he fetched a bottle from the glass case he remembered with odd vividness, an old-fashioned wooden knife that had belonged to his mother. It bore the inscription "Knowledge Is Power."

A strange freedom and confidence came to Mr. Budd; his mind was alert; he removed the razors with an easy, natural movement, and made nonchalant conversation as he skillfully applied the dark-brown tint.

The streets were less crowded when Mr. Budd let his customer out. He watched the tall figure cross Grosvenor Place and climb on to a 24 bus.

Mr. Budd put on his hat and coat and extinguished the lights carefully.

He closed the shop door, shook it, as he always did, to make sure that the lock had caught properly, and in his turn made his way to the police station at Whitehall Street.

The policeman was a little condescending at first when Mr. Budd demanded to see "somebody very high up," but finding the little barber insist so earnestly that he had news of the Manchester murderer, and that

there wasn't any time to lose, he consented to pass him through.

Mr. Budd was interviewed first by an important-looking inspector in uniform, who listened very politely to his story and made him repeat very carefully about the gold tooth and the thumbnail and the hair which had been black before it was gray or red and now dark-brown.

The inspector then touched a bell, and said, "Perkins, I think Sir Andrew would like to see this gentleman at once," and he was taken to another room where sat a very shrewd gentleman who heard him with even greater attention, and called in another inspector to listen too, and to take down a very exact description of—yes, surely the undoubted William Strickland as he now appeared.

"But there's one thing more," said Mr. Budd. "I hope, sir, it is the right man, because if it isn't it'll be the ruin of me—"

Mr. Budd leaned across the table and breathlessly uttered the story of his Great Inspiration.

"Tzee—z-z-z—tzee—tzee—z-z—tzee—z-z—"

"Dzoo—dz-dz-dz—dzoo—dz—dzoo—dzoo—dz."

"Tzee—z—z."

The fingers of the radio operator on the ship *Miranda* bound for Ostend, Belgium, moved swiftly as they jotted down the messages of the buzzing, noisy radio.

One message made him laugh.

"The captain better see this, I suppose," he said.

The captain scratched his head when he read it and rang a little bell for the ship's first officer. The first officer ran down to the office and picked up the passenger list and departed. There was a short discussion, and then the first officer spoke to the radio operator again.

"Tzee—z-z—tzeez-z-z—tzee—tzee—z—tzee."

All down the Channel, all over the North Sea, and out into the Atlantic flashed the message. In ship after ship the radio operator sent his message to the captain, and the captain sent for the first officer. Huge liners, little boats, destroyers, large private yachts—ships in every port in England, France, Holland, Germany, Denmark, Norway—whenever people could interpret the message—heard, between laughter and excitement, the tale of Mr. Budd's Great Inspiration.

The *Miranda* docked at Ostend at 7 A.M. A man burst hurriedly into the cabin where the radio operator was just taking off his headphones.

"Here!" he cried; "send out this message at once. Something has happened and the captain has sent for the police."

The radio operator got to work.

"Tzee—z—tzee—" A message started on its way to the English police.

"There is a man on board answering to the description. Ticket bought in name of Watson. Has locked himself in cabin and refuses to come out. Insists on having hairdresser sent to him. Have contacted Ostend police. Await instructions."

The captain with sharp words and authoritative gestures cleared a way through the excited little group of people gathered about First Class Cabin No. 36. Several passengers had got wind of "something up." He herded them away. The captain and

four or five sailors stood waiting and guarding the cabin door. In the silence, the passenger in No. 36 could be heard pacing up and down the narrow cabin.

Soon somebody arrived, with a message. The captain nodded. Six Belgian police officers soon arrived. The captain glanced at them and nodded.

"Ready?"

"Yes."

The captain knocked at the door of No. 36.

"Who is it?" cried a harsh, sharp voice.

"The barber is here, sir, that you sent for."

"Ah!" There was relief in the voice. "Send him in alone if you please. I—I have had an accident."

"Yes, sir."

At the sound of the lock being turned, the captain stepped forward. The door opened a bit and was slammed shut. But the captain's boot was firmly wedged inside the door. The policemen surged forward. There was a shout and a shot which smashed harmlessly through the window, and the passenger was brought out.

"Look at that! Look at that!" shouted a passenger who had rushed to see what was happening. "Look at his head! It's gone green in the night!"

Green!

Not for nothing had Mr. Budd studied the mutual reactions of chemical dyes. "Knowledge Is Power." In the pride of his knowledge he had set a mark on his man, to distinguish him from everyone else in the world. Was there a port anywhere where a murderer might slip away to with every hair on his head and his mustache a bright, vivid green?

The Inspiration of Mr. Budd

Mr. Budd got his five hundred pounds. The *Evening Messenger* published the full story of his Great Inspiration. Mr. Budd trembled, fearing this sinister fame. Surely no one would ever come to his shop again.

On the next morning an enormous blue limousine rolled up to his door. A lady, magnificent in diamonds, swept into the shop.

"You are Mr. Budd, aren't you?" she cried. "The great Mr. Budd? Isn't it too wonderful? And now, dear Mr. Budd, you must do me a favor. You must dye my hair green at once. Now. I want to be able to say *I'm* the *very first* to be done by you. I'm the Duchess of Winchester, and that awful Lady Melcaster is following me because *she* wants to be the first."

If you want it done, I can give you the number of Mr. Budd's new shop in the best section of London. But I understand it is a very expensive process!

About the Author

Dorothy L. Sayers (1893–1957) was born in Oxford, England, and later attended Oxford University, where she became one of the first women to receive a degree from that university. Sayers's 11 novels and many short stories, most of which feature amateur detective Lord Peter Wimsey, firmly established Sayers as one of the leading authors of detective fiction. Her works are known for clever plots, interesting and complex characters, and witty dialogue, as well as for the use of extensive and fascinating background material. Late in her career, Sayers abandoned mystery stories in favor of writing about religious and scholarly subjects.

THINK ABOUT THE STORY. The following questions help you check your reading comprehension. Put an *x* in the box next to the correct answer.

1. This story is mainly about
   - ☐ a. how a barber uses his knowledge to bring a criminal to justice.
   - ☐ b. the difficulties involved in establishing a profitable business.
   - ☐ c. why one must exercise care in dealing with a dangerous individual.

2. William Strickland asked Mr. Budd to dye his hair
   - ☐ a. black.
   - ☐ b. brown.
   - ☐ c. red.

3. Strickland was wanted by the police for
   - ☐ a. stealing money from a bank.
   - ☐ b. breaking into a store.
   - ☐ c. murdering his aunt.

4. As a result of his efforts, Mr. Budd
   - ☐ a. lost customers and nearly went out of business.
   - ☐ b. made enemies everywhere.
   - ☐ c. eventually opened a successful, expensive shop.

HANDLE NEW VOCABULARY WORDS. The following questions check your vocabulary skills. Put an *x* in the box next to the correct answer. Each vocabulary word appears in the story.

1. Mr. Budd would "gently dissuade" a customer from having his hair dyed a dreadful color. The word *dissuade* means
   - ☐ a. encourage.
   - ☐ b. cooperate with.
   - ☐ c. persuade not to do something.

2. Since he was very eager to satisfy customers, Mr. Budd acted in an obsequious way. What is the meaning of the word *obsequious*?
   - ☐ a. overly eager to please or obey
   - ☐ b. humorous or joking
   - ☐ c. rapid or speedy

3. He had to "do the job very well"; there could be no fiasco. What is a *fiasco*?
   - ☐ a. a kind of festival
   - ☐ b. a change of mind
   - ☐ c. a ridiculous failure

4. Strickland's black hair had turned prematurely gray. Define the word *prematurely*.
   - ☐ a. without warning
   - ☐ b. too early or too soon
   - ☐ c. brightly colored

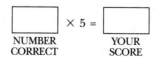

NUMBER CORRECT   × 5 =   YOUR SCORE

NUMBER CORRECT   × 5 =   YOUR SCORE

EXAMINE STORY ELEMENTS. The following questions check your knowledge of story elements. Put an *x* in the box next to each correct answer.

1. Of the following, which happened first in the *plot* of the story?
   ☐ a. Mr. Budd removed Strickland's beard.
   ☐ b. Sir Andrew and another gentleman listened to Strickland's story.
   ☐ c. Mr. Budd read a description of William Strickland.

2. Which of the following is an example of *inner conflict*?
   ☐ a. Mr. Budd wanted to capture Strickland himself but was too fearful to attempt the capture.
   ☐ b. Mr. Budd believed that he was a better barber than his rival.
   ☐ c. As soon as Strickland left, Mr. Budd went to the police.

3. Which statement best *characterizes* Mr. Budd?
   ☐ a. He possessed the courage and determination of all great detectives.
   ☐ b. He was past middle age, a bit heavy, and had thinning hair.
   ☐ c. He was 43 years old and was about six feet tall.

4. The *setting* of the story is
   ☐ a. London.
   ☐ b. the United States.
   ☐ c. ports in Germany, France, and Belgium.

☐ × 5 = ☐
NUMBER CORRECT   YOUR SCORE

MASTER CRITICAL THINKING. The following questions check your critical thinking skills. Put an *x* in the box next to each correct answer.

1. We may infer that Mr. Budd turned Strickland's hair green by
   ☐ a. dying Strickland's hair green in the shop.
   ☐ b. applying a dye that combined with the dye in Strickland's hair to cause it to change colors later.
   ☐ c. accidentally using the wrong dye.

2. Probably Strickland wanted to have his hair dyed because
   ☐ a. he wanted to change his appearance.
   ☐ b. he was tired of the old color.
   ☐ c. his fiancée suggested that he should try a new hair color.

3. Evidence in the story suggests that Strickland concealed his left hand because
   ☐ a. he was holding a gun in it.
   ☐ b. it was swollen and bruised.
   ☐ c. he wished to hide his injured thumbnail.

4. We may conclude that "Watson" sent for a barber to
   ☐ a. deliver a message to a friend.
   ☐ b. do something about his green hair.
   ☐ c. complain about Mr. Budd.

☐ × 5 = ☐
NUMBER CORRECT   YOUR SCORE

EXPLORE THE WRITER'S CRAFT. The following questions check your knowledge of skills related to the craft of writing. Put an *x* in the box next to each correct answer. You may refer to pages 4 and 5.

1. The scarlet border "ran round and round like a kitten chasing its own tail." This sentence contains
   ☐ a. alliteration.
   ☐ b. personification.
   ☐ c. a simile.

2. Mr. Budd heard his customer ask, "Are you prepared to die?" This is a pun, or a play on words, because
   ☐ a. Mr. Budd was not ready to die.
   ☐ b. the customer had recently caused someone to die.
   ☐ c. the customer meant "dye," not "die."

3. Mr. Budd noted that there are "hundreds of people" with smashed left thumbs and gold upper left teeth in the country. Since Mr. Budd did not really mean that, his thoughts were
   ☐ a. ironic.
   ☐ b. symbolic.
   ☐ c. an example of dialect.

4. Mr. Budd said, "That was what Sherlock Holmes would do." This sentence contains
   ☐ a. onomatopoeia.
   ☐ b. a literary allusion.
   ☐ c. a metaphor.

Questions for Writing and Discussion

- What was Mr. Budd's "Great Inspiration"? Explain in detail.
- Mr. Budd did not have to arrest William Strickland himself. Budd just had to provide "information leading to the arrest." Why is this information so important?
- Why did telegraph operators in many ports laugh at the message they received?
- Explain why Strickland became a very easy target to capture.
- Mr. Budd thought of the inscription "Knowledge Is Power." Show how those words proved to be true.

See additional questions for extended writing on pages 124 and 125.

Use the boxes below to total your scores for the exercises. Then record your scores on pages 224 and 225.

☐ **T**HINK ABOUT THE STORY
+
☐ **H**ANDLE NEW VOCABULARY WORDS
+
☐ **E**XAMINE STORY ELEMENTS
+
☐ **M**ASTER CRITICAL THINKING
+
☐ **E**XPLORE THE WRITER'S CRAFT
▼
☐ **Total Score:** Story 8

☐ × 5 = ☐

NUMBER   YOUR
CORRECT   SCORE

Miss Marple decides that something is "too good to be true" in . . .

The Case of the Perfect Maid

by Agatha Christie

"**O**h, if you please, M'am, could I speak to you a moment?"

Miss Marple said promptly, "Certainly, Edna; come in and shut the door. What is it?"

Obediently shutting the door, Miss Marple's little maid advanced into the room, pleated the corner of her apron between her fingers, and swallowed once or twice.

"Yes, Edna?" said Miss Marple encouragingly.

"Oh, please, M'am, it's my cousin Gladdie."

"Dear me," said Miss Marple, her mind leaping to the worst—and, alas, the most usual conclusion. "Not—not in *trouble?*"

Edna hastened to reassure her.

"On, no, M'am, nothing of *that* kind. It's just that she's upset. You see, she's lost her place."[1]

"Dear me, I am sorry to hear that. She was at Old Hall, wasn't she, with the Miss—Miss—Skinners?"

"Yes, M'am, that's right, M'am. And Gladdie's very upset about it—very upset indeed."

"Gladys has changed places rather often before, though, hasn't she?"

"Oh, yes, M'am. She's always one for a change, Gladdie is. She never seems to get really *settled,* if you know that I mean. But she's always been the one to *give* the notice,[2] you see!"

"And this time it's the other way round?" said Miss Marple dryly.

"Yes, M'am, and it's upset Gladdie something awful."

Miss Marple looked slightly surprised. Her recollection of Gladys, who had occasionally come to drink tea in the kitchen on her "days out," was of a stout, giggling girl of unshakably equable[3] temperament.

Edna went on. "You see, M'am, it's the *way* it happened—the way Miss Skinner looked."

"How," inquired Miss Marple patiently, "did Miss Skinner look?"

This time Edna got well away with her news bulletin.

"Oh, M'am, it was ever such a shock to Gladdie. You see, one of Miss Emily's brooches[4] was missing and such a hue and cry for it as never was, and, of course, nobody likes a thing like that to happen—it's upsetting, M'am, if you know what I mean. And Gladdie helped search *everywhere,* and there was Miss Lavinia saying she was going to the police about it, and then it turned up again, pushed right to the back of a drawer in the dressing-table, and *very* thankful Gladdie was. And the very next day as ever was a plate got broken, and Miss Lavinia she bounced out right away and told Gladdie to take a month's notice.[5] And what Gladdie feels is it *couldn't* have been the plate, and that Miss Lavinia was just making an excuse of that, that it must be because of the brooch, and they think as she took it and put it back when the police was mentioned, and Gladdie wouldn't do

---

1. **lost her place:** lost her job

2. **to give the notice:** to say that one is leaving or quitting a job

3. **equable:** calm; not easily disturbed

4. **brooches:** pieces of jewelry; large pins

5. **take a month's notice:** to be notified that one's employment will end in one month

such a thing, and what she feels is as it will get around and tell against her, and it's a very serious thing for a girl, as you know, M'am."

Miss Marple nodded.

Edna said wistfully, "I suppose, M'am, there isn't anything you could do about it? Gladdie's in ever such a state."

"Tell her not to be silly," said Miss Marple crisply. "If she didn't take the brooch—which I'm sure she didn't—then she has no cause to be upset."

"It'll get about," said Edna dismally.

"I—er—am going up that way this afternoon," said Miss Marple. "I'll have a word with the Misses Skinner."

"Oh! *thank* you, M'am," said Edna.

Old Hall was a big Victorian house surrounded by woods and parkland. Since it had proved unlettable[6] and unsalable as it was, an enterprising speculator had divided it into four flats[7] with a central hot-water system, and the use of "the grounds" to be held in common by the tenants.

The experiment had been satisfactory. A rich and eccentric old lady and her maid occupied one flat. The old lady had a passion for birds and entertained a feathered gathering to meals every day. A retired Indian judge and his wife rented a second flat. A very young couple, recently married, occupied the third, and the fourth had been taken only two months ago by two ladies of the name Skinner.

The four sets of tenants were only on the most distant terms with each other, since none of them had anything in common. The landlord had been heard to say that this was an excellent thing. What he dreaded were friendships followed by estrangements and subsequent complaints to him.

Miss Marple was acquainted with all the tenants, though she knew none of them well. The elder Miss Skinner, Miss Lavinia, was what might be termed the working member of the firm. Miss Emily, the younger, spent most of her time in bed suffering from various complaints which, in the opinion of St. Mary Mead, were largely imaginary. Only Miss Lavinia believed devoutly in her sister's martyrdom and patience under affliction, and willingly ran errands and trotted up and down to the village for things that "my sister had suddenly fancied."

It was the view of St. Mary Mead that if Miss Emily suffered half as much as she said she did, she would have sent for Doctor Haydock long ago. But Miss Emily, when this was hinted to her, shut her eyes in a superior way and murmured that her case was not a simple one—the best specialists in London had been baffled by it—and that a wonderful new man had put her on a most revolutionary course of treatment and that she really hoped her health would improve under it. No humdrum G.P.[8] could *possibly* understand her case.

"And it's my opinion," said the outspoken Miss Hartnell, "that she's very wise not to send for him. Dear Doctor Haydock would tell her that there was nothing the matter with her and to get up and not make a fuss. Do her a lot of good!"

---

6. **unlettable:** unable to be rented

7. **flats:** apartments

---

8. **G.P.:** general practitioner; a doctor who treats many kinds of illness

Failing such arbitrary treatment, however, Miss Emily continued to lie on sofas, to surround herself with strange little pillboxes, and to reject nearly everything that had been cooked for her and ask for something else.

The door was opened to Miss Marple by Gladdie, looking more depressed than Miss Marple had ever thought possible. In the sitting room Miss Lavinia rose to greet Miss Marple.

Lavinia Skinner was a tall, gaunt, bony female of fifty. She had a gruff voice and an abrupt manner.

"Nice to see you," she said. "Emily's lying down—feeling low today, poor dear. Hope she'll see you, it would cheer her up, but there are times when she doesn't feel up to seeing *anybody*. Poor dear, she's wonderfully patient."

Miss Marple responded politely. Servants were the main topic of conversation in St. Mary Mead, so it was not difficult to lead the conversation in that direction. Miss Marple said she had heard that that nice girl, Gladys Holmes, was leaving.

Miss Lavinia nodded. "Wednesday week. Broke things, you know. Can't have that."

Miss Marple sighed and said we all had to put up with things nowadays. Did Miss Skinner really think it was wise to part with Gladys?

"Know it's difficult to get servants," admitted Miss Lavinia. "The Devereuxs haven't got *anybody*—but then I don't wonder—always quarreling, jazz on all night—meals any time. Then the Larkins have just lost *their* maid. Of course, what with the judge's temper and his wanting Chota Hazri,[9] as he calls it, at six in the morning, and Mrs. Larkin always fussing, I don't wonder at that, either. Mrs. Carmichael's Janet is a fixture, of course—though in my opinion she's the most disagreeable woman and absolutely *bullies* the old lady."

"Then don't you think you might reconsider your decision about Gladys? She really is a nice girl. I know all her family—very honest and superior."

Miss Lavinia shook her head.

Miss Marple murmured, "You missed a brooch, I understand—"

"Now who has been talking? I suppose the girl has. Quite frankly, I'm almost certain she took it. And then got frightened and put it back—but of course one can't say anything unless one is *sure*." She changed the subject. "Do come and see Miss Emily, Miss Marple, I'm sure it would do her good."

Miss Marple followed meekly to where Miss Lavinia knocked on a door, was bidden enter, and ushered her guest into the best room in the flat, most of the light of which was excluded by half-drawn blinds. Miss Emily was lying in bed.

The dim light showed her to be a thin, indecisive looking creature with a good deal of grayish-yellow hair untidily wound round her head and erupting into curls—the whole thing looking like a bird's nest of which no self-respecting bird could be proud. There was a smell in the room of eau-de-cologne,[10] stale biscuits, and camphor.

With half-closed eyes and in a thin, weak voice, Emily Skinner explained that this was one of her *bad* days.

---

9. Chota Hazri: a light morning snack or refreshment

10. eau-de-cologne: a kind of perfume

"The worst of ill health is," said Miss Emily in a melancholy tone, "that one knows what a *burden* one is to everyone around one."

"No, no, Emily dear, indeed that is not so," protested her sister.

"Lavinia is very good to me," said Miss Emily. "Lavvie dear, I do so hate giving trouble, but if my hot-water bottle could only be filled in the way I like it—*too* full it weighs on me so; on the other hand, if it is not *sufficiently* filled, it gets *cold* immediately!"

"I'm sorry, dear. Give it to me. I will empty a little out."

"Perhaps, if you're doing that, it might be refilled. There are no rusks[11] in the house, I suppose—no, no, it doesn't matter. I can do without. Some weak tea and a slice of lemon—no lemons? No, really, I couldn't drink tea without lemon—I think the milk was slightly turned this morning—it has put me right against milk in my tea. It doesn't matter. I can do without my tea. Only I do feel so weak. Oysters, they say, are nourishing—I wonder if I could fancy a few? No, no, too much bother to get hold of them so late in the day. I can fast until tomorrow."

Lavinia left the room, murmuring something incoherent about bicycling down to the village.

Miss Marple told Edna that evening that she was afraid her embassy[12] had met with no success.

She was rather troubled to find that rumors as to Glady's dishonesty were already going round the village.

In the Post Office Miss Wetherby tackled her. "My dear Jane, they gave her a written reference saying she was willing and sober and respectable, but saying nothing about *honesty*—that seems to me *most* significant! They'll find it *most* difficult to get anyone else. Girls simply *will not* go to Old Hall. You'll see, the Skinners won't find anyone else, and then perhaps that dreadful hypochondriac[13] sister will *have* to get up and do something!"

Great was the chagrin of the village when it was made known that the Misses Skinner had engaged, from an agency, a new maid who, by all accounts, was a perfect paragon.

"A three years' reference recommending her most warmly; she *prefers* the country and actually asks less wages than Gladys. I really feel we have been *most* fortunate."

It then became the opinion of St. Mary Mead that the paragon would cry off at the last minute.

None of these prognostications[14] came true, however, and the village was able to observe the domestic treasure, by name Mary Higgins, driving through the village in Reed's taxi to Old Hall. A most respectable looking woman, very neatly dressed.

When Miss Marple next visited Old Hall, on the occasion of recruiting stallholders for the Vicarage Fête, Mary Higgins opened the door. She was certainly a superior-looking maid, at a guess forty years of age, with neat black hair, rosy cheeks, a plump figure discreetly arrayed in black with a

---

11. **rusks:** biscuits

12. **embassy:** as used here, *embassy* means "mission"

13. **hypochondriac:** a person who continually imagines himself or herself to be sick

14. **prognostications:** predictions

white apron and a cap—"quite the good, old-fashioned type of servant," as Miss Marple explained afterwards, and with the proper, inaudible, respectful voice.

Miss Lavinia was looking far less harassed than usual, and although she regretted that she could not take a stall owing to her preoccupation with her sister, she nevertheless tendered a handsome monetary contribution and promised to produce a consignment of penwipers and babies' socks.

Miss Marple commented on her air of well-being.

"I really feel I owe a great deal to Mary. I am *so thankful* I had the resolution to get rid of that other girl. Mary is really *invaluable.* Cooks nicely and waits beautifully and keeps our little flat scrupulously clean—mattresses turned *every day.* And she is really *wonderful* with Emily!"

Miss Marple hastily inquired after Emily.

"Oh, poor dear, she has been very much under the weather lately. She can't help it, of course, but it really makes things a little *difficult,* sometimes. Wanting certain things cooked and then, when they come, saying she can't eat now—and then wanting them again half an hour later. It makes, of course, a lot of work—but fortunately Mary does not seem to mind *at all.* She's been used to waiting on invalids, she says, and understands them. It is such a *comfort.*"

"Dear me," said Miss Marple. "You *are* fortunate."

"Yes, indeed. I really feel Mary has been sent to us as an answer to a *prayer.*"

"She sounds to me," said Miss Marple, "almost too good to be true. I should—well, I should be a little careful if I were you."

Lavinia Skinner failed to perceive the point of this remark. She said, "Oh! I assure you I do all I can to make her comfortable. I don't know what I should do if she left."

"I don't expect she'll leave until she's ready to leave," said Miss Marple, and stared very hard at her hostess.

"If one has no domestic worries," said Miss Lavinia, "it takes such a load off one's mind, doesn't it? How is your little Edna shaping?"

"She's doing quite nicely. Not much *head,* of course. Not like your Mary. Still, I do know all about Edna, because she's a village girl."

Again she stared hard at Miss Lavinia; then sighed and changed the subject, asking if she should go in and see Miss Emily.

"Not today, I'm afraid," said Lavinia, shaking her head. "Poor Emily is quite unfit for visitors."

Miss Marple expressed polite sympathy and took her leave.

As she went out into the hall she heard the invalid's voice fretfully raised: "This compress has been allowed to get quite dry—Doctor Allerton particularly said moisture *continually* renewed. There, there, leave it. I want a cup of tea and a boiled egg—boiled only three minutes and a half, remember—and send Miss Lavinia to me."

The efficient Mary emerged from the bedroom, and saying to Lavinia, "Miss Emily is asking for you, Madam," proceeded to open the door for Miss Marple, helping her into her coat and handing her her umbrella.

Miss Marple took the umbrella, dropped it, tried to pick it up, and dropped her bag, which flew open. Mary politely retrieved various odds and ends—a handkerchief, an engagement book, an old-fashioned leather purse, two shillings,[15] three pennies, and a striped piece of peppermint rock.[16]

Miss Marple received the last with some signs of confusion.

"Oh, *dear,* that must have been Mrs. Clement's little boy. He *was* sucking it, I remember, and he took my bag to play with. He must have put it inside. It's terribly sticky, isn't it?"

"Shall I take it, Madam?"

"Oh, would you? Thank you so much."

Mary stooped to retrieve the last item, a small mirror, upon recovering which Miss Marple exclaimed fervently, "How lucky now that that isn't broken!"

She thereupon departed, Mary standing politely by the door holding a piece of striped rock with a completely expressionless face.

For ten days longer St. Mary Mead had to endure hearing of the excellencies of Miss Lavinia's and Miss Emily's treasure. On the eleventh day, the village awoke to its big thrill.

Mary, the paragon, was missing. Her bed had not been slept in and the front door was found ajar. She had slipped out quietly during the night.

And not Mary alone was missing! Two brooches and five rings of Miss Lavinia's; three rings, a pendant, a bracelet, and four brooches of Miss Emily's were missing also!

It was the beginning of a chapter of catastrophe.

Young Mrs. Devereaux had lost her diamonds which she kept in an unlocked drawer, and also some valuable furs given to her as a wedding present. The judge and his wife also had had jewelry taken and a certain amount of money. Mrs. Carmichael was the greatest sufferer. Not only had she some very valuable jewels but she also kept in the flat a large sum of money, which had gone. It had been Janet's evening out and her mistress was in the habit of walking round the gardens at dusk calling to the birds and scattering crumbs. It seemed clear that Mary, the perfect maid, had had keys to fit all the flats!

There was, it must be confessed, a certain amount of ill-natured pleasure in St. Mary Mead. Miss Lavinia had boasted so much of her marvelous Mary.

"And all the time, my dear, just a common *thief!*"

Interesting revelations followed. Not only had Mary disappeared into the blue but the agency which had provided her and vouched for her credentials was alarmed to find that the Mary Higgins who had applied to them and whose references they had taken up had, to all intents and purposes, never existed. It was the name of a *bona fide*[17] servant who had lived with the *bona fide* sister of a dean, but the real Mary Higgins was existing peacefully in a place in Cornwall.

"Clever, the whole thing," Inspector Slack was forced to admit. "And if you ask me, that woman works in with a gang. There was a case of much the same kind in Northumberland a year ago. Stuff was never traced and they never caught her. However, we'll do better than that in Much Benham!"

Nevertheless, weeks passed and Mary Higgins remained triumphantly at large. In

---

15. **shillings:** coins worth a certain amount of money in Great Britain

16. **peppermint rock:** peppermint candy

17. *bona fide:* genuine

vain Inspector Slack redoubled the energy that so belied his name.

Miss Lavinia remained tearful. Miss Emily was so upset, and felt so alarmed by her condition, that she actually sent for Doctor Haydock.

The whole of the village was terribly anxious to know what he thought of Miss Emily's claims to ill health, but naturally could not ask him.

Satisfactory data came to hand on the subject, however, through Mr. Meek, the chemist's assistant, who was walking out with Clara, Mrs. Price-Ridley's maid. It was then known that Doctor Haydock had prescribed a mixture of asafœtida and valerian which, according to Mr. Meek, was the stock remedy for malingerers[18] in the Army! It was felt that this settled the question of Miss Emily's health once and for all, and great admiration was felt for Doctor Haydock's masterly handling of the case.

Soon afterwards it was learned that Miss Emily, not relishing the medical attention she had had, was declaring that in the state of her health she felt it her duty to be near the specialist in London who *understood* her case. It was, she said, only fair to Lavinia.

The flat was put up for sub-letting.[19]

It was a few days after that that Miss Marple, rather pink and flustered, called at the police station in Much Benham and asked for Inspector Slack.

Inspector Slack did not like Miss Marple. But he was aware that the Chief Constable,

Colonel Melchett, did not share that feeling. Rather grudgingly, therefore, he received her.

"Good afternoon, Miss Marple; what can I do for you?"

"Oh, dear," said Miss Marple, "I'm afraid you're in a hurry."

"Lot of work on," said Inspector Slack, "but I can spare a few moments."

"Oh, dear," said Miss Marple, "I hope I shall be able to put what I say properly. So difficult, you know, to explain oneself, don't you think? No, perhaps, you don't. But you see, not having been educated in the modern style—just a governess, you know, who taught one the dates of the Kings of England and General Knowledge—Doctor Brewer—three kinds of diseases of wheat—blight, mildew—now what was the third—was it *smut?*"

"Do you want to talk about smut?" asked Inspector Slack, and then blushed.

"On, no, no. Just an *illustration,* you know. It's about Miss Skinner's maid. Gladys, you know."

"Mary Higgins," said Inspector Slack.

"Oh, yes, the *second* maid. But it's Gladys Holmes I mean—rather an impertinent girl and far too pleased with herself, but really strictly honest, and it's so important that that should be *recognized.*"

"No charge against *her* so far as I know," said the Inspector.

"No, I know there isn't a charge—but that makes it worse. Because you see, people go on *thinking* things. Oh dear—I knew I should explain badly. What I really mean is that the important thing is to find Mary Higgins."

"Certainly," said Inspector Slack. "Have you any ideas on the subject?"

18. **malingerers:** people who pretend to be sick in order to avoid work or responsibility

19. **put up for sub-letting:** advertised for rent

The Case of the Perfect Maid

He grudgingly remembered that Miss Marple's ideas had occasionally proved of use in the administration of justice.

"Well, as a matter of fact, I *have*," said Miss Marple. "May I ask you a question? Are fingerprints of no use to you?"

"Ah!" said Inspector Slack, "that's where she was a bit too artful for us. Did most of her work in rubber gloves or housemaid's gloves, it seems. And she'd been careful—wiped off everything in her bedroom and on the sink. Couldn't find a single fingerprint in the place!"

"If you did have her fingerprints, would it help?"

"It might, Madam; they may be known at the Yard.[20] This isn't her first job, I'd say!"

Miss Marple nodded brightly. She opened her bag and extracted a small cardboard box. Inside it, wedged in cotton-wool, was a small mirror.

"From my handbag," said Miss Marple. "The maid's prints are on it. I *think* they should be satisfactory—she touched an extremely sticky substance a moment previously."

Inspector Slack stared. "Did you get her fingerprints on purpose?"

"Of course."

"You suspected her, then?"

"Well, you know, it did strike me that she as a little *too good to be true*. I practically told Miss Lavinia so—but she simply wouldn't take the hint! I'm afraid, you know, Inspector, that I don't believe in *paragons*. Most of us have our faults—and domestic service shows them up very quickly!"

"Well," said Inspector Slack, recovering his balance. "I'm obliged to you, I'm sure. We'll send these up to the Yard and see what they have to say."

He stopped. Miss Marple had put her head a little on one side and was regarding him with a good deal of meaning.

"You wouldn't consider, I suppose, Inspector, looking a little *nearer home?*"

"What do you mean, Miss Marple?"

"It's very difficult to explain, but when you come across a peculiar thing you notice it. Although, often, peculiar things may be the merest trifles. I've felt that all along, you know—I mean, about Gladys and the brooch. She's an honest girl, and she didn't take that brooch—then *why did Miss Skinner think she did?* Miss Skinner's not a fool, far from it! Why was she so anxious to let a girl go who was a good servant, when servants are hard to get? It was *peculiar,* you know. So I wondered . . . I wondered a good deal. And I noticed another peculiar thing! Miss Emily's a hypochondriac—but she's the first hypochondriac who hasn't sent for some doctor or other at once. Hypochondriacs *love* doctors. Miss Emily didn't!"

"What are you suggesting, Miss Marple?" Inspector Slack was still quite fogged.

"Well, I'm suggesting, you know, that Miss Lavinia and Miss Emily are peculiar people. Miss Emily spends nearly all her time in a dark room. And if that hair of hers isn't a wig I—I'll eat my own back switch! And what I say is this—it's perfectly possible for a thin, pale, gray-haired, whining woman to be the same as a black-haired, rosy-cheeked, plump woman. And nobody that *I* can find ever *saw Miss Emily and Mary Higgins at one and the same time.* Plenty of time to get impressions of all the keys, plenty of time to find out all about the

20. the Yard: Scotland Yard, the headquarters of the London police force, especially the branch involved in detective work

other tenants, and then—get rid of the local girl. Miss Emily takes a brisk walk across country one night and arrives at the station as Mary Higgins next day. And then, at the right moment, Mary Higgins disappears, and off goes the hue and cry after *her*.

"I'll tell you where you'll find her, Inspector. On Miss Emily Skinner's sofa! Get *her* fingerprints if you don't believe me, but you'll find I'm right. A couple of clever thieves, that's what the Skinners are—and no doubt in league with a clever post and rails, or fence, or whatever you call it. But they won't get away with it *this* time! I'm not going to have one of our village girl's

character for honesty taken away like that! Gladys Holmes is as honest as the day and everybody's going to know it! Good afternoon!"

Miss Marple had stalked out before Inspector Slack had recovered.

"Whew!" he muttered. "I wonder if she's right?"

He soon found out that Miss Marple was right again.

Colonel Melchett congratulated Slack on his efficiency, and Miss Marple arranged for Gladys to come to tea with Edna and spoke to her seriously on settling down in a good situation when she got one.

About the Author

Agatha Christie (1890–1976) may be the most widely read mystery writer of all time. During a 50-year career, Christie produced more than 65 novels, numerous short story collections, and 16 plays. Countless copies of her works have been sold, and her work has been translated into more than one hundred languages. In addition, her suspense thriller *The Mousetrap* is the longest running play in the history of the theater.

Among Christie's most famous creations are Hercule Poirot, an amusing, bumbling Belgian detective, and Miss Jane Marple, an elderly amateur crime solver who is the main character in "The Case of the Perfect Maid." Born in England, Christie won dozens of awards for her writing, and many prizes for detective fiction bear her name. As critic H. R. F. Keating stated, Christie is "a towering figure in the history of crime literature."

THINK ABOUT THE STORY. The following questions help you check your reading comprehension. Put an *x* in the box next to the correct answer.

1. This story is mainly about how Miss Marple
   - ☐ a. tries to help Gladys find a new job.
   - ☐ b. proves that Inspector Slack is not particularly smart.
   - ☐ c. solves a crime involving two sisters.

2. Miss Lavinia said the reason she fired Gladys was that the maid
   - ☐ a. broke things.
   - ☐ b. did not clean the house well.
   - ☐ c. paid very little attention to her ailing sister, Emily.

3. What did Mary Higgins steal?
   - ☐ a. a letter from the agency that employed her
   - ☐ b. jewelry, furs, and money
   - ☐ c. an item that fell out of Miss Marple's purse

4. Miss Marple obtained Mary's fingerprints on
   - ☐ a. an umbrella.
   - ☐ b. a drinking glass.
   - ☐ c. a mirror.

HANDLE NEW VOCABULARY WORDS. The following questions check your vocabulary skills. Put an *x* in the box next to the correct answer. Each vocabulary word appears in the story.

1. Mary's credentials from the agency proved to be false. The word *credentials* means
   - ☐ a. references or letters of recommendation.
   - ☐ b. supervisors or directors.
   - ☐ c. uniforms that one is required to wear at work.

2. Miss Marple stated, "I don't believe in *paragons*. Most of us have our faults." What is a *paragon*?
   - ☐ a. a person who frequently gets into trouble
   - ☐ b. a very wise teacher
   - ☐ c. a model of perfection

3. The eccentric old lady insisted on eating all her meals while seated among a flock of birds. What is the meaning of the word *eccentric*?
   - ☐ a. pleasant and friendly
   - ☐ b. unusual or odd
   - ☐ c. cheerful or joyous

4. Lavinia stayed home most of the time because of her preoccupation with her sick sister. Which expression best defines *preoccupation*?
   - ☐ a. fear of meeting a stranger
   - ☐ b. the ability to cure an ill person
   - ☐ c. extreme concern with something

☐ × 5 = ☐
NUMBER CORRECT   YOUR SCORE

☐ × 5 = ☐
NUMBER CORRECT   YOUR SCORE

EXAMINE STORY ELEMENTS. The following questions check your knowledge of story elements. Put an *x* in the box next to each correct answer.

1. Of the following events, which happened last in the *plot* of the story?
   ☐ a. Miss Marple visited Inspector Slack at the police station.
   ☐ b. Mary Higgins was hired by Lavinia.
   ☐ c. Edna told Miss Marple that Gladys had been fired.

2. Which of the following *foreshadows* what occurred at the end of the story?
   ☐ a. Inspector Slack said that the police could not find "a single fingerprint."
   ☐ b. Miss Emily said she was "a burden" to those around her.
   ☐ c. Miss Marple stated that Mary was "almost too good to be true."

3. What was Miss Lavinia's *motive* for firing Gladys?
   ☐ a. Lavinia believed that Gladys could not be trusted.
   ☐ b. Lavinia needed a reason to hire Mary Higgins.
   ☐ c. Lavinia discovered that Gladys never stayed very long at a job.

4. Who is the *narrator* of the story?
   ☐ a. Miss Marple
   ☐ b. Miss Lavinia
   ☐ c. the writer

MASTER CRITICAL THINKING. The following questions check your critical thinking skills. Put an *x* in the box next to each correct answer.

1. We may infer that Mary Higgins and Emily Skinner were
   ☐ a. sisters.
   ☐ b. very good friends.
   ☐ c. the same person.

2. It is fair to say that Emily
   ☐ a. truly felt too ill to get out of bed.
   ☐ b. pretended that she was sick as part of a plan.
   ☐ c. did not trust her sister.

3. Evidence in the story suggests that Miss Marple
   ☐ a. really believed that Lavinia was fortunate to find such a fine maid.
   ☐ b. figured out a clever way to get Mary's fingerprints.
   ☐ c. had never been of help to the police before.

4. We may conclude that Lavinia and Emily
   ☐ a. intended to go to London but were arrested before they could leave.
   ☐ b. suspected all along that Miss Marple knew they were thieves.
   ☐ c. were never captured and brought to justice.

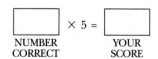

NUMBER CORRECT   × 5 =   YOUR SCORE

EXPLORE THE WRITER'S CRAFT. The following questions check your knowledge of skills related to the craft of writing. Put an *x* in the box next to each correct answer. You may refer to pages 4 and 5.

1. Miss Lavinia boasted and bragged about marvelous Mary. This sentence illustrates
   ☐ a. alliteration.
   ☐ b. onomatopoeia.
   ☐ c. symbolism.

2. Emily Skinner's hair wound untidily around her head, "looking like a bird's nest." This sentence contains
   ☐ a. a metaphor.
   ☐ b. a simile.
   ☐ c. an example of personification.

3. The morning after the daring robbery "the village awoke to its big thrill." As used in this sentence, what is the connotation of the word *thrill*?
   ☐ a. delight
   ☐ b. shock
   ☐ c. fright

4. Miss Marple believed that the Skinners were working with "a clever post and rails, or fence, or whatever you call it." Since *fence* is slang for "a person who takes stolen goods," the author intends the sentence to be
   ☐ a. mysterious.
   ☐ b. humorous.
   ☐ c. helpful in solving the crime.

☐ × 5 = ☐
NUMBER   YOUR
CORRECT   SCORE

Questions for Writing and Discussion

- Briefly explain the plan that the Skinners devised.
- Why did Miss Marple become suspicious when Miss Lavinia fired Gladys? Identify clues in the story that made Miss Marple suspicious of Emily and Mary.
- Describe in detail how Miss Marple tricked Mary into leaving her fingerprints.
- Miss Emily was a fine actress. Support this statement by referring to events in the story.

See additional questions for extended writing on pages 124 and 125.

Use the boxes below to total your scores for the exercises. Then record your scores on pages 224 and 225.

☐ **T**HINK ABOUT THE STORY
+
☐ **H**ANDLE NEW VOCABULARY WORDS
+
☐ **E**XAMINE STORY ELEMENTS
+
☐ **M**ASTER CRITICAL THINKING
+
☐ **E**XPLORE THE WRITER'S CRAFT
▼
☐ **Total Score:** Story 9

The Red-Headed League

by Arthur Conan Doyle

I had called upon my friend, Mr. Sherlock Holmes, one day in the autumn of last year, and found him in deep conversation with a very heavyset, elderly gentleman, with fiery red hair. With an apology for intruding, I was about to withdraw, when Holmes pulled me abruptly into the room, and closed the door behind me.

"You could not possibly have come at a better time, my dear Watson," he said cordially.

"I was afraid that you were busy."

"So I am. Very much so."

"Then I can wait in the next room."

"Not at all." He turned to the others. "This gentleman, Mr. Wilson, has been my partner and helper in many of my most successful cases, and I have no doubt that he will be of the utmost use to me in yours."

The stout gentleman half rose from his chair, and gave a nod of greeting, with a quick little questioning glance.

"Sit on the sofa," said Holmes, relapsing into his armchair, and putting his fingertips together, as was his custom when in thoughtful moods. "I know, my dear Watson, that you share my love of all that is bizarre and outside the humdrum routine of everyday life. You have shown your relish for it by the enthusiasm which has prompted you to chronicle, and, if you will excuse my saying so, to somewhat embellish so many of my own little adventures."

"Your cases have indeed been of the greatest interest to me," I observed.

"Now, Mr. Jabez Wilson here has been good enough to call upon me this morning, and to begin a narrative which promises to be one of the most unusual which I have listened to for some time. As far as I have heard, it is impossible for me to say whether the present case is an instance of crime or not, but the course of events is certainly among the strangest that I have ever listened to. Perhaps, Mr. Wilson, you would have the great kindness to recommence your narrative. I ask you not merely because my friend Dr. Watson has not heard the opening part, but also because the peculiar nature of the story makes me anxious to have every possible detail from your lips. As a rule, when I have heard some slight indication of the course of events I am able to guide myself by the thousands of other similar cases which occur to my memory. In the present instance I am forced to admit that the facts are, to the best of my belief, unique."

The portly client puffed out his chest with an appearance of some little pride, and pulled a dirty and wrinkled newspaper from the inside pocket of his jacket. As he glanced down the advertisement column, with his head thrust forward, and the paper flattened out upon his knee, I took a good look at the man, and endeavored after the fashion of my companion to read the indications which might be presented by his dress or appearance.

I did not gain very much, however, by my inspection. Our visitor bore every mark of being an average tradesman. Altogether, look as I would, there was nothing remarkable about the man except his blazing red head.

Sherlock Holmes shook his head with a smile as he noticed my questioning glances. "Beyond the obvious facts that he has at some time done much physical labor, that he has been in China, and that he has done a considerable amount of writing lately, I can deduce nothing else."

Mr. Jabez Wilson started up in his chair, his eyes upon my companion.

"How, in the name of good fortune, did you know all that, Mr. Holmes?" he asked. "How did you know, for example, that I did manual labor? It's true that I used to work as a ship's carpenter."

"Your hands, my dear sir. Your right hand is at least one size larger than your left. You have worked with it, and the muscles are more developed."

"But the writing?"

"What else can be indicated by that right cuff so very shiny for five inches, and the left one with the smooth patch near the elbow where you rest it upon the desk?"

"Well, but China?"

"The fish which you have tattooed just above your right wrist could only have been done in China. I have made a small study of tattoo marks, and have even contributed to the literature of the subject. That trick of staining the fishes' scales of a delicate pink is done only in China. When, in addition, I see a Chinese coin hanging from your watch-chain, the matter becomes even more simple."

Mr. Jabez Wilson laughed heavily. "Well, I never!" said he. "I thought at first you had done something clever, but I see that there was nothing in it after all."

"I begin to think, Watson," said Holmes, "that I make a mistake in explaining. My poor little reputation, such as it is, will suffer if I am so candid. Can you find the advertisement, Mr. Wilson?"

"Yes, I have got it now," he answered, with his thick, red finger pointed halfway down the column. "Here it is. This is what began it all. You just read it for yourself, sir."

I took the paper from him and read as follows:—

"TO THE RED-HEADED LEAGUE.— Because of the will of the late Ezekiah Hopkins, of Lebanon, Pennsylvania, there is now another vacancy open which entitles a member of the League to a salary of four pounds[1] a week for fairly easy work. All red-headed men who are sound in body and mind, and above the age of twenty-one years, are eligible. Apply in person on Monday, at eleven o'clock, to Duncan Ross, at the offices of the League, 7 Fleet Street."

"What on earth does this mean?" I asked, after I had twice read over the extraordinary announcement.

Holmes chuckled. "It is a little off the beaten track, isn't it?" said he. "And now, Mr. Wilson, tell us all about yourself, your household, and the effect which this advertisement had upon your fortunes. You will first make a note, Doctor, of the paper and the date."

"It is *The Morning Chronicle*, of April 27. Just two months ago."

"Very good. Now, Mr. Wilson?"

"Well, it is just as I have been telling you, Mr. Sherlock Holmes," said Jabez Wilson, mopping his forehead, "I have a small shoe-repair shop at Coburg Street, near the City. It's not a very large place, and of late years it has not done more than just give me a living. I used to be able to keep two assistants, but now I only keep one; and I would have a job to pay him, but that he is willing to work for half pay, so as to learn the business."

"What is the name of this obliging youth?" asked Sherlock Holmes.

"His name is Vincent Spaulding, and he's not such a youth either. It's hard to say his age. I should not wish a smarter assistant, Mr. Holmes; and I know very well that he could better himself, and earn twice what I am able to give him. But after all, if he is satisfied, why should I put ideas in his head?"

"Why, indeed? You seem most fortunate in having an employee who is willing to

---

1. **pound:** a unit of money in the United Kingdom

work cheaply. It is not a common experience among employers in this age.
I don't know that your assistant is not as remarkable as your advertisement."

"Oh, he has his faults, too," said Mr. Wilson. "Never was such a fellow for photography. Snapping away with a camera when he ought to be improving his mind, and then diving down into the cellar like a rabbit into its hole to develop his pictures. That is his main fault; but on the whole, he's a good worker. There's no vice in him."

"He is still with you, I presume?"

"Yes, sir. He and an elderly woman, who does a bit of simple cooking, and keeps the place clean—that's all I have in the house, for I am a widower, and never had any family. We live very quietly, sir, the three of us; and we keep a roof over our heads, and pay our debts, if we do nothing more.

"Spaulding, he came down into the office just this day eight weeks with this very paper in his hand, and he says:

"'I wish, Mr. Wilson, that I was a red-headed man.'

"'Why that?' I asks.

"'Why,' says he, 'here's another vacancy in the League of the Red-Headed Men. It's worth quite a fortune to any man who gets it, and I understand that there are more vacancies than there are men, so that the trustees are at their wits' end what to do with the money. If my hair would only change color, here's a nice easy job all ready for me to step into.'

"'Why, what is it, then?' I asked. You see, Mr. Holmes, I am a very stay-at-home man, and, as my business came to me instead of my having to go to it, I was often weeks on end without putting my foot over the doormat. In that way I didn't know much of

what was going on outside, and I was always glad of a bit of news.

"'Have you never heard of the League of the Red-Headed Men?' he asked, with his eyes open.

"'Never.'

"'Why, I wonder at that, for you are eligible yourself for one of the vacancies.'

"'And what are they worth?' I asked.

"'Oh, merely a couple of hundred pounds a year, but the work is slight, and it need not interfere much with one's other occupations.'

"Well, you can easily think that that interested me a great deal, for the business has not been good for some years, and an extra couple of hundred would have been very handy.

"'Tell me all about it,' said I.

"'Well,' said he, showing me the advertisement, 'you can see for yourself that the League has a vacancy, and there is the address where you should apply for particulars. As far as I can make out, the League was founded by an American millionaire, Ezekiah Hopkins, who was very peculiar in his ways. He was himself red-headed, and he had a great sympathy for all red-headed men; so, when he died, it was found that he had left his enormous fortune in the hands of trustees, with instructions to apply the interest to the providing of easy jobs to men whose hair is of that color. From all I hear it is splendid pay, and very little to do.'

"'But,' said I, 'there would be millions of red-headed men who would apply.'

"'Not so many as you might think,' he answered. 'You see, it is really confined to Londoners and to grown men. This American had started his business in

London when he was young, and he wanted to do the old town a good turn. Then, again, I have heard it is no use your applying if your hair is light red, or dark red, or anything but real, bright, blazing, fiery red. Now, if you cared to apply, Mr. Wilson, you would just walk in; but perhaps it would hardly be worth your while to put yourself out of the way for the sake of a few hundred pounds.'

"Now, it is a fact, gentlemen, as you may see for yourselves, that my hair is of a very full and rich tint, so that it seems to me that, if there was to be any competition in the matter, I stood as good a chance as any man that I had ever met. Vincent Spaulding seemed to know so much about it that I thought he might prove useful, so I just ordered him to close the shop for the day, and to come right away with me. He was very willing to have a holiday, so we shut the business up, and started off for the address that was given us in the advertisement.

"I never hope to see such a sight as that again, Mr. Holmes. From north, south, east, and west every man who had a shade of red in his hair had tramped into the City to answer the advertisement. Fleet Street was choked with red-headed folk. Every shade of red hair they had—orange, brick, clay— but, as Spaulding said, there were not many who had the real vivid flame-colored tint. When I saw how many were waiting, I would have given it up in despair; but Spaulding would not hear of it. How he did it I could not imagine, but he pushed and pulled until he got me through the crowd, and right up to the steps which led to the office. There were many people on the stair, some going up in hope, and some coming back dejected. But we wedged in as well as we

could, and soon found ourselves in the office."

"Your experience has been a most entertaining one," remarked Holmes, as his client paused for a moment. "Please continue your very interesting statement."

"There was nothing in the office but a couple of wooden chairs and a table, behind which sat a small man, with a head that was even redder than mine. He said a few words to each candidate as he came up, and then he always managed to find some fault in them which would disqualify them. Getting a vacancy did not seem to be such a very easy matter at all. However, when our turn came, the little man was more favorable to me than to any of the others, and he closed the door as we entered, so that he might have a private word with us.

"'This is Mr. Jabez Wilson,' said my assistant, 'and he is willing to fill a vacancy in the League.'

"'And he is admirably suited for it,' the other answered. 'He has every requirement. I cannot recall when I have seen anything so fine.' He took a step backwards and gazed at my hair until I felt quite bashful. Then suddenly he plunged forwards, wrung my hand, and congratulated me warmly on my success.

"'It would be injustice to hesitate,' said he. 'You will, however, I am sure, excuse me for taking an obvious precaution.' With that he seized my hair in both his hands, and tugged until I yelled with pain. 'I perceive that all is as it should be. But we have to be careful, for we have twice been deceived by wigs and once by dye.' He stepped over to the window and shouted through it at the top of his voice that the vacancy was filled.

A groan of disappointment came up from below, and the folk all trooped away in different directions, until there was not a red head to be seen except my own and that of the manager.

"'My name,' said he, 'is Mr. Duncan Ross, and I am myself one of the trustees of the fund left by Ezekiah Hopkins. When shall you be able to enter upon your new duties?'

"'Well, it is a little awkward, for I have a business already,' said I.

"'Oh, never mind about that, Mr. Wilson!' said Vincent Spaulding. 'I shall be able to look after that for you.'

"'What would be the hours?' I asked.

"'Ten to two.'

"I knew that my assistant was a good man, and that he would be able to manage anything that had to be done.

"'That would suit me very well,' said I. 'And the pay?'

"'Is four pounds a week.'

"'And the work?'

"'Is fairly simple.'

"'What do you call fairly simple?'

"'Well, you have to be in the office, or at least in the building, the whole time. If you leave, you forfeit your position for ever. The will is very clear upon that point. You don't comply with the conditions if you budge from the office during that time.'

"'It is only four hours a day, and I should not think of leaving,' said I.

"'No excuse will avail,' said Mr. Duncan Ross, 'neither sickness, nor business, nor anything else. There you must stay, or you will lose your job.'

"'And the work?'

"'Is to copy the *Encyclopedia Britannica.* There is the first volume of it on that shelf. You must bring your own ink, pens, and paper, but we provide this table and chair. Will you be ready tomorrow?'

"'Certainly,' I answered.

"'Then, good-bye, Mr. Jabez Wilson, and let me congratulate you once more on the important position which you have been fortunate enough to gain.' He bowed me out of the room, and I went home with my assistant, hardly knowing what to say or do, I was so pleased at my own good fortune."

"Well, I thought over the matter all day, and by evening I was in low spirits again; for I had persuaded myself that the whole thing must be some great hoax or fraud, though what its object might be I could not imagine. It seemed altogether past belief that anyone could make such a will, or that they would pay such a sum for doing anything so simple as copying the *Encyclopedia Britannica.* Vincent Spaulding did what he could to cheer me up, but by bedtime I had reasoned myself out of the whole thing. However, in the morning I determined to have a look at it anyhow, so I bought a bottle of ink, and with a pen, and seven sheets of paper, I started off to the office on Fleet Street.

"Well, to my surprise and delight everything was as right as possible. The table was set out ready for me, and Mr. Duncan Ross was there to see that I got right to work. He started me off on the letter *A*, and then he left me; but he would drop in from time to time to see that all was right with me. At two o'clock he bade me good day, complimented me upon the amount that I had written, and locked the door of the office after me.

"This went on day after day, Mr. Holmes, and on Saturday the manager came in and plunked down four pounds for my week's work. It was the same next week, and the same the week after. Every morning I was there at ten, and every afternoon I left at two. By degrees Mr. Duncan Ross took to coming in only once of a morning, and then, after a time, he did not come in at all. Still, of course, I never dared to leave the room for an instant, for I was not sure when he might come, and the job was such a good one, and suited me so well, that I would not risk the loss of it.

"Eight weeks passed away like this, and I had written about Africa, and Agriculture, and Architecture, and hoped with diligence that I might get on to the *B*'s before very long. I had pretty nearly filled a shelf with my writings. And then suddenly the whole business came to an end."

"To an end?"

"Yes, sir. And no later than this morning. I went to my work as usual at ten o'clock, but the door was shut and locked, with a note hammered on to the middle of the door with a tack. Here it is, and you can read for yourself."

He held up a white card with these words on it:

THE RED-HEADED LEAGUE IS DISSOLVED

Sherlock Holmes and I looked at this card and at the rueful face of Jabez Wilson behind it, until the comical side of the affair so completely overwhelmed us that we both burst out into a roar of laughter.

"I cannot see that there is anything very funny," cried our red-headed client. "If you can do nothing better than laugh at me, I can go elsewhere."

"No, no," cried Holmes, shoving him back into the chair from which he had half risen. "I really wouldn't miss your case for the world. It is most refreshingly unusual. But there is, if you will excuse my saying so, something just a little funny about it. What steps did you take when you found the card upon the door?"

"I was staggered, sir. I did not know what to do. Then I stopped in at the offices in the building, but no one seemed to know anything about it. Finally, I went to the landlord, who is an accountant living on the ground floor, and I asked him if he could tell me what had become of the Red-Headed League. He said that he had never heard of any such organization. Then I asked him who Mr. Duncan Ross was. He answered that the name was new to him.

"'Well,' said I, 'the gentleman at No. 4.'

"'What, the red-headed man?'

"'Yes.'

"'Oh,' said he, 'his name was William Morris. He was a lawyer, and was using my room as a temporary convenience until his new premises were ready. He moved out yesterday.'

"'Where could I find him?'

"'Oh, at his new offices. He did tell me the address. Yes, 17 King Edward Street.'

"I left at once, Mr. Holmes, but when I got to that address it was a factory, and no one in it had ever heard of either Mr. William Morris or Mr. Duncan Ross."

"And what did you do then?" asked Holmes.

"I went home and spoke to my assistant. But he could not help me in any way. He could only say that if I waited I should hear something by mail. But that was not quite good enough, Mr. Holmes. I did not wish to lose such a job without a struggle, so, as I had heard that you were good enough to give advice to poor folk who were in need of it, I came right away to you."

"And you did very wisely," said Holmes. "Your case is an exceedingly remarkable one, and I shall be happy to look into it. From what you have told me I think that it is possible that graver issues hang from it than might at first sight appear."

"It's serious enough!" said Mr. Jabez Wilson. "Why, I have lost four pounds a week."

"As far as you are personally concerned," remarked Holmes, "I do not see that you have any grievance against this extra-ordinary league. On the contrary, you are, as I understand, richer by some thirty pounds, to say nothing of the knowledge which you have gained on every subject which comes under the letter *A*. You have lost nothing by them."

"No, sir. But I want to find out about them, and who they are, and what their object was in playing this prank—if it was a prank—upon me. It was a pretty expensive joke for them, for it cost them thirty-two pounds."

"We shall endeavor to clear up these points for you. And first, one or two questions, Mr. Wilson. This assistant of yours who first called your attention to the advertisement—how long has he been with you?"

"About a month then."

"How did he come?"

"In answer to an advertisement."

"Was he the only applicant?"

"No, I had a dozen."

"Why did you pick him?"

"Because he was handy, and would work cheap."

"At half pay, in fact."

"Yes."

"What is he like, this Vincent Spaulding?"

"Small, strong, very quick in his ways, no hair on his face, though he's at least thirty. Has a scar on his forehead."

Holmes sat up in considerable excitement.

"I thought as much," said he. "He is still with you?"

"Oh, yes, sir; I have only just left him."

"And has your business been attended to in your absence?"

"Nothing to complain of, sir. There's never very much to do."

"That will do, Mr. Wilson. I shall be happy to give you an opinion upon the subject in the course of a day or two. Today is Saturday, and I hope that by Monday we may come to a conclusion."

"Well, Watson," said Holmes, when our visitor had left us, "what do you make of it all?"

"I make nothing of it," I answered frankly. "It is a most mysterious business."

"As a rule," said Holmes, "the more bizarre a thing is the less mysterious it proves to be. It is your common crimes which are really puzzling, just as a common face is the most difficult to identify. But I must be prompt over this matter."

"What are you going to do, then?" I asked.

"I beg that you won't speak to me for fifty minutes." He curled himself up in his chair, with his thin knees drawn up to his hawk-like nose, and there he sat with his eyes closed. I had come to the conclusion that he had dropped asleep, and indeed was nodding myself, when he suddenly sprang out of his chair with the gesture of a man who had made up his mind.

"What do you think, Watson? Could your patients spare you for a few hours?"

"I have no one to see today. My practice is not very large."

"Then put on your hat, and come."

We traveled by bus as far as Aldersgate; and a short walk took us to Coburg Street, the street where our red-headed client carried on his business. Sherlock Holmes stopped in front of Jabez Wilson's shop and looked it all over, with his eyes shining brightly. Then he walked slowly up the street and then down again to the corner, looking keenly at the houses. Finally he returned to the shop, went up to the door, and knocked. It was instantly opened by a bright-looking, clean-shaven young fellow, who asked him to step in.

"Thank you," said Holmes. "I only wished to ask you how you would go from here to the Strand Theatre."

"Fourth block on your left," answered the assistant promptly, closing the door.

"Smart fellow, that," observed Holmes as we walked away. "He is, in my judgment, the fourth smartest man in London, and for daring, he may be the third. I have known something of him before."

"Evidently," said I, "Mr. Wilson's assistant counts for a good deal in this mystery of the Red-Headed League. I am sure that you inquired your way merely in order that you might see him."

"Not him."

"What then?"

"The knees of his trousers."

"And what did you see?"

"What I expected to see. My dear Doctor, this is a time for observation, not for talk."

"Let me see," said Holmes, standing at the corner. "I should like just to remember the order of the houses here. It is a hobby of mine to have an exact knowledge of London. There is Mortimer's grocery, the little newspaper shop, the Coburg branch of the City and Suburban Bank, and the Vegetarian Restaurant. And now, Doctor, you want to go home, no doubt," he remarked.

"Yes, it would be as well."

"And I have some business to do which will take some hours. This business at Coburg Street is serious."

"Why serious?"

"A considerable crime is being con-templated. I have every reason to believe that we shall be in time to stop it. But today being Saturday rather complicates matters. I shall want your help tonight."

"At what time?"

"Ten will be early enough."

"I shall be at your apartment at Baker Street at ten."

"Very well. And, I say, Doctor! There may be some little danger, so kindly put your army revolver in your pocket." He waved his hand, turned on his heel, and disappeared in an instant among the crowd.

I trust that I am not more dense than my neighbors, but I was always oppressed with a sense of my own stupidity in my dealings with Sherlock Holmes. I had heard what he had heard, I had seen what he had seen, and yet from his words it was evident that he saw clearly not only what had happened, but what was about to happen, while to me the whole business was still confusing and grotesque. As I drove home to my house in Kensington I thought over it all, from the extraordinary story of the red-headed copier of the *Encyclopedia* down to the visit to Coburg Street, and the ominous words with which Holmes had parted from me. What was this nocturnal expedition, and why should I go armed? Where were we going, and what were we to do? I had the hint from Holmes that this smooth-faced assistant was a formidable man—a man who might play an important part in this affair. I tried to puzzle it out, but gave it up in despair, and set the matter aside until night should bring an explanation.

It was a quarter past nine when I started from home and made my way to Baker Street. Two cabs were standing at the door, and, as I went up the stairs, I heard the sound of voices from above. On entering his room, I found Holmes conversing with two men, one of whom I recognized as Peter Jones, the official police agent. The other was a long, thin, sad-faced man, with a shiny hat and a very expensive overcoat.

"Ha! our party is complete," said Holmes. "Watson, I think you know Mr. Jones, of Scotland Yard? Let me introduce you to Mr. Merryweather, who is to be our companion in tonight's adventure."

"Our friend Holmes here is a wonderful man for starting a chase," Jones said to me.

"I hope a wild goose may not prove to be the end of our chase," observed Mr. Merryweather gloomily.

"You may place considerable confidence in Mr. Holmes, sir," said the police agent. "He has his own extraordinary methods, and it is not too much to say that often he has been more nearly correct than our entire official force."

"Oh, if you say so, Mr. Jones, it is all right!" said the stranger.

"I think you will find," said Sherlock Holmes, "that the game we will play tonight will be more exciting than any you have ever played before. For you, Mr. Merryweather, the stakes will be some fifty thousand pounds; and for you, Jones, it will be the man upon whom you wish to lay your hands."

"You mean," said Mr. Jones, "John Clay, the murderer, thief, and forger. He's a young man, Mr. Merryweather, but he is at the head of his profession, and I would rather have handcuffs on him than on any criminal in London. He's a remarkable man, is young John Clay. His grandfather was a duke, and he himself has been to Oxford. His brain is as cunning as his fingers, and though we meet signs of him at every turn, we never know where to find the man himself. I've been on his track for years, and have never set eyes on him yet."

"I hope," said Holmes, "that I may have the pleasure of introducing you tonight. I've had one or two little turns with Mr. John Clay, and I agree with you that he is at the head of his profession. It is past ten, however, and quite time that we started. If you two will take the first cab, Watson and I will follow in the second."

Sherlock Holmes was not very communicative during the long drive. He sat in the cab humming some tunes.

"We are close there now," my friend remarked. "This fellow Merryweather is a bank director and personally interested in the matter. I thought it as well to have Jones with us also. The man is a bulldog, and as tenacious as a lobster if he gets his claws upon anyone. Here we are, and they are waiting for us."

We had reached Coburg Street, the same place in which we had found ourselves earlier in the day. Our cabs were dismissed, and, following the guidance of Mr. Merryweather, we passed down a narrow passage, and through a side door, which he opened for us. Within there was a small corridor, which ended in a very massive iron gate. This also was opened, and led down a flight of winding stone steps, which terminated at another formidable gate. Mr. Merryweather stopped to light a lantern, and then conducted us down a dark, earth-smelling passage, and so, after opening a third door, into a huge vault or cellar, which was piled all round with crates and massive boxes.

"You are not very vulnerable from above," Holmes remarked, as he held up the lantern and gazed about him.

"Nor from below," said Mr. Merryweather, striking his stick upon the floor. "Why, dear me, it sounds quite hollow!" he remarked, looking up in surprise.

"I must really ask you to be a little more quiet," said Holmes severely. "You have already endangered the whole success of our plan. Might I beg that you would have the goodness to sit down upon one of those boxes, and not to interfere?"

The solemn Mr. Merryweather perched himself upon a crate, with a very injured expression upon his face, while Holmes fell upon his knees upon the floor, and, with the lantern and a magnifying lens, began to examine carefully the cracks between the stones. A few seconds sufficed to satisfy him, for he sprang to his feet again, and put his glass in his pocket.

"We have at least an hour before us," he remarked, "for they can hardly take any steps until Jabez Wilson is safely in bed.

Then they will not lose a minute, for the sooner they do their work the longer time they will have for their escape. We are at present, Doctor Watson—as no doubt you have guessed—in the cellar of the Coburg branch of the City and Suburban Bank. Mr. Merryweather is the director of the bank, and he will explain to you that there are reasons why the more daring criminals of London should take a considerable interest in this cellar at present."

"It is our gold," whispered the director. "We have had several warnings that an attempt might be made upon it."

"Your gold?"

"Yes. We had occasion some months ago to strengthen our resources, and borrowed, for that purpose, fifty thousand gold pieces from the Bank of France. It has become known that we have not yet had occasion to unpack the money, and that it is still lying in our cellar. The crate upon which I sit contains two thousand gold pieces alone. Our reserve of gold is much larger at present than is usually kept in a single branch office. We have had some anxiety upon the subject."

"Which was very well justified," observed Holmes. "And now it is time that we arranged our little plans. I expect that within an hour matters will come to a head. In the meantime, Mr. Merryweather, we must put a screen over that lantern."

"And sit in the dark?"

"I am afraid so. I see that the enemy's preparations have gone so far that we cannot risk the presence of a light. And, first of all, we must choose our positions. These are daring men, and, though we shall take them at a disadvantage, they may do us some harm, unless we are careful. I shall stand behind this crate, and you conceal yourself behind those. When I flash a light upon them, close in swiftly. If they fire, Watson, you will have to use your revolver."

Holmes slipped a screen across the front of his lantern, and left us in pitch darkness—such an absolute darkness as I have never before experienced. There was something depressing in the sudden gloom, and in the cold, damp air of the vault.

"They have but one retreat," whispered Holmes. "That is back through the house and out into Coburg Street. I hope that you have done what I asked you, Jones?"

"I have two officers waiting at the front door."

"Then there is no way for them to escape. And now we must be silent and wait."

What a time it seemed! It was but an hour and a quarter, yet it appeared to me that we waited half the night. My limbs were weary and stiff, for I feared to change my position. My nerves were worked up to the highest pitch of tension, as I heard the gentle breathing of my companions. Suddenly my eyes caught the glint of light.

At first it was only a bright spark upon the stone pavement. Then it lengthened until it became a yellow line, and then, without any warning or sound, a gash seemed to open and a hand appeared in the center of the little area of light. For a minute or more the hand protruded out of the floor. Then it was withdrawn as suddenly as it appeared, and all was dark again.

Its disappearance, however, was but momentary. With a tearing sound, one of the broad, white stones turned over upon its side, and left a square, gaping hole, through which streamed the light of a lantern. Over

the edge there peeped a clean-cut boyish face, which looked keenly about it, and then, with a hand on either side of the opening, drew itself shoulder high and waist high, until one knee rested upon the edge. In another instant he stood at the side of the hole, and was hauling up after him a companion, lithe and small like himself, with a head of very red hair.

"It's all clear," he whispered. "Do you have the chisel and the bags? Great Scott! Get back! Get back!"

Sherlock Holmes had sprung out and seized the intruder by the collar. The other dived down the hole, and I heard the sound of ripping cloth as Jones clutched at his shirt. The light flashed upon the barrel of a revolver, but Holmes's fist came down on the man's wrist, and the pistol clinked upon the stone floor.

"It's no use, John Clay," said Holmes calmly. "You have no chance at all."

"So I see," the other answered very coolly. "I guess that my pal is all right, though I see you have got a piece of his shirt."

"There are two men waiting for him at the door," said Holmes.

"Oh, indeed. You seem to have thought of everything. I must compliment you."

"And I you," Holmes answered. "Your red-headed idea was very new and effective."

"You'll see your pal again presently," said Jones. "He's quicker at climbing down holes than I am. Just hold out your hands while I put on these cuffs."

"Don't touch me with your filthy hands," remarked our prisoner, as the handcuffs clattered upon his wrists. "You may not be aware that I have royal blood in my veins. Have the goodness also when you address me always to say 'sir' and 'please.'"

"All right," said Jones, with a smile. "Well, would you please, sir, march upstairs, where we can get a cab to carry your highness to the police station."

"That is better," said John Clay serenely. He made a sweeping bow to the three of us, and walked quietly off in the custody of the detective.

"Really, Mr. Holmes," said Mr. Merryweather, as we followed them from the cellar, "I do not know how the bank can thank you or repay you. There is no doubt that you have detected and defeated in the most complete manner one of the most determined attempts at bank robbery that has ever come within my experience."

"I have had one or two little scores of my own to settle with Mr. John Clay," said Holmes. "I have been at some small expense over this matter, which I shall expect the bank to refund, but beyond that I am amply repaid by having had an experience which is in many ways unique."

"You see, Watson," he explained in the early hours of the morning, as we sat in his apartment on Baker Street, "it was perfectly obvious from the first that the only possible object of this rather fantastic business of the advertisement of the League, and the copying of the *Encyclopedia*, must be to get this Jabez Wilson out of the way for a number of hours every day. It was a curious way of managing it, but really it would be difficult to suggest a better. The method was no doubt suggested to Clay's ingenious mind by the color of his accomplice's hair. The four pounds a week was a lure which must draw him, and what was it to them, who were playing for thousands? They put in the advertisement, they incite the man to apply for it, and together they manage to secure his absence every morning in the week. From the time that I heard of the assistant having come for half pay, it was obvious to me that he had some strong motive for taking the job."

"But how could you guess what the motive was?"

"The man's business was a small one, and there was nothing in the house which could account for such elaborate preparations and such an expenditure as they were at. It must then be something out of the house. What could it be? I thought of the assistant's fondness for photography, and his trick of vanishing into the cellar. The cellar! There was the clue! He was doing something in the cellar—something which took many hours a day for months on end. What could it be, once more? I could think of nothing except that he was digging a tunnel to some other building.

"So far I had got when we went to visit the shop. I rang the bell, and, as I hoped, the assistant answered it. We have had some skirmishes, but we had never set eyes on each other before. I hardly looked at his face. His knees were what I wished to see. You must yourself have remarked how worn, wrinkled, and stained they were. They spoke of hours of digging. The only remaining point was what they were burrowing for. I walked round the corner, saw that the City and Suburban Bank was just behind our friend's shop, and felt that I had solved my problem. When you drove home, I called upon Scotland Yard, and upon the bank's director, with the result that you have seen."

"And how could you tell that they would make their attempt tonight?" I asked.

"Well, when they closed their League

offices that was a sign that they cared no longer about Mr. Jabez Wilson's presence; in other words, that they had completed their tunnel. But it was essential that they should use it soon, as it might be discovered, or the gold might be removed. Saturday would suit them better than any other day, as it would give them two days for their escape. For all these reasons I expected them to come tonight."

"You reasoned it out beautifully," I exclaimed in sincere admiration. "It is so long a chain, and yet every link rings true."

"It saved me from boredom," he answered, yawning. "I love to escape boredom. These little problems help me to do so."

"And you, at the same time, help people," said I.

He shrugged his shoulders. "Well, perhaps, I can be of some little use," he noted. "Thus ends the remarkable case of the Red-Headed League," said Holmes with a smile.

About the Author

Sir Arthur Conan Doyle (1859–1930) was born in Edinburgh, Scotland. His great creation, Sherlock Holmes, was patterned after Dr. Joseph Bell, a professor at the University of Edinburgh, where Conan Doyle was studying medicine. Dr. Bell utilized deductive principles (reasoning to draw conclusions) in treating diseases. When Conan Doyle created Sherlock Holmes, generally considered the world's greatest and most famous detective, the author had Holmes employ the same deductive principles that guided Dr. Bell's work. Conan Doyle created his character's name by combining the name of a star cricket player named Sherlock and that of the famous American writer and physician, Oliver Wendell Holmes: Sherlock Holmes. It would be difficult to overstate the popularity of Sherlock Holmes. The character has appeared in 54 short stories and four novels by Conan Doyle, and in stage plays, movies, and television programs. In fact, many people do not believe that Sherlock Holmes was an imaginary sleuth. They think that he once lived and resided at 221B Baker Street, his home in the stories. Sherlock Holmes is truly one of the most beloved characters in detective fiction.

THINK ABOUT THE STORY. The following questions help you check your reading comprehension. Put an *x* in the box next to the correct answer.

1. This story is mainly about
   - ☐ a. why Ezekiah Hopkins established the Red-Headed League.
   - ☐ b. how Sherlock Holmes foiled an elaborate plan to rob a bank.
   - ☐ c. the lives of Jabez Wilson and Vincent Spaulding.

2. Mr. Wilson "never dared to leave the room" for fear of
   - ☐ a. receiving less pay.
   - ☐ b. losing the job.
   - ☐ c. getting a letter of warning from his employer.

3. Holmes realized that the assistant kept disappearing into the cellar to
   - ☐ a. dig a tunnel.
   - ☐ b. develop photographs.
   - ☐ c. relax for a while.

4. The Coburg branch of the City and Suburban Bank was a particularly appealing target because it
   - ☐ a. was not protected by a guard.
   - ☐ b. was in the center of town.
   - ☐ c. had received a large supply of gold.

HANDLE NEW VOCABULARY WORDS. The following questions check your vocabulary skills. Put an *x* in the box next to the correct answer. Each vocabulary word appears in the story.

1. Sherlock Holmes wondered whether he should be "so candid" in explaining how he reached his conclusions. A person who is *candid*
   - ☐ a. does not tell the truth.
   - ☐ b. tries to impress others.
   - ☐ c. speaks openly and sincerely.

2. Jabez Wilson always arrived at the office promptly and did the job steadily; he demonstrated diligence. What is the definition of the word *diligence*?
   - ☐ a. actions that reveal annoyance
   - ☐ b. actions that reveal hard work
   - ☐ c. actions that reveal little thought or effort

3. He was using the room "until his new premises were ready." As used in this sentence, the word *premises* means
   - ☐ a. statements of fact.
   - ☐ b. instructions or orders.
   - ☐ c. a home or part of a building.

4. Holmes described the police agent as being "as tenacious as a lobster if he gets his claws upon anyone." What is the meaning of the word *tenacious*?
   - ☐ a. able to hold tightly
   - ☐ b. capable of setting a trap
   - ☐ c. not especially intelligent

☐ × 5 = ☐
NUMBER CORRECT   YOUR SCORE

☐ × 5 = ☐
NUMBER CORRECT   YOUR SCORE

EXAMINE STORY ELEMENTS. The following questions check your knowledge of story elements. Put an *x* in the box next to each correct answer.

1. Of the following, which happened first in the *plot* of the story?
   - ☐ a. Sherlock Holmes and Dr. Watson visited Jabez Wilson's shop.
   - ☐ b. Holmes knocked Clay's pistol down.
   - ☐ c. Wilson showed Holmes an advertisement for the Red-Headed League.

2. Which of the following statements best *characterizes* Sherlock Holmes?
   - ☐ a. He was overly cautious and unable to make important decisions.
   - ☐ b. He possessed keen powers of observation and remarkable ability to reach conclusions by reasoning.
   - ☐ c. He was impatient and was therefore not a good listener.

3. What was Vincent Spaulding's *motive* for accepting very low pay?
   - ☐ a. He wanted to make certain that he would get the job.
   - ☐ b. He knew that Jabez Wilson could not afford to pay higher wages.
   - ☐ c. He had great sympathy for Mr. Wilson and wished to be kind.

4. As in all Sherlock Holmes stories, the *narrator* is
   - ☐ a. Dr. Watson.
   - ☐ b. Sherlock Holmes.
   - ☐ c. the writer.

☐ × 5 = ☐

NUMBER CORRECT · YOUR SCORE

MASTER CRITICAL THINKING. The following questions check your critical thinking skills. Put an *x* in the box next to each correct answer.

1. It is fair to say that the purpose of the Red-Headed League was to
   - ☐ a. provide easy jobs for men with red hair.
   - ☐ b. get Jabez Wilson away from his shop.
   - ☐ c. obey the wishes of the League's founder, Ezekiah Hopkins.

2. We may infer that when Mr. Wilson applied for a position with the Red-Headed League, it
   - ☐ a. had already been determined that he would get the job.
   - ☐ b. was possible that he might not have been accepted for the job.
   - ☐ c. was through luck that he managed to find Duncan Ross.

3. Evidence in the story suggests that one reason Holmes went to Coburg Street was to
   - ☐ a. visit Jabez Wilson at his shop.
   - ☐ b. have a meal with Watson.
   - ☐ c. see what stores and businesses were near Wilson's shop.

4. We may infer that Clay and Spaulding
   - ☐ a. had never heard of Holmes.
   - ☐ b. were both members of the Red-Headed League.
   - ☐ c. had planned the bank robbery some months earlier.

☐ × 5 = ☐

NUMBER CORRECT · YOUR SCORE

EXPLORE THE WRITER'S CRAFT. The following questions check your knowledge of skills related to the craft of writing. Put an *x* in the box next to each correct answer. You may refer to pages 4 and 5.

1. In referring to Peter Jones, Sherlock Holmes stated, "The man is a bulldog." This sentence contains
   ☐ a. a simile.
   ☐ b. a metaphor.
   ☐ c. an example of alliteration.

2. Spaulding's worn, stained knees "spoke of hours of digging." Since knees cannot speak, this sentence provides an illustration of
   ☐ a. dialect.
   ☐ b. a flashback.
   ☐ c. figurative language.

3. Merryweather "conducted us down a dark, earth-smelling passage, . . . into a huge vault or cellar, which was piled all round with crates and massive boxes." This is an example of
   ☐ a. personification.
   ☐ b. the author's ability to create character.
   ☐ c. a descriptive passage.

4. During the course of the story, Holmes refers to his "poor little reputation." Since Holmes actually was famous, his words are
   ☐ a. ironic.
   ☐ b. symbolic.
   ☐ c. an example of imagery.

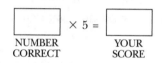

| NUMBER CORRECT | × 5 = | YOUR SCORE |

Questions for Writing and Discussion

- At the beginning of the story, Sherlock Holmes rapidly inferred some facts about Jabez Wilson. Explain how this serves to reveal important character traits and abilities of the detective.
- Name three details in Jabez Wilson's story that aroused Holmes's suspicion.
- Jabez Wilson's most striking feature was his fiery red hair. Explain why this characteristic is vital to the story.
- How did Holmes know that it was essential to act immediately to prevent the bank robbery? How did he know exactly where to go and what assistance he needed?

See additional questions for extended writing on pages 124 and 125.

Use the boxes below to total your scores for the exercises. Then record your scores on pages 224 and 225.

	THINK ABOUT THE STORY
+	HANDLE NEW VOCABULARY WORDS
+	EXAMINE STORY ELEMENTS
+	MASTER CRITICAL THINKING
+	EXPLORE THE WRITER'S CRAFT
▼	**Total Score:** Story 10

Masters of Mystery

Questions for Discussion and Extended Writing

The following questions provide you with opportunities to express your thoughts and feelings about the selections in this unit. Your teacher may assign selected questions. When you write your responses, remember to state your point of view clearly and to support your position by presenting specific details—examples, illustrations, and references drawn from the story and, in some cases, from your life. Organize your writing carefully and check your work for correct spelling, capitalization, punctuation, and grammar.

1. The theme of this unit is "Masters of Mystery." Briefly explain why each story in the unit may be considered the work of a "master."

2. The color of a character's hair plays a vital role in two stories in this unit. Support this statement by referring to the mysteries involved.

3. Dr. Watson stated, "I trust that I am not more dense than my neighbors, but I was always oppressed with a sense of my own stupidity in my dealings with Sherlock Holmes. Here I had heard what he had heard, I had seen what he had seen, and yet from his words it was evident that he saw clearly not only what had happened, but what was about to happen, while to me the whole business was still confusing." Write a paper entitled "A Character Study of Sherlock Holmes." Be sure to describe in detail the character traits that Holmes possessed that so amazed Dr. Watson.

4. Read Dr. Watson's statement above. By referring to the story in which she appears, explain why Watson's words might well be applied to Miss Marple.

5. In many ways "The Inspiration of Mr. Budd" is different from the other stories in this unit. Do you agree or disagree with this statement? Support your position by referring to the selections.

6. In which story do you think conflict played the most important role? Identify the conflict or conflicts in the story you selected.

7. Clues may be considered the "building blocks" upon which mysteries are constructed. Illustrate, by referring to the story, how clues in "The Case of the Perfect Maid" helped Miss Marple solve the crime.

8. Identify and describe five clues that helped Sherlock Holmes solve the case of "The Red-Headed League."

9. In which story in the unit does the setting play the most significant role? Provide details and examples to support your opinion.

10. It would be difficult to overestimate the fame of the three "Masters of Mystery" whose works appear in this unit. (Sherlock Holmes is undoubtedly the most famous fictional detective of all time.) What are your thoughts about fame? What are some advantages and disadvantages of being famous? Would you enjoy being famous? Are some things more important than fame? Discuss your ideas in an essay entitled "Fame." Your essay should have an introduction, a body, and a conclusion.

Something Unexpected

"Expect the unexpected."

—*ancient proverb*

Previewing the Unit

Few would dispute the traditional wisdom, "Expect the unexpected." But some things are more easily said than done, and one cannot always follow this sensible recommendation. You have heard that truth is stranger than fiction. Still, the best fiction resounds with truth. This observation applies to the stories in this unit. In each, "Something Unexpected" occurs.

THE PIANO Aníbal Monteiro Machado's fascinating story revolves around the ordeals that a family experiences in disposing of an antique piano. There are many striking features that distinguish this tale. One is the remarkable way in which the piano assumes the characteristics of a living creature—one that possesses strong feelings. Another is the wide range of emotions that the story stirs in the reader. You'll see what we mean—but expect the unexpected.

THE WIDOW AND THE PARROT Cynics like to sneer and proclaim, "No good deed goes unpunished." "The Widow and the Parrot" revolves around a good deed. Will that good deed be punished? You will discover the answer when you have completed the story. Virginia Woolf is famous for writing great novels. Although she produced relatively few stories, "The Widow and the Parrot" is probably her most enjoyable.

THE SCARLET IBIS James Hurst's touching tale concerns a man who is consumed with guilt over an incident that occurred many years before. You will seldom read a short story that so effectively combines beautiful language, strong characterization, and flawless construction. The main characters are indelibly drawn. Many passages are poetic, and the image of the scarlet ibis is, in every way, perfect. The story contains everything we've promised—and perhaps something more.

THE POSSIBILITY OF EVIL Shirley Jackson has outdone even herself with "The Possibility of Evil." Every sentence contributes to the total effect of the story. In Miss Adela Strangeworth, Jackson has etched a portrait with acid, and the author's description of life in a small town is incredibly vivid. We defy you to forget Miss Strangeworth—or how the story concludes.

As you read, try to anticipate how each story will end. The conclusions to the selections may not be so unexpected after all.

To João, it was a dearly beloved old friend, but to everyone else it was merely . . .

The Piano

by Aníbal Monteiro Machado

"Rosália!" shouted João de Oliveira to his wife, who was upstairs. "I told the guy to get out. What a nerve! He laughed at it. He said it wasn't worth even five hundred cruzeiros."[1]

"It's an old trick," she replied. "He wants to get it for nothing and then sell it to somebody else. That's how these fellows get rich."

But Rosália and Sara looked somewhat alarmed as they came downstairs. The family approached the old piano respectfully, as if to console it after the insult.

"We'll get a good price for it, you'll see," asserted Oliveira, gazing at the piano with a mixture of affection and apprehension. "They don't make them like this any more."

"Put an ad in the paper," said Rosália, "and they'll come flocking. The house will

---

1. **cruzeiros:** a unit of money in Brazil

be like *this* with people." She joined the tips of the fingers of her right hand in customary token of an immense crowd. "It's a pity to have to give it up."

"Ah, it's a love of a piano!" said João. "Just looking at it you think you hear music." He caressed its oaken case.

"Well, come on, João. Let's put the ad in."

It had to be sold so that the little parlor could be made into a bedroom for Sara and her intended, a lieutenant in the artillery. Besides, the price would pay for her trousseau.[2]

Three mornings later, the piano was adorned with flowers for the sacrifice, and the house was ready to receive prospective buyers.

The first to arrive were a lady and her daughter. The girl opened the piano and played a few chords.

"It's no good at all, mama."

The lady stood up, looked at it, and noticed that the ivory was missing from some of the keys. She took her daughter by the hand and walked out, muttering as she went:

"Think of coming all this distance to look at a piece of junk."

The Oliveira family had no time to feel resentment, for three new candidates appeared, all at the same time: an elderly lady who smelled like a rich widow, a young girl wearing glasses and carrying a music portfolio, and a redheaded man in a worn, wrinkled suit.

"I was here ahead of you," said the young girl to the old lady. "It doesn't really matter. I only came because my mother wanted me to. There must be plenty others for sale. But

I'd just like to say that I was ringing the doorbell while you were still getting off the bus. We came in together but I got here first."

The young girl went over to the piano, while the redheaded man stood at a distance and evaluated it with a cool eye. At this moment a lady entered holding a schoolgirl by the hand. They sat down distrustfully.

Suddenly the young girl began to play, and the whole room hung on the notes that she extracted from the keyboard. Off-pitch, metallic, horrible notes. The Oliveiras anxiously studied the faces of their visitors. The redheaded man remained utterly impassive. The others glanced at one another as if seeking a common understanding. The newly arrived lady made a wry face. The perfumed old lady seemed more tolerant and looked indulgently at the old piano case.

It was a jury trial and the piano was the accused. The young girl continued to play, as if she were wringing a confession from it. The timbre[3] suggested that of a decrepit, cracked-voiced soprano with stomach trouble. Some of the notes did not play at all. Doli joined in with her barking, a well-considered verdict. A smile passed around the room. No one was laughing, however. The girl seemed to be playing now out of pure malice, hammering at the dead keys. It was a dreadful situation.

"There's something you ought to know about this piano," explained João de Oliveira. "It's very sensitive to the weather, it changes a great deal with variations in temperature."

---

2. **trousseau:** possessions—usually clothes and linen—that a bride brings to a marriage

3. **timbre:** the quality of sound

The young girl stopped abruptly. She rose, put on some lipstick, and picked up her music portfolio.

"I don't know how you had the nerve to advertise this horror," she said, speaking to João but looking disdainfully at Rosália as if she had been the horror.

And she left.

João said nothing for a moment. After all, the insult had been directed at the old piano, not at him. Nevertheless, he felt constrained to declare that it was a genuine antique.

"They don't make them like this any more," he said emphatically. "They just don't make them."

There was a long silence. Finally, the redheaded man spoke:

"What are you asking for it?"

In view of what had happened, João de Oliveira lowered substantially the price he had had in mind.

"Five contos," he said timidly.

He looked at everyone to see the effect. There was a silent response. Oliveira felt cold. Was the price monstrously high? Only the old lady showed any delicacy at all: she said she would think it over. But, through her veil of mercy, João perceived her decision.

As they all were leaving, a man about to enter stepped out of their way.

"Did you come about the piano?" asked one of them. "Well, you'll . . . "

But Oliveira interrupted.

"Come in," he said cheerfully. "It's right here. Lots of people have been looking at it."

The man was middle-aged, with a shock of grayish hair. He lifted the lid of the piano and examined the instrument at length. "Probably a music teacher," thought João.

The man did not ask the price. "Thank you," he said and left.

The house was empty again. Sara returned to her room. Rosália and João looked at each other in disappointment.

"Nobody understands its value," commented João sadly. "If I can't get a decent price for it, I'd rather not sell it at all."

"But how about Sara's trousseau?" said Rosália.

"I'll borrow the money."

"You'd never be able to pay it back out of your salary."

"We'll postpone the marriage."

"They love each other, João. They'll want to get married no matter what, trousseau or no trousseau . . . "

At this moment, Sara could be heard shouting from her room that she could not possibly get married without two new slips and so forth.

"The thing is," Rosália went on, "this house is about the size of a matchbox. Where can we put the newlyweds? We'll have to give up the piano to make room for them. Nobody nowadays has enough room."

Sara's voice was heard again:

"No, don't sell the piano. It's so pretty . . . "

"It's also so silent," interrupted her mother. "You never play it any more."

She went to her daughter's room to speak further with her. Strange that Sara should talk like that. Rosália put the dilemma flatly:

"A husband or a piano. Choose."

"Oh, a husband!" replied Sara with conviction. "Of course."

"So . . . ?"

"You're always against it, Rosália," shouted João de Oliveira.

"Against what?"

"Our piano."

"Oh, João, how can you say such a thing!"

The next day, as soon as he got back from work, João de Oliveira asked about the piano.

"Did any people answer the ad, Rosália?"

Yes, there had been several telephone calls for information about the piano, and an old man had come and looked at it. Also, the redheaded man had come again.

"Did any of them say anything about buying it?" asked João.

"No. But the two men who came to the house looked at it a long time."

"They did? Did they look at it with interest? With admiration?"

"It's hard to say."

"Yes, they admired it," said Sara. "Especially the old man. He almost ate it with his eyes."

João de Oliveira was touched. It was no longer a matter of price. He just wanted his piano to be treated with consideration and respect, that's all. Maybe it wasn't worth a lot of money but it certainly deserved some courteous attention. He was sorry he hadn't been there, but what his daughter told him of the old man's respectful attitude consoled him. That man must understand the soul of antique furniture.

"Did he leave his address, Sara? No? Oh, well . . . he'll probably be back."

He rose from his chair and walked around the old instrument. He smiled at it lovingly.

"My piano," he said softly. He ran his hand over the varnished wood as if he were caressing an animal.

No candidate the next day. Only a voice with a foreign accent asking if it was new. Rosália replied that it wasn't but that they had taken such good care of it that it almost looked like new.

"Tomorrow is Saturday," thought Oliveira. "There's bound to be a lot of people."

There were two, a man and a little girl, and they came in a limousine. The man looked at the modest house of the Oliveira family and considered it useless to go in. Nevertheless, he went to the door and asked the make and age of the piano.

"Thank you. There's no need for me to see it," he replied to João's insistence that he look at it. "I thought it would be a fairly new piano. Good luck . . . "

And he went away.

João was grief-stricken. Ever since he had inherited the piano he had prized it dearly. He had never thought he would have to part with it. Worst of all, no one appreciated it, no one understood its value.

No one, except possibly the fellow who came the next Wednesday. He praised the piano in the most enthusiastic terms, said it was marvelous, and refused to buy. He said that if he paid so low a price for it he would feel he was stealing it, and that João and Rosália were virtually committing a crime in letting this precious thing get out of their hands. Oliveira did not exactly understand.

"Does he mean what he says?" he asked Rosália.

"I think he's just trying to be funny," she replied.

"I don't know. Maybe not."

Rosália was the first to lose hope. Her main concern now, when her husband came home from work, was to alleviate his suffering.

"How many today?"

"Nobody. Two telephone calls. They didn't give their names but they said they'd probably come and look at it."

Her voice was calm, soothing.

"How about the redheaded fellow?"

"I'm sure he'll be back."

For several days no one came or telephoned. João de Oliveira's feelings may be compared to those of a man who sees his friend miss a train: he is sad for his friend's sake and he is happy because he will continue for a time to have the pleasure of his company. João sat down near the piano and enjoyed these last moments with it. He admired its dignity. He confided his thoughts to it. Three generations had played it. How many people it had induced to dream or to dance! All this had passed away, but the piano remained. It was sort of eternal.

"Sara, come and play that little piece by Chopin. See if you remember it."

"I couldn't, Papa. The piano sounds terrible."

"Don't say that," Rosália whispered. "Can't you see how your father feels?"

For days and days no prospective buyer appeared. Nothing but an occasional telephone call from the redheaded man, as if he had been a doctor verifying the progress of a terminal case. The advertisement was withdrawn.

"Well, João, what are we going to do about it?"

"What are we going to do about what, Rosália?"

"The piano!"

"I'm not going to sell it," João shouted. "Those leeches just want a bargain. I'd rather give it away to someone who'll take good care of it, who knows what it represents."

He was walking back and forth agitatedly. Suddenly the expression of his face changed.

"Listen, Rosália. Let's phone our relatives in Tijuca."

Rosália understood his purpose and was pleased.

"Hello! Is Messias there? He went out? Oh, is this Cousin Miquita? Look . . . I want to give you our piano as a present. . . . Yes, as a present. . . . No, it's not a joke. . . . Really. . . . Right. . . . Exactly. . . . So it won't go out of the family. . . . Fine. Have it picked up here sometime soon. . . . You're welcome. I'm glad to do it. . . . "

After he had hung up he turned to his wife.

"You know what? She didn't believe me at first. She thought it was All Fools' Day."

Rosália was delighted. João walked over to the old piano as if to confer with it about what he had just done.

"My conscience is clear," he thought. "You will not be rejected. You will stay in the family, with people of the same blood. My children's children will know and respect you; you will play for them. I'm sure you understand and won't be angry with us."

"When will they come for it?" interrupted Rosália, eager to get the room ready for the bridal couple.

The next day Messias telephoned his relatives in Ipanema. Did they really mean to give him a piano? It was too much. He was grateful but they really shouldn't. When his wife told him, he could hardly believe it.

"No, it's true, Messias. You know, our house is about as big as a nutshell. We can't keep the piano here, and João doesn't want it to fall into the hands of strangers. If you people have it, it's almost the same as if it was still with us. Are you going to send for it soon?"

Several days went by. No moving van came. Mr. and Mrs. Oliveira thought the silence of their relatives in Tijuca extremely odd.

"Something's wrong. Telephone them, Rosália."

Cousin Miquita answered. She was embarrassed. The moving men asked a fortune for the job.

"I guess it's the gasoline shortage. . . . Wait a few more days. Messias will arrange something. We're delighted about getting the piano. We think of nothing else, Rosália."

This last sentence struck a false note, thought Rosália. After a week João de Oliveira telephoned again.

"Do you want it or don't you, Messias?"

"João, you can't imagine how terrible we feel about this," came the stammered reply. "You give us a fine present and we can't accept it. They're asking an arm and a leg to move it here. And, anyway, we really have no room for it. We haven't even got enough room for the stuff we have now. We should have thought of this before. Miquita feels awful about it."

"In short, you don't want the piano."

"We want it. . . . But we don't . . . we can't . . . "

João de Oliveira hung up. He was beginning to understand.

"You see, Rosália? We can't even give the piano away. We can't even give it away."

"What can you do, João! Everything ends up with nobody wanting it."

After a few minutes of silent despondence, they were aroused by Sara, who interspersed her sobs with words of bitter desperation. Her mother comforted her.

"Don't worry, child. It'll be all right. We'll sell it for whatever we can get."

"I want it out right away, Mama. In a few days I'm to be married and my room isn't even ready yet. None of our things are in here. Only that terrible piano ruining my life, that piano that nobody wants."

"Speak softly, dear. Your father can hear you."

"I want him to hear me," she cried, with another sob. She wiped her eyes.

João de Oliveira slept little that night. He was meditating about life. His thoughts were confused and generally melancholy. They induced in him a fierce rage against both life and the piano. He left the house early.

Oliveira came back accompanied by two husky Portuguese in work clothes. He showed them the piano. They hefted it and said they doubted if they could handle it.

Rosália and Sara looked on in amazement.

"Have you found a buyer?" asked Rosália.

"No, wife. Nobody will buy this piano."

"You're giving it away?"

"No, wife. Nobody wants it even for free."

"Then what are you doing, João? What in the world are you doing?"

João's eyes watered but his face hardened.

"I'm going to throw it in the ocean."

"Oh, no, Papa!" exclaimed Sara. "That's crazy!"

The Oliveiras could not see the ocean from their windows, but they could smell it and hear it, for they were only three blocks from the avenue that ran along the beach.

The men were waiting, talking among themselves.

"What a courageous thing to do, João!" said his wife. "But shouldn't we talk it over first? Is there no other way out? People will think it funny, throwing a piano into the water."

"What else can we do, Rosália? Lots of ships go to the bottom of the ocean. Some of them have pianos on board."

This logic silenced his wife. João seemed to take heart.

"You fellows," he cried. "Up with it! Let's go!"

One of the Portuguese came forward and said humbly that they couldn't do it. They hoped he would excuse them, but it would hurt their conscience to throw something like that in the sea. It almost seemed like a crime.

"Why don't you put an ad in the paper? The piano is in such good condition."

"Yes, I know," replied Oliveira ironically. "You may go."

The men left.

Rosália rested her head on her husband's shoulder and fought back the tears.

"Ah, João, what a decision you have made!"

"But if nobody wants it, and if it can't stay here . . . "

"I know, João. But I can't help feeling sad. It's always been with us. Doesn't it seem cruel, after all these years, to throw it in the ocean? Look at it, standing there, knowing nothing about what's going to happen to it. It's been there almost twenty years, in that corner, never doing any harm . . . "

"We must try to avoid sentimentality, Rosália."

She looked at him with admiration. "All right, João. Do what you must."

Groups of boys, ragged but happy, start out from the huts at Pinto and Latolandia where they live, and stroll through the wealthy neighborhoods. One can always find them begging nickels for ice cream, gazing in rapture at the posters outside the movie houses, or rolling on the sand in Leblon.

That morning a southwester was whipping the Atlantic into a fury. The piano, needless to say, remained as tranquil as ever.

Preparations for the departure were under way. Without mentioning it to his family, João de Oliveira had recruited a bunch of boys. They were waiting impatiently outside the door. Oliveira now told them to come in, the strongest ones first.

It was twenty after four in the afternoon when the funeral cortege[4] started out. A small crowd on the sidewalk made way for it. The piano moved slowly and irregularly. Some people came up to observe it more closely. Rosália and her daughter contemplated it sadly from the porch, their arms around each other's shoulders. They could not bring themselves to accompany it.

"Which way?" asked the boys when the procession reached the corner. They were all trying to hold the piano at the same time, with the result that it almost fell.

"Which way?" they repeated.

"To the sea!" cried João de Oliveira. And with the grand gesture of a naval commander he pointed toward the Atlantic.

---

4. **funeral cortege:** a funeral procession; a group of attendants

The Piano

"To the sea! To the sea!" echoed the boys in chorus.

They began to understand that the piano was going to be destroyed, and this knowledge excited them. They laughed and talked animatedly among themselves. The hubbub inspired little Doli to leap in the air and bark furiously.

The balconies of the houses were crowded, chiefly with young girls.

"What is it?" And, incredulously, "A piano!"

"It came from ninety-nine."

"Why, that's where Sara lives."

"It's João de Oliveira's house."

An acquaintance ran out to learn the facts from Oliveira himself.

"What's wrong, João?"

"Nothing's wrong. I know what I'm doing. Just everybody keep out of the way."

"But why don't you sell it?"

"I'll sell it, all right. I'll sell it to the Atlantic Ocean. See it there? The ocean . . . "

With the air of a somewhat flustered executioner, he resumed his command.

"More to the left, fellows. . . . Careful, don't let it drop. . . . Just the big boys now, everybody else let go."

From time to time one of the boys would put his arm inside the piano and run his hand along the strings. The sound was a sort of death rattle.

A lady on a balcony shouted at João, "Would you sell it?"

"No, madam, it's not for sale. I'll give it away. You want it?"

The lady reddened, felt offended, and went into her house. João made his offer more general.

"Anyone around here want a piano?"

At number forty-three a family accepted. They were astounded, but they accepted.

"Then it's yours," shouted João de Oliveira.

The family came down and stood around the piano.

"We'll take it, all right. . . . But . . . our house is very small. Give us a couple of days to get ready for it."

"Now or never!" replied Oliveira. "Here it is, right outside your house. You don't want it? Fellows, let's go."

The piano moved closer and closer to the sea. It swayed like a dead cockroach carried by ants.

João de Oliveira distinguished only a few of the exclamations coming from the doors, windows, and balconies of the houses.

"This is the craziest thing I ever heard of," someone shouted from a balcony.

"Crazy?" replied João de Oliveira, looking up at the speaker. "Then you take it. Take it. . . . "

Further on, the scene was repeated. Everyone thought it was a crazy thing to do and everyone wanted the piano; but as soon as the owner offered immediate possession, there was just embarrassed silence. After all, who is prepared to receive a piano at a moment's notice?

A group of motorcycle policemen stopped the procession and surrounded the old piano. João de Oliveira gave a detailed explanation. They asked to see his documents. He went back to the house and got them. He resented having had to give an explanation. He certainly had a right to throw away his own property. This thought reawakened his affection for the instrument. Placing his hand on the piano as if on the forehead of a deceased friend, he felt deeply moved.

"It's an antique, one of the oldest pianos in Brazil."

It had belonged to his grandparents.

"It was a fine piano, you may believe me. Famous musicians played on it. They say that Chopin preferred it over all others. But what does this matter? No one appreciates it any more. Times have changed. . . . Sara, my daughter, is getting married. She'll live with us. The house is small. What can I do? No one wants it. This is the only way out."

And he nodded toward the sea.

The boys were growing impatient with the interruptions. They were eager to see the piano sink beneath the waves. Almost as impatient as these improvised movers were the people who had joined the procession, including delivery men, messenger boys, a few women, and a great many children.

The police examined the interior of the piano but found nothing suspicious. They returned Oliveira's papers and suggested that he hurry so that traffic would not be impeded.

A photographer asked some of the people to form a group and snapped their picture. João de Oliveira was on the left side in a pose expressing sadness. Then he became annoyed with all these interruptions that prolonged the agony of his piano.

Night fell rapidly. A policeman observed that after six o'clock they would not be permitted to go on. They would have to wait till the next day.

The boys dispersed.

The piano remained there on the street where they had left it, keeled over against the curb. A ridiculous position. Young men and women on their evening promenade soon surrounded it and made comments.

When he got home, João de Oliveira found some of Sara's girl friends there, eagerly questioning her about the piano.

It was still dark when João and his wife awoke to the loud sound of rain. Wind, rain, and the roar of the surf. They lit the light and looked at each other.

"I was thinking about the piano, Rosália."

"So was I, João. Poor thing! Out in the rain there . . . and it's so cold!"

"The water must be getting into the works and ruining everything . . . the felt, the strings. It's terrible, isn't it, Rosália."

"We did an ungrateful thing, João."

"I don't even like to think about it, Rosália."

João de Oliveira looked out the window. Flashes of lightning illuminated the trees, revealing branches swaying wildly in the wind. João went back to bed and slept fitfully. He woke again and told his wife that he had been listening to the piano.

"I heard everything that was ever played on it. Many different hands. My grandmother's hands, my mother's, yours, my aunt's, Sara's. More than twenty hands, more than a hundred fingers were pressing the keys. I never heard such pretty music. It was sublime, Rosália. The dead hands sometimes played better than the live ones. Lots of young girls from earlier generations were standing around the piano, listening. Couples who later got married were sitting nearby, holding hands. I don't know why, but after a while they all looked at me—with contempt. Suddenly the hands left the piano, but it kept on playing. The Funeral March. Then the piano shut by itself. . . . There was a torrent of water. The piano let itself get swept along . . . toward the ocean. I shouted to it but it wouldn't listen to me. It seemed to be offended, Rosália, and it just kept on going. . . . I stood there in the street, all alone. I began to cry. . . . "

The Piano

João de Oliveira was breathing hard. The mysterious concert had left him in a state of emotion. He felt remorseful.

The rain stopped. As soon as it was light, João went out to round up the boys. All he wanted now was to get the thing over with as quickly as possible.

The wind was still strong, and the ocean growled as if it were digesting the storm of the night before. The boys came, but in smaller number than before. Several grown men were among them. João de Oliveira, in a hoarse voice, assumed command again.

On the beach the piano moved more slowly. Finally the long tongues of the waves began to lick it.

Some families stood on the sidewalk, watching the spectacle. Oliveira's crew carried and pushed the piano far enough for the surf to take charge and drag it out to sea. Two enormous waves broke over it without effect. The third made it tremble. The fourth carried it away forever.

João de Oliveira stood there, knee deep in water, with his mouth open. The sea seemed enormously silent. No one could tell that he was crying, for the tears on his cheeks were indistinguishable from the drops of spray.

Far off, he saw Sara with her head resting on the lieutenant's shoulder. João was glad that Rosália had not come.

Many people appeared later on the beach, asking one another what had happened. It seemed at first that an entire family had drowned. Subsequently, it was learned that only one person had drowned. Some said it was a child. Others insisted that it was a lady who had had an unhappy love affair. Only later was it generally known that the person who had drowned was a piano.

People posted themselves at their windows to watch João de Oliveira come back from the beach.

"That's the man!" someone announced.

Oliveira walked slowly, staring at the ground. Everyone felt respect for him.

"It's gone, Rosália," he said as he entered the house. "It has passed the point of no return."

"Before we talk about it, João, go change your clothes."

"Our piano will never come back, Rosália."

"Of course it won't come back. That's why you threw it in the sea."

"Who knows," said Sara. "Maybe it'll be washed up on a beach somewhere."

"Let's not think about it any more. It's over. It's finished. Sara, it's time you did your room."

There was a pause, after which João resumed his lamentation.

"I saw the waves swallow it."

"Enough, my husband. Enough!"

"It came back to the surface twice."

"It's all over! Let's not think about it any more."

"I didn't mention it to anybody so they wouldn't think I went crazy . . . though they're beginning to think I'm crazy anyway. . . . The fact is, I'm probably the most rational man in the whole neighborhood. . . . But a little while ago I clearly heard the piano play the Funeral March."

"That was in your dream last night," Rosália reminded him.

"No, it was there by the sea, in broad daylight. Didn't you hear it, Sara? Right afterwards, it was covered all over with foam, and the music stopped."

He nodded his head. He was talking as if to himself.

"It must be far away by now. Under the water, moving along past strange sights. The wrecks of ships. Submarines. Fishes. Until yesterday it had never left this room. . . . Years from now it will be washed up on some island in an ocean on the other side of the world. And when Sara, Rosália, and I are dead, it will still remember the music it made in this house."

He left the room. Sara, alone, looked at the place where the piano had been. She felt a little guilty.

Doli was sniffing the area where the piano had been. She wailed a little and fell asleep.

The doorbell rang. A man entered and drew some papers from a briefcase. He said he came from the Port Captain's office.

"Are you João de Oliveira?"

"Yes, I am João de Oliveira."

"What did you cast in the sea this morning?"

Oliveira was stupefied.

"Out here we're not in the port, my dear sir. It's ocean."

"Are you going to give me a vocabulary lesson, Mr. Oliveira?"

The man repeated his previous question and explained that regulations now forbade the placing of objects in or on the sea without a license.

"Have you a license?"

Oliveira humbly asked whether what he had done was in any way offensive or bad.

"That's not the question."

"But it was just a piano, sir."

"It's still a violation. Anyway, was it really a piano? Are you absolutely sure?"

"I think I am," João blurted, looking at his daughter and his wife. "Wasn't it a piano, Rosália? Wasn't it, Sara?"

"Where's your head, João!" exclaimed Rosália. "You know it was a piano."

Her husband's doubt surprised everyone. He seemed to be musing.

"I thought a person could throw anything in the ocean that he wanted to."

"No, indeed! That's all we need. . . . "

João arose. He looked delirious.

Sara broke into the smile with which she always greeted the lieutenant, who had just come in. She ran to kiss him.

"See our room, darling. It looks good now, doesn't it?"

"Yes, real good. Where are you going to put the new one?"

"The new one?"

"Yes. Aren't you going to get another?"

Sara and her mother exchanged glances of amazement.

"I'm crazy for a piano," said Sara's fiancé. "You have no idea how it relaxes me. A little soft music in the evening . . . "

Sara had a fit of coughing. João de Oliveira went out the door. He felt suffocated; he needed to breathe.

Who else would come out of the night and make new demands of him? How could he have known that a piano hidden from the world, living in quiet anonymity, was really an object of public concern? Why hadn't he just left it where it was?

It was miles away now, traveling. . . . Far away, riding the southern seas. . . . And free. More so than he or Sara or Rosália. It was he, João de Oliveira, who now felt abandoned. For himself and for his family. It wasn't their piano any more. It was a creature loose in the world. Full of life and of pride, moving boldly through the seven seas. Sounding forth. Embraced by all the waters of the world.

The Piano

Free to go where it wished, to do what it wished.

Beneath the trees in front of the house, the boys were waiting for their second day's pay. They had worked hard. In the midst of them he saw a vaguely familiar form. The person opened the garden gate and asked permission to enter.

With some difficulty João recognized the redheaded man, but he was wholly unprepared for what the man was about to say:

"I've come back about the piano. I think I can make you a reasonable offer."

About the Author

Aníbal Monteiro Machado (1895–1964) was born in Brazil and lived most of his life in the area around Rio de Janeiro. Machado received a law degree and held a number of public offices, but he also worked as a teacher of high school English. Machado wrote two books and a number of short stories, essays, and poems, as well as two plays, one of which is based on "The Piano." Machado's first book was *Vila Feliz,* from which "The Piano" is taken.

THINK ABOUT THE STORY. The following questions help you check your reading comprehension. Put an *x* in the box next to the correct answer.

1. This story is mainly about
    - ☐ a. what happens when a family tries to dispose of an old piano.
    - ☐ b. why some people are not interested in buying an "antique" piano.
    - ☐ c. the difficulties involved in transporting a piano to the sea.

2. Messias said that his family could not accept the piano because
    - ☐ a. they did not like the way the piano looked.
    - ☐ b. it cost too much to move the piano.
    - ☐ c. they already owned a piano.

3. When a wave carried the piano out to sea, João de Oliveira began to
    - ☐ a. applaud.
    - ☐ b. laugh.
    - ☐ c. cry.

4. The man from the Port Captain's office told João
    - ☐ a. that he was under arrest.
    - ☐ b. that people had complained about him.
    - ☐ c. that one needed a license to put objects into the sea.

HANDLE NEW VOCABULARY WORDS. The following questions check your vocabulary skills. Put an *x* in the box next to the correct answer. Each vocabulary word appears in the story.

1. "I don't know how you had the nerve to advertise this horror," a young woman said as she looked disdainfully at Rosália. The word *disdainfully* means
    - ☐ a. expressing interest or fascination.
    - ☐ b. exhibiting great concern.
    - ☐ c. showing scorn or contempt.

2. Rosália's main concern was to alleviate her husband's suffering. What is the meaning of the word *alleviate*?
    - ☐ a. ignore or overlook
    - ☐ b. relieve or lessen
    - ☐ c. change or transform

3. Sara was crying, but her sobs were interspersed with bitter words. Define the word *interspersed*.
    - ☐ a. scattered here and there
    - ☐ b. unable to be heard
    - ☐ c. of little value

4. The group carrying the piano had to move quickly "so that traffic would not be impeded." The word *impeded* means
    - ☐ a. hindered or obstructed.
    - ☐ b. injured or hurt.
    - ☐ c. looked at or stared at.

☐ × 5 = ☐

NUMBER CORRECT   YOUR SCORE

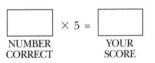

☐ × 5 = ☐

NUMBER CORRECT   YOUR SCORE

EXAMINE STORY ELEMENTS. The following questions check your knowledge of story elements. Put an *x* in the box next to each correct answer.

1. Of the following, which happened last in the *plot* of the story?
   - ☐ a. An official from the Port Captain's office came to see João.
   - ☐ b. The family decided to put an ad in the newspaper.
   - ☐ c. A mother and her daughter came to look at the piano.

2. One *motive* for getting rid of the piano was to
   - ☐ a. obtain enough money to pay for the wedding.
   - ☐ b. provide more room for the couple who planned to get married.
   - ☐ c. throw out an object that was worthless and meaningless.

3. The *mood* of "The Piano" is unusual in that it
   - ☐ a. is both mysterious and suspenseful.
   - ☐ b. combines touches of humor with bittersweet sadness.
   - ☐ c. is extraordinarily joyous.

4. What is the *theme* of the story?
   - ☐ a. Most people do not recognize or appreciate the virtues of an old piano.
   - ☐ b. Something is worth only what someone is willing to pay for it.
   - ☐ c. Disposing of the family piano brings its owner hardship and remorse.

	× 5 =	
NUMBER CORRECT		YOUR SCORE

MASTER CRITICAL THINKING. The following questions check your critical thinking skills. Put an *x* in the box next to each correct answer.

1. Evidence in the story suggests that João
   - ☐ a. didn't care much about the piano.
   - ☐ b. was not a good father to his daughter.
   - ☐ c. loved the piano.

2. We may infer from the story that
   - ☐ a. almost anyone would be willing to buy a piano for a low price.
   - ☐ b. although a piano may be old, it can still be in perfect condition.
   - ☐ c. few people are prepared to accept a piano at a moment's notice.

3. João's guilt and sorrow over giving up the piano are expressed in
   - ☐ a. his dream.
   - ☐ b. the documents he gave to the policemen.
   - ☐ c. his statement that he was "probably the most rational man in the whole neighborhood."

4. It is likely that the redheaded man
   - ☐ a. was not really interested in the piano.
   - ☐ b. was a famous music teacher who loved old pianos.
   - ☐ c. would have bought the piano if it were still available.

	× 5 =	
NUMBER CORRECT		YOUR SCORE

E<small>XPLORE THE</small> W<small>RITER'S</small> C<small>RAFT</small>. The following questions check your knowledge of skills related to the craft of writing. Put an *x* in the box next to each correct answer. You may refer to pages 4 and 5.

1. João wanted to give the piano to someone "who knows what it represents." What does the piano represent, or symbolize, to João?
   ☐ a. something that has outlived its usefulness
   ☐ b. the future
   ☐ c. a piece of the family history

2. The expression "the ocean growled" is an example of
   ☐ a. personification.
   ☐ b. alliteration.
   ☐ c. an illusion.

3. Sara said that an old man "almost ate [the piano] with his eyes." This sentence
   ☐ a. contains a simile.
   ☐ b. contains an example of figurative language.
   ☐ c. illustrates onomatopoeia.

4. At the end of the story, Sara's fiancé, the lieutenant, said that he was "crazy for a piano." He asked, "Aren't you going to get another?" This is an example of
   ☐ a. symbolism.
   ☐ b. irony.
   ☐ c. a flashback.

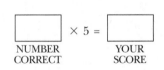

NUMBER CORRECT × 5 = YOUR SCORE

Questions for Writing and Discussion

● Explain why the family tried to sell the piano. Give two reasons.
● João had mixed feelings about disposing of the piano. Offer several examples from the story to support this statement.
● Throughout the story, the piano is described as though it were a living being. Illustrate this fact by referring to the story. Why do you think the author chose to portray the piano in that manner?
● At the end of the story, João seemed suffocated and confused. Why do you think he felt that way? Read the last two lines of the story again. Why are they so powerful?

See additional questions for extended writing on pages 178 and 179.

Use the boxes below to total your scores for the exercises. Then record your scores on pages 224 and 225.

☐ **T**<small>HINK ABOUT THE STORY</small>
   +
☐ **H**<small>ANDLE NEW VOCABULARY WORDS</small>
   +
☐ **E**<small>XAMINE STORY ELEMENTS</small>
   +
☐ **M**<small>ASTER CRITICAL THINKING</small>
   +
☐ **E**<small>XPLORE THE WRITER'S CRAFT</small>
   ▼
☐ **Total Score:** Story 11

A fortune is waiting to be found—if you know where to look, in . . .

THE WIDOW AND THE PARROT

by Virginia Woolf

Some fifty years ago Mrs. Gage, an elderly widow, was sitting in her cottage in a village called Spilsby in Yorkshire.[1] Although lame and rather short sighted she was doing her best to mend a pair of clogs,[2] for she had only a few shillings[3] a week to live on. As she hammered at the clog, the postman opened the door and threw a letter into her lap.

It bore the address "Messrs. Stagg and Beetle, 67 High Street, Lewes, Sussex."

Mrs. Gage opened it and read:

"Dear Madam: We have the honor to inform you of the death of your brother Mr. Joseph Brand."

"Lawk a mussy," said Mrs. Gage. "Old brother Joseph gone at last!"

---

1. **Yorkshire:** a county in northeastern England

2. **clogs:** shoes with thick wooden soles

3. **shilling:** coin worth a certain amount of money in the United Kingdom

"He has left you his entire property," the letter when on, "which consists of a dwelling house, stable, cucumber frames, mangles, wheelbarrows, etc., etc., in the village of Rodmell, near Lewes. He also bequeaths to you his entire fortune; viz: £3,000 (three thousand pounds[4]) sterling."

Mrs. Gage almost fell into the fire with joy. She had not seen her brother for many years, and, as he did not even acknowledge the Christmas card which she sent him every year, she thought that his miserly habits, well known to her from childhood, made him grudge even a penny stamp for a reply. But now it had turned out to her advantage. With three thousand pounds, to say nothing of house, etc., etc., she and her family could live in great luxury forever.

She determined that she must visit Rodmell at once. The village clergyman, the Rev. Samuel Tallboys, lent her two pound ten, to pay her fare, and by next day all preparations for her journey were complete. The most important of these was the care of her dog Shag during her absence, for in spite of her poverty she was devoted to animals, and often went short herself rather than stint her dog of his bone.

She reached Lewes late on Tuesday night. In those days, I must tell you, there was no bridge over the river at Southease, nor had the road to Newhaven yet been made. To reach Rodmell it was necessary to cross the river Ouse by a ford,[5] traces of which still exist, but this could only be attempted at low tide, when the stones on the river bed appeared above the water. Mr. Stacey, the farmer, was going to Rodmell in his cart, and he kindly offered to take Mrs. Gage with him. They reached Rodmell about nine o'clock on a November night and Mr. Stacey obligingly pointed out to Mrs. Gage the house at the end of the village which had been left her by her brother. Mrs. Gage knocked at the door. There was no answer. She knocked again. A very strange high voice shrieked out "Not at home." She was so much taken aback that if she had not heard footsteps coming she would have run away. However, the door was opened by an old village woman, by name Mrs. Ford.

"Who was that shrieking out 'Not at home'?" said Mrs. Gage.

"Drat the bird!" said Mrs. Ford very peevishly, pointing to a large grey parrot. "He almost screams my head off. There he sits all day humped up on his perch like a monument screeching 'Not at home' if ever you go near his perch." He was a very handsome bird, as Mrs. Gage could see; but his feathers were sadly neglected. "Perhaps he is unhappy, or he may be hungry," she said. But Mrs. Ford said it was temper merely; he was a seaman's parrot and had learnt his language in the east. However, she added, Mr. Joseph was very fond of him, had called him James; and, it was said, talked to him as if he were a rational being. Mrs. Ford soon left. Mrs. Gage at once went to her box and fetched some sugar which she had with her and offered it to the parrot, saying in a very kind tone that she meant him no harm, but was his old master's sister, come to take possession of the house, and she would see to it that he

---

4. **pound:** a unit of money in the United Kingdom

5. **ford:** a shallow place in the river

was as happy as a bird could be. Taking a lantern she next went round the house to see what sort of property her brother had left her. It was a bitter disappointment. There were holes in all the carpets. The bottoms of the chairs had fallen out. Rats ran along the mantelpiece. There were large toadstools growing through the kitchen floor. There was not a stick of furniture worth seven pence halfpenny; and Mrs. Gage only cheered herself by thinking of the three thousand pounds that lay safe and snug in Lewes Bank.

She determined to set off to Lewes next day in order to claim her money from Messrs. Stagg and Beetle the solicitors,[6] and then to return home as quick as she could. Mr. Stacey, who was going in to market with some fine Berkshire pigs, again offered to take her with him, and told her some terrible stories of young people who had been drowned through trying to cross the river at high tide, as they drove. A great disappointment was in store for the poor old woman directly she got in to Mr. Stagg's office.

"Pray take a seat, Madam," he said, looking very solemn and grunting slightly. "The fact is," he went on, "that you must prepare to face some very disagreeable news. Since I wrote to you I have gone carefully through Mr. Brand's papers. I regret to say that I can find no trace whatever of the three thousand pounds. Mr. Beetle, my partner, went himself to Rodmell and searched the premises with the utmost care. He found absolutely nothing—no gold, silver, or valuables of any kind—except a fine grey parrot which I advise you

to sell for whatever he will fetch. His language, Benjamin Beetle said, is very extreme. But that is neither here nor there. I much fear you have had your journey for nothing. The premises are dilapidated; and of course our expenses are considerable." Here he stopped, and Mrs. Gage well knew that he wished her to go. She was almost crazy with disappointment. Not only had she borrowed two pound ten from the Rev. Samuel Tallboys, but she would return home absolutely empty handed, for the parrot James would have to be sold to pay her fare. It was raining hard, but Mr. Stagg did not press her to stay, and she was too beside herself with sorrow to care what she did. In spite of the rain she started to walk back to Rodmell across the meadows.

Mrs. Gage, as I have already said, was lame in her right leg. At the best of times she walked slowly, and now, what with her disappointment and the mud on the bank, her progress was very slow indeed. As she plodded along, the day grew darker and darker, until it was as much as she could do to keep on the raised path by the river side. You might have heard her grumbling as she walked, and complaining of her crafty brother Joseph, who had put her to all this trouble "Express," she said, "to plague me. He was always a cruel little boy when we were children," she went on. "He liked worrying the poor insects, and I've known him trim a hairy caterpillar with a pair of scissors before my very eyes. He was such a miserly varmint too. He used to hide his pocket money in a tree, and if anyone gave him a piece of iced cake for tea, he cut the sugar off and kept it for his supper. "I make no doubt he's all aflame at this very moment

---

6. **solicitors:** lawyers

in Hell fire, but what's the comfort of that to me?" she asked, and indeed it was very little comfort, for she ran slap into a great cow which was coming along the bank, and rolled over and over in the mud.

She picked herself up as best as she could and trudged on again. It seemed to her that she had been walking for hours. It was now pitch dark and she could scarcely see her own hand before her nose. Suddenly she bethought her of Farmer Stacey's words about the ford. "Lawk a mussy," she said, "however shall I find my way across? If the tide's in, I shall step into deep water and be swept out to sea in a jiffy! Many's the couple that been drowned here; to say nothing of horses, carts, herds of cattle, and stacks of hay."

Indeed what with the dark and the mud she had got herself into a pretty pickle. She could hardly see the river itself, let alone tell whether she had reached the ford or not. No lights were visible anywhere, for, as you may be aware, there is no cottage or house on that side of the river nearer than Asheham House, lately the seat of Mr. Leonard Woolf.[7] It seemed that there was nothing for it but to sit down and wait for the morning. But at her age, with the rheumatics in her system, she might well die of cold. On the other hand, if she tried to cross the river it was almost certain that she would be drowned. So miserable was her state that she would gladly have changed places with one of the cows in the field. No more wretched old woman could have been found in the whole county of Sussex; standing on the river bank, not knowing

whether to sit or to swim, or merely to roll over in the grass, wet though it was, and sleep or freeze to death, as her fate decided.

At that moment a wonderful thing happened. An enormous light shot up into the sky, like a gigantic torch, lighting up every blade of grass, and showing her the ford not twenty yards away. It was low tide, and the crossing would be an easy matter if only the light did not go out before she had got over.

"It must be a Comet or some such wonderful monstrosity," she said as she hobbled across. She could see the village of Rodmell brilliantly lit up in front of her.

"Bless us and save us!" she cried out. "There's a house on fire—thanks to the Lord"—for she reckoned that it would take some minutes at least to burn a house down, and in that time she would be well on her way to the village.

"It's an ill wind that blows nobody any good," she said as she hobbled along the Roman road. Sure enough, she could see every inch of the way, and was almost in the village street when for the first time it struck her: "Perhaps it's my own house that's blazing to cinders before my very eyes!"

She was perfectly right.

A small boy in his nightgown came capering up to her and cried out, "Come and see old Joseph Brand's house ablaze!"

All the villagers were standing in a ring round the house handing buckets of water which were filled from the well in Monk's house kitchen, and throwing them on the flames. But the fire had got a strong hold, and just as Mrs. Gage arrived, the roof fell in.

"Has anybody saved the parrot?" she cried.

"Be thankful you're not inside yourself, Madam," said the Rev. James Hawkesford,

---

7. **the seat of Mr. Leonard Woolf:** the home of Leonard Woolf (actually the author's husband)

the clergyman. "Do not worry for the dumb creatures. I make no doubt the parrot was mercifully suffocated on his perch."

But Mrs. Gage was determined to see for herself. She had to be held back by the village people, who remarked that she must be crazy to hazard her life for a bird.

"Poor old woman," said Mrs. Ford, "she has lost all her property, save one old wooden box, with her night things in it. No doubt we should be crazed in her place too."

So saying, Mrs. Ford took Mrs. Gage by the hand and led her off to her own cottage, where she was to sleep the night. The fire was now extinguished, and everybody went home to bed. But poor Mrs. Gage could not sleep. She tossed and tumbled thinking of her miserable state, and wondering how she could get back to Yorkshire and pay the Rev. Samuel Tallboys the money she owed him. At the same time she was even more grieved to think of the fate of the poor parrot James. She had taken a liking to the bird, and thought that he must have an affectionate heart to mourn so deeply for the death of old Joseph Brand, who had never done a kindness to any human creature. It was a terrible death for an innocent bird, she thought; and if only she had been in time, she would have risked her own life to save his.

She was lying in bed thinking these thoughts when a slight tap at the window made her start. The tap was repeated three times over. Mrs. Gage got out of bed as quickly as she could and went to the window. There, to her utmost surprise, sitting on the window ledge, was an enormous parrot. The rain had stopped and it was a fine moonlight night. She was greatly alarmed at first, but soon recognized the grey parrot, James, and was overcome with joy at his escape. She opened the window, stroked his head several times, and told him to come in. The parrot replied by gently shaking his head from side to side, then flew to the ground, walked away a few steps, looked back as if to see whether Mrs. Gage were coming, and then returned to the window sill, where she stood in amazement.

"The creature has more meaning in its acts than we humans know," she said to herself. "Very well, James," she said aloud, talking to him as though he were a human being. "I'll take your word for it. Only wait a moment while I make myself decent."

So saying she pinned on a large apron, crept as lightly as possible downstairs, and let herself out without rousing Mrs. Ford.

The parrot James was evidently satisfied. He now hopped briskly a few yards ahead of her in the direction of the burnt house. Mrs. Gage followed as fast as she could. The parrot hopped, as if he knew his way perfectly, round to the back of the house, where the kitchen had originally been. Nothing now remained of it except the brick floor, which was still dripping with the water which had been thrown to put out the fire. Mrs. Gage stood still in amazement while James hopped about, pecking here and there, as if he were testing the bricks with his beak. It was a very uncanny sight, and had not Mrs. Gage been in the habit of living with animals, she would have lost her head, very likely, and hobbled back home. But stranger things yet were to happen. All this time the parrot had not said a word. He suddenly got into a state of the greatest excitement, fluttering his wings, tapping the floor repeatedly with his beak, and crying so shrilly, "Not at home! Not at home!" that Mrs. Gage feared that the whole village would be roused.

"Don't take on so, James; you'll hurt yourself," she said soothingly. But he repeated his attack on the bricks more violently than ever.

"Whatever can be the meaning of it?" said Mrs. Gage, looking carefully at the kitchen floor. The moonlight was bright enough to show her a slight unevenness in the laying of the bricks, as if they had been taken up and then relaid not quite flat with the others. She had fastened her apron with a large safety pin, and she now prized this pin between the bricks and found that they were only loosely laid together. Very soon she had taken one up in her hands. No sooner had she done this than the parrot hopped onto the brick next to it, and, tapping it smartly with his beak, cried, "Not at home!" which Mrs. Gage understood to mean that she was to move it. So they went on taking up the bricks in the moonlight until they had laid bare a space some six feet by four and a half. This the parrot seemed to think was enough. But what was to be done next?

Mrs. Gage now rested, and determined to be guided entirely by the behavior of the parrot James. She was not allowed to rest for long. After scratching about in the sandy foundations for a few minutes, as you may have seen a hen scratch in the sand with her claws, he unearthed what at first looked like a round lump of yellowish stone. His excitement became so intense that Mrs. Gage now went to his help. To her amazement she found that the whole space which they had uncovered was packed with long rolls of these round yellow stones, so neatly laid together that it was quite a job to move them. But what could they be? And for what purpose had they been hidden here? It was not until they had removed the entire layer on the top, and next a piece of oil cloth which lay beneath them, that a most miraculous sight was displayed before their eyes—there, in row after row, beautifully polished, and shining brightly in the moonlight, were thousands of brand new sovereigns!!!![8]

This, then, was the miser's hiding place; and he had made sure that no one would detect it by taking two extraordinary precautions. In the first place, as was proved later, he had build a kitchen range over the spot where his treasure lay hid, so that unless the fire had destroyed it, no one could have guessed its existence; and secondly he had coated the top layer of sovereigns with some sticky substance, then rolled them in the earth, so that if by any chance one had been laid bare no one would have suspected that it was anything but a pebble such as you may see for yourself any day in the garden. Thus, it was only by the extraordinary coincidence of the fire and the parrot's sagacity that old Joseph's craft was defeated.

Mrs. Gage and the parrot now worked hard and removed the whole hoard—which numbered three thousand pieces, neither more nor less—placing them in her apron which was spread upon the ground. As the three thousandth coin was placed on top of the pile, the parrot flew up into the air in triumph and alighted very gently on the top of Mrs. Gage's head. It was in this fashion that they returned to Mrs. Ford's cottage, at a very slow pace, for Mrs. Gage was lame, as I

---

8. **sovereign:** a gold coin worth one British pound

have said, and now she was almost weighted to the ground by the contents of her apron. But she reached her room without any one knowing of her visit to the ruined house.

Next day she returned to Yorkshire. Mr. Stacey once more drove her into Lewes and was rather surprised to find how heavy Mrs. Gage's wooden box had become. But he was a quiet sort of man, and merely concluded that the kind people at Rodmell had given her a few odds and ends to console her for the dreadful loss of all her property in the fire. Out of sheer goodness of heart Mr. Stacey offered to buy the parrot off her for half a crown; but Mrs. Gage refused his offer with such indignation, saying that she would not sell the bird for all the wealth of the Indies, that he concluded that the old woman had been crazed by her troubles.

It now only remains to be said that Mrs. Gage got back to Spilsby in safety; took her black box to the Bank; and lived with James the parrot and her dog Shag in great comfort and happiness to a very great age.

It was not till she lay on her death bed that she told the clergyman (the son of the Rev. Samuel Tallboys) the whole story, adding that she was quite sure that the house had been burnt on purpose by the parrot James, who, being aware of her danger on the river bank, flew into the scullery,[9] and upset the oil stove which was keeping some scraps warm for her dinner. By this act, he not only saved her from drowning, but brought to light the three thousand pounds, which could have been found in no other manner. Such, she said, is the reward of kindness to animals.

The clergyman thought that she was wandering in her mind. But it is certain that the very moment the breath was out of her body, James the parrot shrieked out, "Not at home! Not at home!" and fell off his perch stone dead. The dog Shag had died some years previously.

Visitors to Rodmell may still see the ruins of the house, which was burnt down fifty years ago, and it is commonly said that if you visit it in the moonlight you may hear a parrot tapping with his beak upon the brick floor, while others have seen an old woman sitting there in a white apron.

---

9. **scullery:** a workroom next to the kitchen

About the Author

Virginia Woolf (1882–1941) was born in London, England, to a family interested in literature, politics, and the arts. Her father was a famous scholar and philosopher who introduced her to great books as well as to his famous friends. Woolf wrote short stories, essays, and articles, but it is her novels that have distinguished her as one of the most influential writers of the twentieth century. In what has come to be known as the technique of "stream-of-consciousness," Woolf explored the inner thoughts of characters. *Mrs. Dalloway* and *To the Lighthouse* are among Woolf's best-known novels. The latter established Woolf as one of the most significant writers of her day.

THINK ABOUT THE STORY. The following questions help you check your reading comprehension. Put an *x* in the box next to the correct answer.

1. This story is mainly about
   - ☐ a. the will of Joseph Brand, brother of the main character.
   - ☐ b. how a parrot repays an elderly widow for her kindness.
   - ☐ c. a house that is destroyed by a raging fire.

2. When Mrs. Gage first received the letter from Mr. Stagg and Mr. Beetle, she was
   - ☐ a. greatly saddened by the death of her dear brother.
   - ☐ b. unconcerned and unmoved by the news.
   - ☐ c. filled with joy because of the fortune she expected to receive.

3. Mrs. Gage discovered that her brother's house was
   - ☐ a. filled with lovely and expensive articles.
   - ☐ b. in unexpectedly good condition.
   - ☐ c. in terrible condition, containing nothing of real value.

4. Where had the miser hidden his gold?
   - ☐ a. under bricks in the kitchen where the stove had once stood
   - ☐ b. in a large heavy wooden box
   - ☐ c. deep in the earth behind the house

HANDLE NEW VOCABULARY WORDS. The following questions check your vocabulary skills. Put an *x* in the box next to the correct answer. Each vocabulary word appears in the story.

1. The dilapidated house had holes in the carpets and toadstools growing through the floor. Define the word *dilapidated*.
   - ☐ a. falling apart or in a state of ruin
   - ☐ b. located in the countryside
   - ☐ c. no longer new

2. "A small boy . . . came capering up to [Mrs. Gage] and cried out, 'Come and see old Joseph's house ablaze.'" The word *capering* means
   - ☐ a. crawling very slowly.
   - ☐ b. crying with grief.
   - ☐ c. playfully jumping about.

3. The bird kept pecking at the bricks with its beak; "it was a very uncanny sight." What is the meaning of the word *uncanny*?
   - ☐ a. dreadful or horrible
   - ☐ b. weird or highly unexpected
   - ☐ c. typical or routine

4. "It was only by the parrot's sagacity" that the gold was discovered. The word *sagacity* means
   - ☐ a. wisdom.
   - ☐ b. strength.
   - ☐ c. ability to speak.

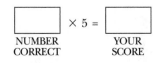

NUMBER CORRECT   × 5 =   YOUR SCORE

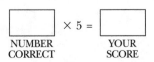

NUMBER CORRECT   × 5 =   YOUR SCORE

EXAMINE **S**TORY **E**LEMENTS. The following questions check your knowledge of story elements. Put an *x* in the box next to each correct answer.

1. Of these events, which happened first in the *plot* of the story?
   - ☐ a. Mrs. Gage borrowed some money and set out for Rodmell.
   - ☐ b. The parrot unearthed what looked like a lump of yellow stone.
   - ☐ c. Mrs. Gage discovered that Joseph Brand's house was on fire.

2. Which of the following best *characterizes* Mrs. Gage?
   - ☐ a. She was greedy and enjoyed living a life of luxury.
   - ☐ b. She was an old woman who had been crazed by her troubles.
   - ☐ c. She was an elderly widow who was devoted to animals.

3. The *climax* of the story occurred when
   - ☐ a. Mrs. Gage was permitted to sleep at Mrs. Ford's cottage.
   - ☐ b. the parrot tapped on the window and beckoned Mrs. Gage to follow it.
   - ☐ c. Mrs. Gage told the whole story as she lay on her deathbed.

4. "I regret to say that I can find no trace whatever of the three thousand pounds." This line of *dialogue* was uttered by
   - ☐ a. Mrs. Gage.
   - ☐ b. Mr. Stagg.
   - ☐ c. Rev. Samuel Tallboys.

☐ × 5 = ☐

NUMBER
CORRECT

YOUR
SCORE

MASTER **C**RITICAL **T**HINKING. The following questions check your critical thinking skills. Put an *x* in the box next to each correct answer.

1. We may infer from evidence in the story that Mrs. Gage
   - ☐ a. thought highly of her brother.
   - ☐ b. had a long and close relationship with Joseph Brand.
   - ☐ c. did not have a close relationship with her brother.

2. Which of these statements is true?
   - ☐ a. Mrs. Gage was not fond of animals.
   - ☐ b. Joseph Brand took extraordinary measures to hide his treasure.
   - ☐ c. Mrs. Gage informed the lawyers that she had found the money.

3. The author suggests that Mrs. Gage's good fortune was due to
   - ☐ a. the assistance the lawyers gave her in finding the gold.
   - ☐ b. the great concern she showed for the parrot.
   - ☐ c. the fact that she was extremely lucky.

4. The affection that the parrot felt for Mrs. Gage is indicated by the fact that
   - ☐ a. a moment after Mrs. Gage died, the parrot died too.
   - ☐ b. the parrot refused to live with anyone else in the village.
   - ☐ c. The parrot shrieked, "Not at home! Not at home!" to whoever came near.

☐ × 5 = ☐

NUMBER
CORRECT

YOUR
SCORE

EXPLORE THE WRITER'S CRAFT. The following questions check your knowledge of skills related to the craft of writing. Put an *x* in the box next to each correct answer. You may refer to pages 4 and 5.

1. Mrs. Ford peevishly pointed at the poor parrot. This sentence illustrates
   ☐ a. alliteration.
   ☐ b. personification.
   ☐ c. figurative language.

2. The parrot sat all day on his perch "like a monument." This sentence contains
   ☐ a. a metaphor.
   ☐ b. a simile.
   ☐ c. an example of irony.

3. Mrs. Gage exclaimed, "Lawk a mussy. Old brother Joseph gone at last!" This sentence provides an example of
   ☐ a. symbolism
   ☐ b. dialect.
   ☐ c. imagery.

4. According to Mrs. Ford, Joseph had been fond of the parrot and had "talked to him as if he were a rational being." This is the author's way of suggesting that
   ☐ a. it may be profitable to be kind to animals.
   ☐ b. the parrot understood things; its actions were intended.
   ☐ c. some parrots are as intelligent as people.

Questions for Writing and Discussion

- What did Mrs. Gage do and then say to the parrot upon first meeting the bird? Why was Mrs. Gage so disappointed in her brother's house?
- On her return to Rodmell, Mrs. Gage "got herself into a pretty pickle," or a difficult situation. Explain why the circumstances presented danger.
- At a point in the story, Mrs. Gage decided "to be guided entirely by the behavior of the parrot." Was this a wise decision? Why? Explain in detail what happened.
- Do you think that Mrs. Gage's eventual good fortune was just a coincidence, or was it a reward? Support your opinion.

See additional questions for extended writing on pages 178 and 179.

Use the boxes below to total your scores for the exercises. Then record your scores on pages 224 and 225.

☐ **T**HINK ABOUT THE STORY
+
☐ **H**ANDLE NEW VOCABULARY WORDS
+
☐ **E**XAMINE STORY ELEMENTS
+
☐ **M**ASTER CRITICAL THINKING
+
☐ **E**XPLORE THE WRITER'S CRAFT
▼
☐ **Total Score:** Story 12

☐ × 5 = ☐
NUMBER   YOUR
CORRECT   SCORE

The injured bird came tumbling down through the limbs of the tree. But even death
could not mar the beauty of . . .

The Scarlet Ibis

by James Hurst

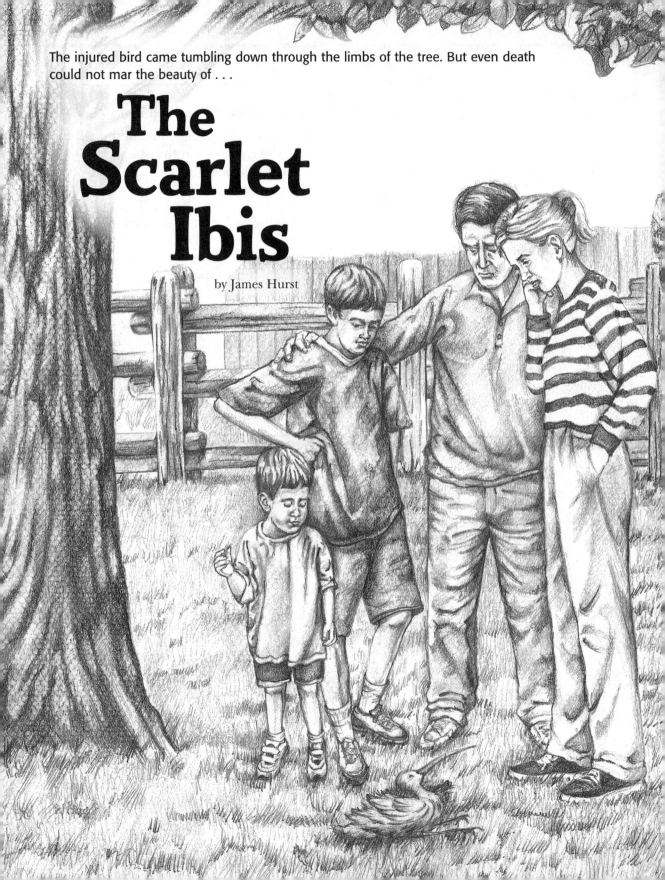

It was in the clove of seasons,[1] summer was dead but autumn had not yet been born. The flower garden was stained with rotting brown magnolia petals and the oriole nest in the elm was untenanted[2] and rocked back and forth like an empty cradle. The last graveyard flowers were blooming, and their smell drifted across the cotton field and through every room of our house, speaking softly the names of our dead.

It's strange that all this is still so clear to me, now that that summer has long since fled and time has had its way. A grindstone stands just outside the kitchen door, and now if an oriole sings in the elm, its song seems to die up in the leaves, a silvery dust. The flower garden is prim, the house a gleaming white, and the pale fence across the yard stands straight and spruce. But sometimes (like right now), as I sit in the cool, green-draped parlor, the grindstone begins to turn, and time with all its changes is ground away—and I remember Doodle.

Doodle was just about the craziest brother a boy ever had. Of course, he wasn't a crazy crazy, but was a nice crazy, like someone you meet in your dreams. He was born when I was six and was, from the outset, a disappointment. He seemed all head, with a tiny body which was red and shriveled like an old man's. Everybody thought he was going to die—everybody except Aunt Nicey, who had delivered him. She said he would live. Daddy had Mr. Heath, the carpenter, build a little mahogany coffin for him. But he didn't die, and when he was three months old Mama and Daddy decided they might as well name him. They named him William Armstrong, which was like tying a big tail on a small kite. Such a name sounds good only on a tombstone.

I thought myself pretty smart at many things, like holding my breath, running, jumping, or climbing the vines in Old Woman Swamp, and I wanted more than anything else someone to race to Horsehead Landing, someone to box with, and someone to perch with in the top fork of the great pine behind the barn, where across the fields and swamps you could see the sea. I wanted a brother. But Mama, crying, told me that even if William Armstrong lived, he would never do these things with me. He might not, she sobbed, even be "all there." He might, as long as he lived, lie on the sheet in the center of the bed in the front bedroom.

It was bad enough having an invalid brother, but having one who possibly was not all there was unbearable. However, one afternoon as I watched him, my head poked

---

1. **clove of seasons:** the time between two seasons

2. **untenanted:** unoccupied

between the iron posts of the foot of the bed, he looked straight at me and grinned. I skipped through the rooms, down the echoing halls, shouting, "Mama, he smiled. He's all there! He's all there!" and he was.

When he was two, if you laid him on his stomach, he began to try to move himself, straining terribly. The doctor said that with his weak heart this strain would probably kill him, but it didn't. Trembling, he'd push himself up, turning first red, then a soft purple, and finally collapse back onto the bed like an old-worn out doll. I can still see Mama watching him, her hand pressed tight across her mouth, her eyes wide and unblinking. But he learned to crawl (it was his third winter), and we brought him out of the front bedroom, putting him on the rug before the fireplace. For the first time he became one of us.

As long as he lay all the time in bed, we called him William Armstrong, even though it was formal and sounded as if we were referring to one of our ancestors, but with his creeping around on the deerskin rug and beginning to talk, something had to be done about his name. It was I who renamed him. When he crawled, he crawled backwards, as if he were in reverse and couldn't change gears. If you called him, he'd turn around as if he were going in the other direction, then he'd back right up to you to be picked up. Crawling backward made him look like a doodlebug, so I began to call him Doodle, and in time even Mama and Daddy thought it was a better name than William Armstrong. Renaming my brother was perhaps the kindest thing I ever did for him, because nobody expects much from someone called Doodle.

Although Doodle learned to crawl, he showed no signs of walking, but he wasn't idle. He talked so much that we all quit listening to what he said. It was about this time that Daddy built him a go-cart and I had to pull him around. At first I just paraded him up and down, but then he started crying to be taken out into the yard and it ended up by my having to lug him wherever I went. If I so much as picked up my cap, he'd start crying to go with me and Mama would call from wherever she was, "Take Doodle with you."

He was a burden in many ways. The doctor had said that he mustn't get too excited, too hot, too cold, or too tired and that he must always be treated gently. A long list of don'ts went with him, all of which I ignored once we got out of the house. To discourage his coming with me, I'd run with him across the ends of the cotton rows and careen him around corners on two wheels. Sometimes I accidentally turned him over, but he never told Mama. His skin was very sensitive, and he had to wear a big straw hat whenever he went out. When the going got rough and he had to cling to the sides of the go-cart, the hat slipped all the way down over his ears. He was a sight. Finally, I could see I was licked. Doodle was my brother and he was going to cling to me forever, no matter what I did, so I dragged him across the burning cotton field to share with him the only beauty I knew, Old Woman Swamp. I pulled the go-cart through the fern, down into the green dimness by the stream. I lifted him out and set him down in the soft grass beside a tall pine. His eyes were round with wonder as he gazed about him, and his little hands began to stroke the grass. Then he began to cry.

"What's the matter?" I asked, annoyed.

"It's so pretty," he said. "So pretty, pretty, pretty."

After that day Doodle and I often went down into Old Woman Swamp. I would gather wild flowers, wild violets, honeysuckle, yellow jasmine, snakeflowers, and water lilies, and with wire grass we'd weave them into necklaces and crowns. We'd bedeck ourselves with our handiwork and loll about thus beautified, beyond the touch of the everyday world. Then when the slanted rays of the sun burned orange in the tops of the pines, we'd drop our jewels into the stream and watch them float away toward the sea.

There is within me (and with sadness I have watched it in others) a knot of cruelty borne by the stream of love, much as our blood sometimes bears the seed of our destruction, and at times I was mean to Doodle. One day I took him up to the barn loft and showed him his casket, telling him how we all had believed he would die. Owls had built a nest inside it.

Doodle studied the mahogany box for a long time, then said, "It's not mine."

"It is," I said. "And before I'll help you down from the loft, you're going to have to touch it."

"I won't touch it," he said sullenly.

"Then I'll leave you here by yourself," I threatened, and made as if I were going down.

Doodle was frightened of being left. "Don't go leave me, Brother," he cried, and he leaned toward the coffin. His hand, trembling, reached out, and when he touched the casket he screamed. A screech owl flapped out of the box into our faces, scaring us. Doodle was paralyzed, so I put him on my shoulder and carried him down the ladder, and even when we were outside in the bright sunshine, he clung to me, crying, "Don't leave me. Don't leave me."

When Doodle was five years old, I was embarrassed at having a brother of that age who couldn't walk, so I set out to teach him. We were down in Old Woman Swamp and it was spring and the sick-sweet smell of bay flowers hung everywhere like a mournful song. "I'm going to teach you to walk, Doodle," I said.

He was sitting comfortably on the soft grass, leaning back against the pine. "Why?" he asked.

I hadn't expected such an answer. "So I won't have to haul you around all the time."

"I can't walk, Brother," he said.

"Who says so?" I demanded.

"Mama, the doctor—everybody."

"Oh, you can walk," I said, and I took him by the arms and stood him up. He collapsed onto the grass like a half-empty flour sack. It was as if he had no bones in his little legs.

"Don't hurt me, Brother," he warned.

"Shut up. I'm not going to hurt you. I'm going to teach you to walk." I heaved him up again, and again he collapsed.

This time he did not lift his face up out of the grass. "I just can't do it."

"Oh yes you can, Doodle," I said. "All you got to do is try. Now come on," and I hauled him up once more.

It seemed so hopeless from the beginning that it's a miracle I didn't give up. But all of us must have something or someone to be proud of, and Doodle had become mine. I did not know then that pride is a wonderful, terrible thing, a seed that bears two vines, life and death.

Every day that summer we went to the pine beside the stream of Old Woman Swamp, and I put him on his feet at least a hundred times each afternoon. Occasionally I too became discouraged because it didn't seem as if he was trying, and I would say, "Doodle, don't you *want* to learn to walk?"

He'd nod his head, and I'd say, "Well, if you don't keep trying, you'll never learn." Then I'd paint for him a picture of us as old men, white-haired, him with a long white beard and me still pulling him around in the go-cart. This never failed to make him try again.

Finally one day, after many weeks of practicing, he stood alone for a few seconds. When he fell, I grabbed him in my arms and hugged him, our laughter pealing through the swamp like a ringing bell. Now we knew it could be done. Hope no longer hid in the dark thicket but perched brilliantly visible. "Yes, yes," I cried, and he cried it too, and the grass beneath us was soft and the smell of the swamp was sweet.

With success so imminent, we decided not to tell anyone until he could actually walk. Each day, barring rain, we sneaked into Old Woman Swamp, and by cotton-picking time Doodle was ready to show what he could do. He still wasn't able to walk far, but we could wait no longer. Keeping a nice secret is very hard to do, like holding your breath. We chose to reveal all on October eighth, Doodle's sixth birthday, and for weeks ahead we mooned around the house, promising everybody a most spectacular surprise.

At breakfast on our chosen day, when Mama, Daddy, and Aunt Nicey were in the dining room, I brought Doodle to the door in the go-cart just as usual and had them turn their backs. I helped Doodle up, and when he was standing alone I let them look. There wasn't a sound as Doodle walked slowly across the room and sat down at his place at the table. Then Mama began to cry and ran over to him, hugging him and kissing him. Daddy hugged him too, so I went to Aunt Nicey and began to waltz her around.

Doodle told them it was I who had taught him to walk, so everyone wanted to hug me, and I began to cry.

"What are you crying for?" asked Daddy, but I couldn't answer. They did not know that I did it for myself; that pride, whose slave I was, spoke to me louder than all their voices; and that Doodle walked only because I was ashamed of having a crippled brother.

Within a few months Doodle had learned to walk well, and his go-cart was put up in the barn loft (it's still there) beside his little mahogany coffin. Now, when we roamed off together, resting often, we never turned back until our destination had been reached, and to help pass the time, we took up lying. From the beginning Doodle was a terrible liar and he got me in the habit.

My lies were scary, involved, and usually pointless; but Doodle's were twice as crazy. People in his stories all had wings and flew wherever they wanted to go. His favorite lie was about a boy named Peter who had a pet peacock with a ten-foot tail. Peter wore a golden robe that glittered so brightly that when he walked through the sunflowers they turned away from the sun to face him. When Peter was ready to go to sleep, the peacock spread his magnificent tail, enfolding the boy gently like a closing go-to-sleep flower. Yes, I must admit it, Doodle could beat me lying.

Doodle and I spent lots of time thinking
out our future. We decided that when we
re grown we'd live in Old Woman
wamp. Beside the stream, he planned,
e'd build us a house. All day long we'd
wing through the cypresses on the rope
vines, and if it rained we'd huddle beneath
an umbrella tree and play stickfrog. Of
course, I was old enough to know this
wouldn't work out, but the picture he
painted was so beautiful and serene that
all I could do was whisper Yes, yes.

Once I had succeeded in teaching
Doodle to walk, I began to believe in my
own infallibility, and I prepared a terrific
development program for him, unknown to
Mama and Daddy, of course. I would teach
him to run, to swim, to climb trees, and
to fight. He, too, now believed in my
infallibility, so we set the deadline for these
accomplishments less than a year away,
when, it had been decided, Doodle could
start to school.

That winter we didn't make much
progress, for I was in school and Doodle
suffered from one bad cold after another.
But when spring came, rich and warm, we
raised our sights again. Success lay at the
end of summer like a pot of gold, and
our campaign got off to a good start. On
hot days, Doodle and I went down to
Horsehead Landing and I gave him
swimming lessons or showed him how to
row a boat. Sometimes we descended into
the cool greenness of Old Woman Swamp
and climbed the rope vines or boxed
scientifically beneath the pine where
he had learned to walk. Promise hung
about us like the leaves, and wherever we
looked, ferns unfurled and birds broke
into song.

So we came to th
School was only a few
Doodle was far behind
barely clear the ground
the rope vines and his sw
certainly not passable. We
double our efforts, to make
and reach our pot of gold. I
until he turned blue and row
couldn't lift an oar. Whenever
purposefully walked fast, and alt
kept up, his face turned red and
became glazed. Once, he could go
further, so he collapsed on the grou
began to cry.

"Aw, come on, Doodle," I urged. "
can do it. Do you want to be different
everybody else when you start school?"

"Does it make any difference?"

"It certainly does," I said. "Now, come
on," and I helped him up.

As we slipped through dog days, Doodle
began to look feverish, and Mama felt his
forehead, asking him if he felt ill. At night
he didn't sleep well, and sometimes he had
nightmares, crying out until I touched him
and said, "Wake up, Doodle. Wake up."

It was Saturday noon, just a few days
before school was to start. I should have
already admitted defeat, but my pride
wouldn't let me. The excitement of our
program had now been gone for weeks, but
we still kept on with a tired doggedness. It
was too late to turn back, for we had both
wandered too far into a net of expectations
and had left no crumbs behind.

Daddy, Mama, Doodle, and I were seated
at the dining-room table having lunch. It
was a hot day, with all the windows and
doors open in case a breeze should come.
In the kitchen Aunt Nicey was humming

After a long silence, Daddy spoke.
calm, I wouldn't be surprised if we
storm this afternoon."

haven't heard a rain frog," said Mama
served the bread around the table.
did," declared Doodle. "Down in the
p."

He didn't," I said contrarily.

"You did, eh?" said Daddy, ignoring my
nial.

"I certainly did." Doodle reiterated,
owling at me over the top of his iced-tea
lass, and we were quiet again.

Suddenly, from out in the yard, came a
strange croaking noise. Doodle stopped
eating, with a piece of bread poised ready
for his mouth, his eyes popped round
like two blue buttons. "What's that?" he
whispered.

I jumped up, knocking over my chair,
and had reached the door when Mama
called, "Pick up the chair, sit down again,
and say excuse me."

By the time I had done this, Doodle had
excused himself and had slipped out into
the yard. He was looking up into the tree.
"It's a great big red bird!" he called.

The bird croaked loudly again, and
Mama and Daddy came out into the yard.
We shaded our eyes with our hands against
the hazy glare of the sun and peered up
through the still leaves. On the topmost
branch a bird the size of a chicken, with
scarlet feathers and long legs, was perched
precariously. Its wings hung down loosely,
and as we watched, a feather dropped away
and floated slowly down through the green
leaves.

"It's not even frightened of us," Mama said.

"It looks tired," Daddy added. "Or maybe
sick."

Doodle's hands were clasped at
throat, and I had never seen him sta
so long. "What is it?" he asked.

Daddy shook his head. "I don't kn
maybe it's—"

At that moment the bird began to flu
but the wings were uncoordinated, and
amid much flapping and a spray of flying
feathers, it tumbled down, bumping
through the limbs of the tree and landing a
our feet with a thud. Its long, graceful neck
jerked twice into an S, then straightened
out, and the bird was still. A white veil came
over the eyes and the long white beak
unhinged. Its legs were crossed and its
clawlike feet were delicately curved at rest.
Even death did not mar its grace, for it lay
on the earth like a broken vase of red
flowers, and we stood around it, awed by its
exotic beauty.

"It's dead," Mama said.

"What is it?" Doodle repeated.

"Go bring me the bird book," said Daddy.

I ran into the house and brought back
the bird book. As we watched, Daddy
thumbed through its pages. "It's a scarlet
ibis," he said, pointing to a picture. "It lives
in the tropics—South America to Florida. A
storm must have brought it here."

Sadly, we all looked back at the bird. A
scarlet ibis! How many miles it had traveled
to die like this, in *our* yard, beneath the
tree.

"Let's finish lunch," Mama said, nudging
us back toward the dining room.

"I'm not hungry," said Doodle, and he
knelt down beside the ibis.

"We've got peach cobbler for dessert,"
Mama tempted from the doorway.

Doodle remained kneeling. "I'm going
to bury him."

"Don't you dare touch him," Mama warned. "There's no telling what disease he might have had."

"All right," said Doodle. "I won't."

Daddy, Mama, and I went back to the dining room table, but we watched Doodle through the open door. He took out a piece of string from his pocket and, without touching the ibis, looped one end around its neck. Slowly, he carried the bird around to the front yard and dug a hole in the flower garden, next to the petunia bed. Now we were watching him through the front window, but he didn't know it. His awkwardness at digging a hole with a shovel whose handle was twice as long as he was made us laugh, and we covered our mouths with our hands so he wouldn't hear.

When Doodle came into the dining room, he found us seriously eating our cobbler. He was pale and lingered just inside the screen door. "Did you get the scarlet ibis buried?" asked Daddy.

Doodle didn't speak but nodded his head.

"Go wash your hands, and then you can have some peach cobbler," said Mama.

"I'm not hungry," he said.

"Dead birds is bad luck," said Aunt Nicey poking her head from the kitchen door. "Specially *red* dead birds!"

As soon as I had finished eating, Doodle and I hurried off to Horsehead Landing. Time was short, and Doodle still had a long way to go if he was going to keep up with the other boys when he started school. The sun, gilded with the yellow cast of autumn, still burned fiercely, but the dark green woods through which we passed were shady and cool. When we reached the landing, Doodle said he was too tired to swim, so we got into a skiff[3] and floated down the creek with the tide. Doodle did not speak and kept his head turned away, letting one hand trail limply in the water.

After we had drifted a long way, I put the oars in place and made Doodle row back against the tide. Black clouds began to gather in the southwest, and he kept watching them, trying to pull the oars a little faster. When we reached Horsehead Landing, lightning was playing across half the sky and thunder roared out, hiding even the sound of the sea. The sun disappeared and darkness descended, almost like night. Flocks of marsh crows flew by, heading inland to their roosting trees.

Doodle was both tired and frightened, and when he stepped from the skiff he collapsed onto the mud. I helped him up, and as he wiped the mud off his trousers, he smiled at me ashamedly. He had failed and we both knew it, so we started back home, racing the storm. We never spoke (What are the words that can solder[4] cracked pride?); but I knew he was watching me, watching for a sign of mercy. The lightning was near now, and from fear he walked so close behind me he kept stepping on my heels. The faster I walked, the faster he walked; so I began to run. The rain was coming, roaring through the pines; and then a tree ahead of us was shattered by a bolt of lightning. When the deafening peal of thunder had died, and in the moment before the rain arrived, I heard Doodle, who had fallen behind, cry out, "Brother, Brother, don't leave me! Don't leave me!"

---

3. **skiff:** a small boat

4. **solder:** (pronounced as *sodder*) fasten, mend, or join together

The Scarlet Ibis

The knowledge that Doodle's and my plans had come to naught was bitter, and that streak of cruelty within me awakened. I ran as fast as I could, leaving him far behind with a wall of rain dividing us. The drops stung my face and the wind flared the wet glistening leaves of the bordering trees. Soon I could hear his voice no more.

I hadn't run too far before I became tired, and the flood of childish spite evanesced[5] as well. I stopped and waited for Doodle. The sound of rain was everywhere, but the wind had died and it fell straight down in parallel paths like ropes hanging from the sky. As I waited, I peered through the downpour, but no one came. Finally I went back and found him huddled beneath a bush beside the road. He was sitting on the ground, his face buried in his arms, which were resting on his drawn-up knees. "Let's go, Doodle," I said.

He didn't answer, so I placed my hand on his forehead and lifted his head. Limply, he fell backwards onto the earth. He had been bleeding from the mouth, and his neck and the front of his shirt were stained a brilliant red.

"Doodle! Doodle!" I cried, shaking him; but there was no answer but the ropy rain. He lay very awkwardly, with his head thrown far back, making his vermilion[6] neck appear unusually long and slim. His little legs, bent sharply at the knees, had never before seemed so fragile, so thin.

I began to weep, and the tear-blurred vision in red before me looked very familiar. "Doodle!" I screamed above the pounding storm and threw my body to the earth above his. For a long, long time, it seemed forever, I lay there crying, sheltering my fallen scarlet ibis from the rain.

---

5. **evanesced:** faded away; disappeared

6. **vermilion:** bright red

About the Author

James Hurst (1922–) grew up on a farm in South Carolina. As a young man, he studied chemical engineering but subsequently went to the Julliard School of Music in New York City, where he took voice lessons in the hope of pursuing a career in opera. Hurst later continued his musical studies in Italy. After three years, he returned to the United States and began a long career in the international department of a large bank. Hurst wrote in his spare time and had several short stories and a play published in small literary magazines. "The Scarlet Ibis" was published in *The Atlantic Monthly* in July 1960. The story won the "Atlantic First" award that year, as well as many other prizes. Over time, "The Scarlet Ibis" has gained recognition as a classic and has appeared in numerous texts and anthologies.

THINK ABOUT THE STORY. The following questions help you check your reading comprehension. Put an *x* in the box next to the correct answer.

1. "The Scarlet Ibis" is mainly about
   - ☐ a. a man's sad recollection of his role in the growth and the death of his brother.
   - ☐ b. why the narrator gave his brother the nickname Doodle.
   - ☐ c. a program that the narrator developed to help his younger brother run, swim, and climb.

2. After the scarlet ibis died, Doodle insisted on
   - ☐ a. having his father remove the bird.
   - ☐ b. staying far away from the bird because dead birds mean bad luck.
   - ☐ c. digging a hole and burying the bird.

3. The narrator wanted Doodle to
   - ☐ a. be different from everybody else at school.
   - ☐ b. keep up with the other boys when school began.
   - ☐ c. read and write better than any of the other students.

4. At the end of the story, the narrator
   - ☐ a. left his brother far behind during a storm.
   - ☐ b. rushed back to help Doodle when he heard his cries for help.
   - ☐ c. tripped and injured himself during the downpour.

☐ × 5 = ☐

NUMBER CORRECT   YOUR SCORE

HANDLE NEW VOCABULARY WORDS. The following questions check your vocabulary skills. Put an *x* in the box next to the correct answer. Each vocabulary word appears in the story.

1. Often Doodle and his older brother would loll around the countryside. Which of the following best defines the word *loll*?
   - ☐ a. to rush about at top speed
   - ☐ b. to yell, shout, and jump
   - ☐ c. to move about in a relaxed, easy manner

2. The narrator's great success made him believe in his own infallibility. What is the meaning of the word *infallibility*?
   - ☐ a. inability to be wrong
   - ☐ b. good luck or good fortune
   - ☐ c. greater strength or power than that of any other individual

3. "I did it," Doodle declared. "I certainly did," he reiterated. The word *reiterated* means
   - ☐ a. to speak softly.
   - ☐ b. to be pleased.
   - ☐ c. to say over again.

4. The poor bird was "perched precariously" on the top branch; a moment later, it fell to the ground. What is the meaning of the word *precariously*?
   - ☐ a. safely
   - ☐ b. dangerously
   - ☐ c. comfortably

☐ × 5 = ☐

NUMBER CORRECT   YOUR SCORE

EXAMINE STORY ELEMENTS. The following questions check your knowledge of story elements. Put an *x* in the box next to each correct answer.

1. Which of the following best illustrates the narrator's *inner conflict*?
   - ☐ a. He was disappointed in Doodle's shortcomings, or lack of ability.
   - ☐ b. He felt love and tenderness for his brother, but he also felt anger.
   - ☐ c. He thought that his brother was "nice crazy, like someone you meet in your dreams."

2. Identify the narrator's *motive* for teaching his brother to walk.
   - ☐ a. He wanted his parents to be proud of what he had done.
   - ☐ b. He was eager to prove that the doctor was wrong.
   - ☐ c. He was ashamed of having a "crippled brother."

3. Which sentence best expresses the *theme* of the story?
   - ☐ a. Pride can produce positive results, but it can also be highly destructive.
   - ☐ b. Sometimes it is difficult to forget things that happened long ago.
   - ☐ c. If at first you don't succeed, you must try, try again.

4. The *mood* of "The Scarlet Ibis" is
   - ☐ a. mysterious.
   - ☐ b. joyful.
   - ☐ c. sad.

☐ × 5 = ☐

NUMBER CORRECT   YOUR SCORE

MASTER CRITICAL THINKING. The following questions check your critical thinking skills. Put an *x* in the box next to each correct answer.

1. The words "dead," "rotting," and "empty" in the first paragraph suggest that the story
   - ☐ a. will be short or have few characters.
   - ☐ b. will be about loss or a sad event.
   - ☐ c. will eventually end happily.

2. The people in Doodle's stories "flew wherever they wanted to go." Probably Doodle told stories like that because
   - ☐ a. he wished that he could move swiftly and effortlessly.
   - ☐ b. he often said that he loved creatures that could fly.
   - ☐ c. Doodle lacked imagination; those were the only stories he knew.

3. The scarlet ibis's death is intended to
   - ☐ a. point out that people should respect all living things.
   - ☐ b. remind the reader of Mama's warning: a dying animal may carry disease.
   - ☐ c. foreshadow Doodle's death.

4. In death, the scarlet ibis lay on the ground like a "vase of red flowers" and Doodle was a "vision in red." We may infer that the color red is stressed
   - ☐ a. to emphasize bravery or courage.
   - ☐ b. to bring more excitement to the story.
   - ☐ c. because it was the author's favorite color.

☐ × 5 = ☐

NUMBER CORRECT   YOUR SCORE

EXPLORE THE WRITER'S CRAFT. The following questions check your knowledge of skills related to the craft of writing. Put an *x* in the box next to each correct answer. You may refer to pages 4 and 5.

1. In the story, the scarlet ibis—wounded, strange, beautiful, and far from its natural home—is intended to be
   ☐ a. a symbol.
   ☐ b. an allusion.
   ☐ c. an example of personification.

2. The bird "tumbled down, bumping through the limbs of the tree and landing at our feet with a thud." This sentence contains
   ☐ a. a flashback.
   ☐ b. conflict.
   ☐ c. onomatopoeia.

3. "The sun, gilded with the yellow cast of autumn, still burned fiercely, but the dark green woods through which we passed were shady and cool." Since this sentence appeals to our senses, it is an example of
   ☐ a. irony.
   ☐ b. alliteration.
   ☐ c. imagery.

4. The rain "fell straight down in parallel paths like ropes hanging from the sky." This sentence
   ☐ a. contains a metaphor.
   ☐ b. contains a simile.
   ☐ c. is an illustration of symbolism.

☐ × 5 = ☐

NUMBER CORRECT   YOUR SCORE

Questions for Writing and Discussion

- What was the narrator's purpose in teaching Doodle to walk and in preparing "a terrific development program for him"?
- Explain in detail the importance of the scarlet ibis in the story. Discuss the many ways in which the bird and Doodle were alike.
- The narrator said that "pride is a wonderful, terrible thing, a seed that bears two vines, life and death." What does this statement mean? Explain its significance to the story.
- Although Doodle's body was weak and frail, he possessed strength of spirit. Find examples from the story to support this statement.

See additional questions for extended writing on pages 178 and 179.

Use the boxes below to total your scores for the exercises. Then record your scores on pages 224 and 225.

☐ **T**HINK ABOUT THE STORY
+
☐ **H**ANDLE NEW VOCABULARY WORDS
+
☐ **E**XAMINE STORY ELEMENTS
+
☐ **M**ASTER CRITICAL THINKING
+
☐ **E**XPLORE THE WRITER'S CRAFT
▼
☐ **Total Score:** Story 13

The Possibility of Evil

by Shirley Jackson

Miss Adela Strangeworth came daintily along Main Street on her way to the grocery. The sun was shining, the air was fresh and clear after the night's heavy rain, and everything in Miss Strangeworth's little town looked washed and bright. Miss Strangeworth took deep breaths and thought that there was nothing in the world like a fragrant summer day.

She knew everyone in town, of course; she was fond of telling strangers—tourists who sometimes passed through the town and stopped to admire Miss Strangeworth's roses— that she had never spent more than a day outside this town in all her long life. She was seventy-one, Miss Strangeworth told the tourists, with a pretty little dimple showing by her lip, and she sometimes found herself thinking that the town belonged to her. "My grandfather built the first house on Pleasant Street," she would say, opening her blue eyes wide with the wonder of it. "This house, right here. My family has lived here for better than a hundred years. My grandmother planted these roses, and my mother tended them, just as I do. I've watched my town grow; I can remember when Mr. Lewis, Senior, opened the grocery store, and the year the river flooded out the shanties[1] on the low road, and the excitement when some young folks wanted to move the park over to the space in front of where the new post office is today. They wanted to put up a statue of Ethan Allen"[2]— Miss Strangeworth would frown a little and sound stern—"but it should have been a statue of my grandfather. There wouldn't have been

1. **shanties:** roughly built cabins or shacks
2. **Ethan Allen:** patriot and soldier during the American Revolutionary War

a town here at all if it hadn't been for my grandfather and the lumber mill."

Miss Strangeworth never gave away any of her roses, although the tourists often asked her. The roses belonged on Pleasant Street, and it bothered Miss Strangeworth to think of people wanting to carry them away, to take them into strange towns and down strange streets. When the new minister came, and the ladies were gathering flowers to decorate the church, Miss Strangeworth sent over a great basket of gladioli; when she picked the roses at all, she set them in bowls and vases around the inside of the house her grandfather had built.

Walking down Main Street on a summer morning, Miss Strangeworth had to stop every minute or so to say good morning to someone or to ask after someone's health. When she came into the grocery, half a dozen people turned away from the shelves and the counters to wave at her or call out good morning.

"And good morning to you, too, Mr. Lewis," Miss Strangeworth said at last. The Lewis family had been in the town almost as long as the Strangeworths; but the day young Lewis left high school and went to work in the grocery, Miss Strangeworth had stopped calling him Tommy and started calling him Mr. Lewis, and he had stopped calling her Addie and started calling her Miss Strangeworth. They had been in high school together, and had gone to picnics together, and to high-school dances and basketball games; but now Mr. Lewis was behind the counter in the grocery, and Miss Strangeworth was living alone in the Strangeworth House on Pleasant Street.

"Good morning," Mr. Lewis said, and added politely, "Lovely day."

"It is a very nice day," Miss Strangeworth said, as though she had only just decided that it would do after all. "I would like a chop, please, Mr. Lewis, a small, lean veal chop. Are those strawberries from Arthur Parker's garden? They're early this year."

"He brought them in this morning." Mr. Lewis said.

"I shall have a box," Miss Strangeworth said. Mr. Lewis looked worried, she thought, and for a minute she hesitated, but then she decided that he surely could not be worried over the strawberries. He looked very tired indeed. He was usually so chipper, Miss Strangeworth thought, and almost commented; but it was far too personal a subject to be introduced to Mr. Lewis, the grocer, so she only said, "And a can of cat food and, I think, a tomato."

Silently, Mr. Lewis assembled her order on the counter, and waited. Miss Strangeworth looked at him curiously and then said, "It's Tuesday, Mr. Lewis. You forgot to remind me."

"Did I? Sorry."

"Imagine your forgetting that I always buy my tea on Tuesday," Miss Strangeworth said gently. "A quarter pound of tea, please, Mr. Lewis."

"Is that all, Miss Strangeworth?"

"Yes thank you, Mr. Lewis. Such a lovely day, isn't it?"

"Lovely," Mr. Lewis said.

Miss Strangeworth moved slightly to make room for Mrs. Harper at the counter. "Morning, Adela," Mrs. Harper said, and Miss Strangeworth said, "Good morning, Martha."

"Lovely day," Mrs. Harper said, and Miss Strangeworth said, "Yes, lovely," and Mr. Lewis, under Mrs. Harper's glance, nodded.

"Ran out of sugar for my cake frosting," Mrs. Harper explained. Her hand shook slightly as she opened her pocketbook. Miss Strangeworth wondered, glancing at her quickly, if she had been taking proper care of herself. Martha Harper was not as young as she used to be, Miss Strangeworth thought. She probably could use a good strong tonic.

"Martha," she said, "you don't look well."

"I'm perfectly all right," Mrs. Harper said shortly. She handed her money to Mr. Lewis, took her change and her sugar, and went out without speaking again. Looking after her, Miss Strangeworth shook her head slightly. Martha definitely did *not* look well.

Carrying her little bag of groceries, Miss Strangeworth came out of the store into the bright sunlight and stopped to smile down on the Crane baby. Don and Helen Crane were really the two most infatuated young parents she had ever known, she thought indulgently, looking at the delicately embroidered baby cap and the lace-edged carriage cover.

"That little girl is going to grow up expecting luxury all her life," she said to Helen Crane.

Helen laughed. "That's the way we want her to feel," she said. "Like a princess."

"A princess can see a lot of trouble sometimes," Miss Strangeworth said dryly. "How old is Her Highness now?"

"Six months next Tuesday," Helen Crane said, looking down with rapt wonder at her child. "I've been worrying, though, about her. Don't you think she ought to move around more? Try to sit up, for instance?"

"For plain and fancy worrying," Miss Strangeworth said, amused, "give me a new mother every time."

"She just seems—slow," Helen Crane said.

"Nonsense. All babies are different. Some of them develop much more quickly than others."

"That's what my mother says." Helen Crane laughed, looking a little bit ashamed.

"I suppose you've got young Don all upset about the fact that his daughter is already six months old and hasn't yet begun to learn to dance?"

"I haven't mentioned it to him. I suppose she's just so precious that I worry about her all the time."

"Well, apologize to her right now," Miss Strangeworth said. "*She* is probably worrying about why you keep jumping around all the time." Smiling to herself and shaking her old head, she went on down the sunny street, stopping once to ask little Billy Moore why he wasn't out riding in his daddy's shiny new car; and talking for a few minutes outside the library with Miss Chandler, the librarian, about the new novels to be ordered and paid for by the annual library appropriation. Miss Chandler seemed absent-minded and very much as though she were thinking about something else. Miss Strangeworth noticed that Miss Chandler had not taken much trouble with her hair that morning, and sighed. Miss Strangeworth hated sloppiness.

Many people seemed disturbed recently, Miss Strangeworth thought. Only yesterday the Stewarts' fifteen-year-old Linda had run crying down her own front walk and all the way to school, not caring who saw her. People around town thought she might have had a fight with the Harris boy, but they showed up together at the soda shop after school as usual, both of them looking grim and bleak. Trouble at home, people concluded, and sighed over the problems of trying to raise kids right these days.

From halfway down the block, Miss

Strangeworth could catch the heavy scent of her roses, and she moved a little more quickly. The perfume of roses meant home, and home meant the Strangeworth House on Pleasant Street. Miss Strangeworth stopped at her own front gate, as she always did, and looked with deep pleasure at her house, with the red and pink and white roses massed along the narrow lawn, and the rambler[3] going up along the porch; and the neat, the unbelievably trim lines of the house itself, with its slimness and its washed white look. Every window sparkled, every curtain hung stiff and straight, and even the stones of the front walk were swept and clear. People around town wondered how old Miss Strangeworth managed to keep the house looking the way it did, and there was a legend about a tourist once mistaking it for the local museum and going all through the place without finding out about his mistake. But the town was proud of Miss Strangeworth and her roses and her house. They had all grown together.

Miss Strangeworth went up her front steps, unlocked her front door with her key, and went into the kitchen to put away her groceries. She debated about having a cup of tea and then decided that it was too close to midday dinnertime; she would not have the appetite for her little chop if she had tea now. Instead she went in to the light, lovely sitting room, which still glowed from the hands of her mother and her grandmother, who had covered the chairs with bright chintz[4] and hung the curtains. All the furniture was spare and shining, and the round hooked rugs on the floor had been the work of Miss Strangeworth's grandmother and her mother. Miss Strangeworth had a bowl of her red roses on the low table before the window, and the room was full of their scent.

Miss Strangeworth went to the narrow desk in the corner and unlocked it with her key. She never knew when she might feel like writing letters, so she kept her notepaper inside and the desk locked. Miss Strangeworth's usual stationery was heavy and cream-colored, with STRANGEWORTH HOUSE engraved across the top; but, when she felt like writing her other letters, Miss Strangeworth used a pad of various-colored paper bought from the local newspaper shop. It was almost a town joke, that colored paper, layered in pink and green and blue and yellow; everyone in town bought it and used it for odd, informal notes and shopping lists. It was usual to remark, upon receiving a note written on a blue page, that so-and-so would be needing a new pad soon—here she was, down to the blue already. Everyone used the matching envelopes for tucking away recipes, or keeping odd little things in, or even to hold cookies in the school lunchboxes. Mr. Lewis sometimes gave them to the children for carrying home penny candy.

Although Miss Strangeworth's desk held a trimmed quill pen that had belonged to her grandfather, and a gold-frosted fountain pen that had belonged to her father, Miss Strangeworth always used a dull stub of pencil when she wrote her letters; and she printed them in a childish block print. After thinking for a minute, although she had been phrasing the letter in the back of her mind all the way home, she wrote on a pink

---

3. **rambler:** a climbing rose

4. **chintz:** brightly colored cotton fabric

sheet: DIDN'T YOU EVER SEE AN IDIOT CHILD BEFORE? SOME PEOPLE JUST SHOULDN'T HAVE CHILDREN SHOULD THEY?

She was pleased with the letter. She was fond of doing things exactly right. When she made a mistake, as she sometimes did, or when the letters were not spaced nicely on the page, she had to take the discarded page to the kitchen stove and burn it at once. Miss Strangeworth never delayed when things had to be done.

After thinking for a minute, she decided that she would like to write another letter, perhaps to go to Mrs. Harper, to follow up the ones she had already mailed. She selected a green sheet this time and wrote quickly: HAVE YOU FOUND OUT YET WHAT THEY WERE ALL LAUGHING ABOUT AFTER YOU LEFT THE BRIDGE CLUB ON THURSDAY? OR IS THE WIFE REALLY ALWAYS THE LAST ONE TO KNOW?

Miss Strangeworth never concerned herself with facts; her letters all dealt with the more negotiable stuff of suspicion. Mr. Lewis would never have imagined for a minute that his grandson might be lifting petty cash from the store register if he had not had one of Miss Strangeworth's letters. Miss Chandler, the librarian, and Linda Stewart's parents would have gone unsuspectingly ahead with their lives, never aware of possible evil lurking nearby, if Miss Strangeworth had not sent letters opening their eyes. Miss Strangeworth would have been genuinely shocked if there *had* been anything between Linda Stewart and the Harris boy; but, as long as evil existed unchecked in the world, it was Miss Strangeworth's duty to keep her town alert to it. It was far more sensible for Miss Chandler to wonder what Mr. Shelley's first wife had really died of than to take a chance on not knowing. There were so many wicked people in the world and only one Strangeworth left in the town. Besides, Miss Strangeworth liked writing her letters.

She addressed an envelope to Don Crane after a moment's thought, wondering curiously if he would show the letter to his wife, and using a pink envelope to match the pink paper. Then she addressed a second envelope, green, to Mrs. Harper. Then an idea came to her and she selected a blue sheet and wrote: YOU NEVER KNOW ABOUT DOCTORS. REMEMBER THEY'RE ONLY HUMAN AND NEED MONEY LIKE THE REST OF US. SUPPOSE THE KNIFE SLIPPED ACCIDENTALLY. WOULD DR. BURNS GET HIS FEE AND A LITTLE EXTRA FROM THAT NEPHEW OF YOURS?

She addressed the blue envelope to old Mrs. Foster, who was having an operation next month. She had thought of writing one more letter, to the head of the school board, asking how a chemistry teacher like Billy Moore's father could afford a new convertible, but, all at once, she was tired of writing letters. The three she had done would do for one day. She could write more tomorrow; it was not as though they all had to be done at once.

She had been writing her letters—sometimes two or three every day for a week, sometimes no more than one in a month—for the past year. She never got any answers, of course, because she never signed her name. If she had been asked, she would have said that her name, Adela Strangeworth, a name honored in the town for so many years, did not belong on such trash. The town where she lived had to be kept clean and sweet, but people everywhere were lustful and evil and degraded, and needed to be watched; the world was so large, and there was only one Strangeworth left in it. Miss Strangeworth sighed, locked her desk, and put the letters into her big black leather pocketbook, to be mailed when she took her evening walk.

She broiled her little chop nicely, and had a sliced tomato and a good cup of tea ready when she sat down to her midday dinner at the table in her dining room, which could be opened to seat twenty-two, with a second table, if necessary, in the hall. Sitting in the warm sunlight that came through the tall windows of the dining room, seeing her roses massed outside, handling the heavy, old silverware and the fine, translucent china, Miss Strangeworth was pleased; she would not have cared to be doing anything else. People must live graciously, after all, she thought, and sipped her tea. Afterward, when her plate and cup and saucer were washed and dried and put back onto the shelves where they belonged, and her silverware was back in the mahogany silver chest, Miss Strangeworth went up the graceful staircase and into her bedroom, which was the front room overlooking the roses, and had been her mother's and her grandmother's. Their Crown Derby dresser set and furs had been kept there, their fans and silver-backed brushes and their own bowls of roses; Miss Strangeworth kept a bowl of white roses on the bed table.

She drew the shades, took the rose satin spread from the bed, slipped out of her dress and her shoes, and lay down tiredly. She knew that no doorbell or phone would ring; no one in town would dare to disturb Miss Strangeworth during her afternoon nap. She slept, deep in the rich smell of roses.

After her nap she worked in her garden for a little while, sparing herself because of the heat; then she came in to her supper. She ate asparagus from her own garden, with sweet-butter sauce and a soft-boiled egg; and, while she had her supper, she listened to a late-evening news broadcast and then to a program of classical music on her small radio. After her dishes were done and her kitchen set in order, she took up her hat—Miss Strangeworth's hats were proverbial[5] in the town; people believed she had inherited them from her mother and her grandmother—and, locking the front door of her house behind her, set off on her evening walk, pocketbook under her arm. She nodded to Linda Stewart's father, who was washing his car in the pleasantly cool evening. She thought that he looked troubled.

There was only one place in town where she could mail her letters, and that was the new post office, shiny with red brick and silver letters. Although Miss Strangeworth had never given the matter any particular thought, she had always made a point of mailing her letters very secretly; it would, of course, not have been wise to let anyone see her mail them. Consequently, she timed her walk so she could reach the post office just as darkness was starting to dim the outlines of the trees and the shapes of people's faces, although no one could ever mistake Miss Strangeworth, with her dainty walk and her rustling skirts.

There was always a group of young people around the post office, the very youngest roller-skating upon its driveway, which went all the way around the building and was the only smooth road in town; and the slightly older ones already knowing how to gather in small groups and chatter and laugh and make great, excited plans for going across the street to the soda shop in a minute or two. Miss Strangeworth had never had any

---

5. proverbial: well-known or commonly referred to

self-consciousness before the children. She did not feel that any of them were staring at her unduly or longing to laugh at her; it would have been most reprehensible for their parents to permit their children to mock Miss Strangeworth of Pleasant Street. Most of the children stood back respectfully as Miss Strangeworth passed, silenced briefly in her presence, and some of the older children greeted her, saying soberly, "Hello, Miss Strangeworth."

Miss Strangeworth smiled at them and quickly went on. It had been a long time since she had known the name of every child in town. The mail slot was in the door of the post office. The children stood away as Miss Strangeworth approached it, seemingly surprised that anyone should want to use the post office after it had been officially closed up for the night and turned over to the children. Miss Strangeworth stood by the door, opening her black pocketbook to take out the letters, and heard a voice which she knew at once to be Linda Stewart's. Poor little Linda was crying again, and Miss Strangeworth listened carefully. This was, after all, her town, and these were her people; if one of them was in trouble she ought to know about it.

"I can't tell you, Dave," Linda was saying—so she was talking to the Harris boy, as Miss Strangeworth had supposed—"I just *can't*. It's just *nasty*."

"But why won't your father let me come around any more? What on earth did I do?"

"I can't tell you. I just wouldn't tell you for *any*thing. You've got to have a dirty, dirty mind for things like that."

"But something's happened. You've been crying and crying, and your father is all

upset. Why can't *I* know about it, too? Aren't I like one of the family?"

"Not any more, Dave, not any more. You're not to come near our house again; my father said so. He said he'd horsewhip you. That's all I can tell you: You're not to come near our house any more."

"But I didn't *do* anything."

"Just the same, my father said . . . "

Miss Strangeworth sighed and turned away. There was so much evil in people. Even in a charming little town like this one, there was still so much evil in people.

She slipped her letters into the slot, and two of them fell inside. The third caught on the edge and fell outside, onto the ground at Miss Strangeworth's feet. She did not notice it because she was wondering whether a letter to the Harris boy's father might not be of some service in wiping out this potential badness. Wearily Miss Strangeworth turned to go home to her quiet bed in her lovely house, and never heard the Harris boy calling to her to say that she had dropped something.

"Old lady Strangeworth's getting deaf," he said, looking after her and holding in his hand the letter he had picked up.

"Well, who cares?" Linda said. "Who cares any more, anyway?"

"It's for Don Crane," the Harris boy said, "this letter. She dropped a letter addressed to Don Crane. Might as well take it on over. We pass his house anyway." He laughed. "Maybe it's got a check or something in it, and he'd be just as glad to get it tonight instead of tomorrow."

"Catch old lady Strangeworth sending anybody a check," Linda said. "Throw it in the post office. Why do anyone a favor?" She sniffled. "Doesn't seem to me anybody around here cares about us," she said. "Why should we care about them?"

"I'll take it over anyway," the Harris boy said. "Maybe it's good news for them. Maybe they need something happy tonight, too. Like us."

Sadly, holding hands, they wandered off down the dark street, the Harris boy carrying Miss Strangeworth's pink envelope in his hand.

Miss Strangeworth awakened the next morning with a feeling of intense happiness and, for a minute wondered why, and then remembered that this morning three people would open her letters. Harsh, perhaps, at first, but wickedness was never easily banished, and a clean heart was a scoured heart. She washed her soft old face and brushed her teeth, still sound in spite of her seventy-one years, and dressed herself carefully in her sweet, soft clothes and buttoned shoes. Then, coming downstairs and reflecting that perhaps a little waffle would be agreeable for breakfast in the sunny dining room, she found the mail on the hall floor and bent to pick it up. A bill, the morning paper, a letter in a green envelope that looked oddly familiar. Miss Strangeworth stood perfectly still for a minute, looking down at the green envelope with the penciled printing, and thought: It looks like one of my letters. Was one of my letters sent back? No, because no one would know where to send it. How did this get here?

Miss Strangeworth was a Strangeworth of Pleasant Street. Her hand did not shake as she opened the envelope and unfolded the sheet of green paper inside. She began to cry silently for the wickedness of the world when she read the words:
LOOK OUT AT WHAT USED TO BE YOUR ROSES.

About the Author

Shirley Jackson (1919–1965) was born in San Francisco, but she spent most of her adult life in Vermont with her husband, author and critic Stanley Edgar Hyman, and their four children. The range of Jackson's writing is truly amazing. Some of her stories and novels are light and amusing, while others are eerie and terrifying. When Jackson's most famous short story, "The Lottery," first appeared in *The New Yorker,* the magazine received hundreds of letters—more than it had ever received in response to a story. Most letters expressed outrage at Jackson's horrifying portrayal of human behavior. The story firmly established Jackson's reputation as a writer. Among Jackson's spine-tingling novels are *The Haunting of Hill House* and *We Have Always Lived in the Castle.* However, not all her work is shocking or frightening. *Life Among the Savages* and *Raising Demons* are humorous, autobiographical books about family life.

THINK ABOUT THE STORY. The following questions help you check your reading comprehension. Put an *x* in the box next to the correct answer.

1. This story is mainly about
   □ a. the evils—known and unknown—that exist in a small town.
   □ b. a woman who is a self-appointed guardian of virtue in a small town.
   □ c. the importance of making sure that people act in a decent and proper manner.

2. For how long had Miss Strangeworth been sending unsigned letters?
   □ a. the past year
   □ b. about five years
   □ c. a very long time—for as long as she could remember

3. Mrs. Strangeworth always mailed her unsigned letters
   □ a. early in the morning.
   □ b. in the afternoon when she took her walk.
   □ c. when it was beginning to get dark.

4. Why didn't Miss Strangeworth notice that one letter had fallen to the ground?
   □ a. She had difficulty seeing.
   □ b. She was beginning to become deaf.
   □ c. She was busy thinking about writing a letter to Dave Harris's father.

HANDLE NEW VOCABULARY WORDS. The following questions check your vocabulary skills. Put an *x* in the box next to the correct answer. Each vocabulary word appears in the story.

1. Don and Helen Crane were infatuated with their daughter and wanted her to grow up feeling "like a princess." Which best defines the word *infatuated*?
   □ a. deeply troubled
   □ b. unconcerned about
   □ c. completely carried away by love

2. The new novels were "to be ordered and paid for by the annual library appropriation." The word *appropriation* means
   □ a. a sum of money set aside for a specific purpose.
   □ b. a committee that establishes rules in a town or city.
   □ c. a contribution or an act of charity.

3. She believed that people were "evil and degraded, and needed to be watched." As used here, the word *degraded* means
   □ a. capable of great achievements.
   □ b. worthy or deserving of merit.
   □ c. disgraceful or dishonorable.

4. "It would have been reprehensible" for the children "to mock Miss Strangeworth." One who acts in a *reprehensible* manner
   □ a. should be complimented.
   □ b. deserves to be criticized or blamed.
   □ c. does not know what she or he is doing.

□ × 5 = □
NUMBER CORRECT   YOUR SCORE

□ × 5 = □
NUMBER CORRECT   YOUR SCORE

EXAMINE STORY ELEMENTS. The following questions check your knowledge of story elements. Put an *x* in the box next to each correct answer.

1. Of these events, which happened last in the *plot* of the story?
   ☐ a. Miss Strangeworth dropped two letters in the mail slot.
   ☐ b. Miss Strangeworth found a green envelope on the hall floor.
   ☐ c. Miss Strangeworth bought tea.

2. Miss Strangeworth may best be *characterized* as a person who believes that
   ☐ a. people are basically good.
   ☐ b. people are basically evil.
   ☐ c. people are self-sufficient and capable of running their own lives.

3. What was Miss Strangeworth's *motive* for writing the letters in pencil "in a childish block print"?
   ☐ a. She wanted to conceal her identity.
   ☐ b. She wanted to make certain that they would be easy to read.
   ☐ c. She wanted to show the people who received them that she thought they were acting childishly.

4. What is the *theme* of the story?
   ☐ a. Evil exists everywhere and must be rooted out.
   ☐ b. Someone who tries to do good is ultimately treated very badly.
   ☐ c. A woman who thinks she is fighting evil is, herself, doing evil things.

☐ × 5 = ☐
NUMBER   YOUR
CORRECT   SCORE

MASTER CRITICAL THINKING. The following questions check your critical thinking skills. Put an *x* in the box next to each correct answer.

1. Evidence in the story indicates that Miss Strangeworth was the kind of person who
   ☐ a. always gave people the benefit of a doubt.
   ☐ b. made everybody's business her own business.
   ☐ c. enjoyed taking trips to distant and interesting places.

2. We may conclude that the green letter was sent to Miss Strangeworth by
   ☐ a. one of the children who found it at the post office.
   ☐ b. a friend of Miss Strangeworth.
   ☐ c. a furious Don Crane.

3. The last line of the story suggests that Miss Strangeworth's roses
   ☐ a. were as beautiful and fragrant as ever.
   ☐ b. had been given to tourists who admired them.
   ☐ c. had been destroyed.

4. We may infer that Miss Strangeworth will eventually
   ☐ a. be regarded as a local hero.
   ☐ b. be revealed to the entire town as the writer of the letters.
   ☐ c. apologize to those who believe her actions were wicked.

☐ × 5 = ☐
NUMBER   YOUR
CORRECT   SCORE

EXPLORE THE WRITER'S CRAFT. The following questions check your knowledge of skills related to the craft of writing. Put an *x* in the box next to each correct answer. You may refer to pages 4 and 5.

1. As a result of the author's detailed descriptions of Miss Strangeworth and her actions, the story may best be described as a
   ☐ a. myth.
   ☐ b. story-within-a-story.
   ☐ c. character study.

2. Miss Strangeworth's roses
   ☐ a. are a symbol of power, position, and tradition.
   ☐ b. are an example of the author's use of personification.
   ☐ c. illustrate allusion.

3. Mrs. Strangeworth believed that she was acting in a positive way, but her actions, in fact, proved highly destructive. This is an example of
   ☐ a. figurative language.
   ☐ b. irony.
   ☐ c. the moral of a story.

4. Often an author gives a character a particular name in order to associate the character with a quality, characteristic, or point of view. The name "Strangeworth" is most closely associated with
   ☐ a. sound judgment.
   ☐ b. an open-minded attitude.
   ☐ c. unusual values.

☐ × 5 = ☐
NUMBER CORRECT   YOUR SCORE

Questions for Writing and Discussion

● Miss Strangeworth "sometimes found herself thinking that the town belonged to her." Why did Miss Strangeworth feel that way?
● Miss Strangeworth believed "as long as evil existed unchecked in the world, it was [her] duty to keep the town alerted to it." Do you approve of her methods? Explain.
● What do Miss Strangeworth's roses represent? What is their significance in the last lines of the story?
● Suppose that Miss Strangeworth had not dropped a letter. Would the people in the town have eventually figured out who had been writing the letters? Explain.

See additional questions for extended writing on pages 178 and 179.

Use the boxes below to total your scores for the exercises. Then record your scores on pages 224 and 225.

☐ **T**HINK ABOUT THE STORY
+
☐ **H**ANDLE NEW VOCABULARY WORDS
+
☐ **E**XAMINE STORY ELEMENTS
+
☐ **M**ASTER CRITICAL THINKING
+
☐ **E**XPLORE THE WRITER'S CRAFT
▼
☐ **Total Score:** Story 14

Something Unexpected

Questions for Discussion and Extended Writing

The following questions provide you with opportunities to express your thoughts and feelings about the selections in this unit. Your teacher may assign selected questions. When you write your responses, remember to state your point of view clearly and to support your position by presenting specific details—examples, illustrations, and references drawn from the story and, in some cases, from your life. Organize your writing carefully and check your work for correct spelling, capitalization, punctuation, and grammar.

1. The theme of this unit is "Something Unexpected." Select three stories and show how each is related to the theme.

2. The Roman general Julius Caesar stated, "No one is so brave that he is not disturbed by something unexpected." Select a character from each of two stories in the unit and describe how the characters you chose were affected by "something unexpected."

3. In which two selections does the setting of the story play the most important role? Give titles and authors and present reasons for your answer.

4. Compare and contrast Mrs. Gage in "The Widow and the Parrot" with Miss Adela Strangeworth in "The Possibility of Evil." In what ways are they similar? How are they different?

5. Which character did you most care about or admire? Explain why.

6. João in "The Piano" and Doodle's older brother in "The Scarlet Ibis" each experience a wide range of emotions. Prove that this statement is true by referring to the stories.

7. Draw upon material found in one selection to write a descriptive essay about a character or setting.

8. In "The Scarlet Ibis" and "The Possibility of Evil," it is not clear what the main characters will do following the conclusion of the story. Write an essay in which you discuss the actions you think the characters will take. Give your essay an appropriate title.

9. In which story do you think a character's inner conflict played a significant role? Describe in detail the inner conflict of the character you selected.

10. About 2,500 years ago, the Greek philosopher Heraclitus wrote, "Everything gives way and nothing stays fixed. . . . Nothing endures but change." What are some changes that have taken place in your life? How have these changes affected you? What changes do you envision, or picture, for your future? Write an essay entitled "Changes in My Life." Your essay should have an introduction, a body, and a conclusion.

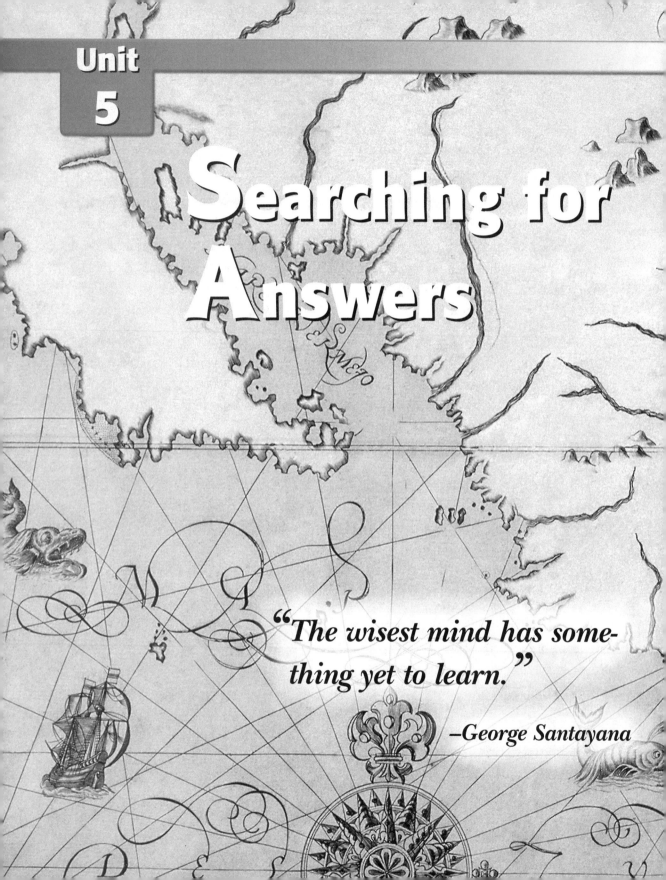

Unit
5

Searching for Answers

"The wisest mind has something yet to learn."

–George Santayana

Previewing the Unit

In a book titled *Discoveries,* it seems altogether fitting that the final unit is "Searching for Answers." The search for answers is a quest that can have neither an end nor too many beginnings. In the words of the philosopher and writer George Santayana, "The wisest mind has something yet to learn." We can never afford to stop searching for answers.

THE FORCE OF LUCK In a charming retelling of a folktale by Rudolfo A. Anaya, two wealthy friends get into a heated argument. Since each holds a different point of view, they decide to enlist the services of a poor but honorable miller in the hope that his actions may help them determine which point of view is correct. The wild and improbable things that the miller experiences are the stuff of which folktales are made. Unlikely occurrences, coincidences, and tricks of fate rule the day. The subsequent "search for answers" proves far more complicated than either man might have anticipated. After all is said and done, what is finally decided? The answer to *that* may—or may *not*—be revealed as you finish reading the story.

THE GOOD DEED Mr. Pan is relieved when he finally succeeds in bringing his mother from a potentially dangerous village in China to the United States. But old Mrs. Pan is unhappy and disillusioned. She feels useless and finds Chinese customs and traditions far different from those in her strange new country. Ultimately old Mrs. Pan decides that it is her responsibility to do a particular "good deed" for a young woman she has befriended. But how can an elderly woman who speaks no English succeed in the difficult task she has undertaken? Old Mrs. Pan starts searching for answers.

BY THE WATERS OF BABYLON Stephen Vincent Benét's brilliant tale "By the Waters of Babylon" calls to mind the words of the great Italian scientist and mathematician Galileo: "All truths are easy to understand once they are discovered; the point is to discover them." In "By the Waters of Babylon," you will embark on an incredible voyage of discovery as you enter the mind of a character burning for knowledge and searching for answers. We hesitate to say a word more. You must experience it all for yourself. An unforgettable journey awaits you!

We all search for answers. As you read, be aware of the ways in which the characters conduct *their* searches.

There's no telling how far a man can go if he is blessed with . . .

THE FORCE OF LUCK

by Rudolfo A. Anaya

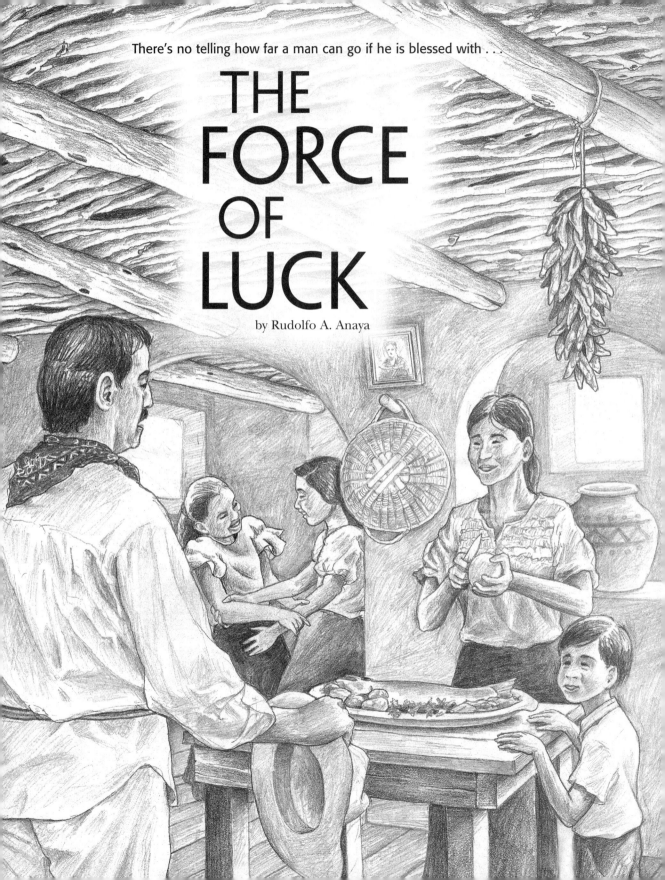

Once two wealthy friends got into a heated argument. One said that it was money which made a man prosperous, and the other maintained that it wasn't money, but luck. They argued for some time and finally decided that if they could find an honorable man, then perhaps they could prove their respective points of view.

One day while they were passing through a small village they came upon a miller who was grinding corn and wheat. They paused to ask the man how he ran his business. The miller replied that he worked for a master and that he earned only four bits[1] a day, and with that he had to support a family of five.

The friends were surprised. "Do you mean to tell us you can maintain a family of five on only fifteen dollars a month?" one asked.

"I live modestly to make ends meet," the humble miller replied.

The two friends privately agreed that if they put this man to a test perhaps they could resolve their argument.

"I am going to make you an offer," one of them said to the miller. "I will give you two hundred dollars and you may do whatever you want with the money."

"But why would you give me this money when you've just met me?" the miller asked.

"Well, my good man, my friend and I have a long-standing argument. He contends that it is luck which elevates a man to high position, and I say it is money. By giving you this money perhaps we can settle our argument. Here, take it, and do with it what you want!"

So the poor miller took the money and spent the rest of the day thinking about the strange meeting which had presented him with more money than he had ever seen.

What could he possibly do with all this money? Be that as it may, he had the money in his pocket and he could do with it whatever he wanted.

When the day's work was done, the miller decided the first thing he would do would be to buy food for his family. He took out ten dollars and wrapped the rest of the money in a cloth and put the bundle in his bag. Then he went to the market and bought supplies and meat to take home.

On the way home he was attacked by a hawk that had smelled the meat which the miller carried. The miller fought off the bird but in the struggle he lost the bundle of money. Before the miller knew what was happening the hawk grabbed the bag and flew away with it. When he realized what had happened he fell into deep thought.

"Ah," he moaned, "now I'm in the same poverty as before! And worse, because now those two men will say I am a thief! I should have thought carefully and bought nothing. Yes, I should have gone straight home and this wouldn't have happened!"

So he gathered what was left of his provisions and continued home, and when he arrived he told his family the entire story.

When he was finished telling his story his wife said, "It has been our lot to be poor, but maybe someday our luck will change."

Three months after he had lost the money to the hawk, it happened that the two wealthy men returned to the village. As soon as they saw the miller they approached him to ask if his luck had changed. When the miller saw them he felt ashamed and afraid that they would think that he had

---

1. **four bits:** fifty cents

squandered the money on worthless things. But he decided to tell them the truth and as soon as they had greeted each other he told his story. The men believed him. In fact, the one who insisted that it was money and not luck which made a man prosper took out another two hundred dollars and gave it to the miller.

"Let's try again," he said, "and let's see what happens this time."

The miller didn't know what to think. "Kind sir, maybe it would be better if you put this money in the hands of another man," he said.

"No," the man insisted. "I want to give it to you because you are an honest man, and if we are going to settle our argument you have to take the money!"

The miller thanked them and promised to do his best. Then as soon as the two men left he began to think what to do with the money so that it wouldn't disappear as it had the first time. The thing to do was to take the money straight home. He took out ten dollars, wrapped the rest in a cloth, and headed home.

When he arrived his wife wasn't at home. At first, he didn't know what to do with the money. He went to the pantry where he had stored a large earthenware jar filled with bran.[2] That was as safe a place as any to hide the money, he thought, so he emptied out the grain and put the bundle of money at the bottom of the jar, then covered it up with the grain. Satisfied that the money was safe he returned to work.

That afternoon when he arrived home from work he was greeted by his wife.

---

2. **bran:** partly ground husks of grain

"Look, my husband, today I bought some good clay with which to whitewash the entire house."

"And how did you buy the clay if we don't have any money?" he asked.

"Well, the man who was selling the clay was willing to trade for jewelry, money, or anything of value," she said. "The only thing we had of value was the jar full of bran, so I traded it for the clay. Isn't it wonderful, I think we have enough clay to whitewash these two rooms!"

The man groaned and pulled his hair.

"What have you done? We're ruined again!"

"But why?" she asked, unable to understand his anguish.

"Today I met the same two friends who gave me the two hundred dollars three months ago," he explained, "and after I told them how I lost the money they gave me another two hundred. And I, to make sure the money was safe, came home and hid it inside the jar of bran—the same jar you have traded for dirt! Now we're as poor as we were before! And what am I going to tell the two men? They'll think I'm a liar and a thief for sure!"

"Let them think what they want," his wife said calmly.

So the miller was consoled and the next day he went to work as usual. Time came and went, and one day the two wealthy friends returned to ask the miller how he had done with the second two hundred dollars. When the poor miller saw them he was afraid they would accuse him of being a liar and a spendthrift. But he decided to be truthful and as soon as they had greeted each other he told them what had happened to the money.

"That is why poor men remain honest," the man who had given him the money said, "because they don't have money they can't get into trouble. But I find your stories hard to believe. I think you gambled and lost the money. That's why you're telling us these wild stories."

"Either way," he continued, "I still believe that it is money and not luck which makes a man prosper."

"Well, you certainly didn't prove your point by giving the money to this poor miller," his friend reminded him. "Good evening, you luckless man," he said to the miller.

"Thank you, friends," the miller said.

"Oh, by the way, here is a worthless piece of lead I've been carrying around. Maybe you can use it for something," said the man who believed in luck. Then the two men left, still debating their points of view on life.

Since the lead was practically worthless, the miller thought nothing of it and put it in his jacket pocket. He forgot all about it until he arrived home. When he threw his jacket on a chair he heard a thump and he remembered the piece of lead. He took it out of the pocket and threw it under the table. Later that night after the family had eaten and gone to bed, they heard a knock at the door.

"Who is it? What do you want?" the miller asked.

"It's me, your neighbor," a voice answered. The miller recognized the fisherman's wife. "My husband sent me to ask you if you have any lead you can spare. He is going fishing tomorrow and he needs the lead to weight down the nets."

The miller remembered the lead he had thrown under the table. He got up, found it, and gave it to the woman.

"Thank you very much, neighbor," the woman said. "I promise you the first fish my husband catches will be yours."

"Think nothing of it," the miller said and returned to bed. The next day he got up and went to work without thinking any more of the incident. But in the afternoon when he returned home he found his wife cooking a big fish for dinner.

"Since when are we so well off we can afford fish for supper?" he asked his wife.

"Don't you remember that our neighbor promised us the first fish her husband caught?" his wife reminded him. "Well this was the fish he caught the first time he threw his net. So it's ours, and it's a beauty. But you should have been here when I gutted[3] him! I found a large piece of glass in his stomach!"

"And what did you do with it?"

"Oh, I gave it to the children to play with," she shrugged.

When the miller saw the piece of glass he noticed it shone so brightly it appeared to illuminate the room, but because he knew nothing about jewels he didn't realize its value and left it to the children. But the bright glass was such a novelty that the children were soon fighting over it and raising a terrible fuss.

Now it so happened that the miller and his wife had other neighbors who were jewelers. The following morning when the miller had gone to work the jeweler's wife visited the miller's wife to complain about all the noise her children had made.

"We couldn't get any sleep last night," she moaned.

"I know, and I'm sorry, but you know how it is with a large family," the miller's wife

---

3. gutted: cut open for cleaning

explained. "Yesterday we found a beautiful piece of glass and I gave it to my youngest one to play with and when the others tried to take it from him he raised a storm."

The jeweler's wife took interest. "Won't you show me that piece of glass?" she asked.

"But of course. Here it is."

"Ah, yes, it's a pretty piece of glass. Where did you find it?"

"Our neighbor gave us a fish yesterday and, when I was cleaning it, I found the glass in its stomach."

"Why don't you let me take it home for just a moment. You see, I have one just like it and I want to compare them."

"Yes, why not? Take it," answered the miller's wife.

So the jeweler's wife ran off with the glass to show it to her husband. When the jeweler saw the glass he instantly knew it was one of the finest diamonds he had ever seen.

"It's a diamond!" he exclaimed.

"I thought so," his wife nodded eagerly. "What shall we do?"

"Go tell the neighbor we'll give her fifty dollars for it, but don't tell her it's a diamond!"

"No, no," his wife chuckled, "of course not." She ran to her neighbor's house. "Ah, yes, we have one exactly like this," she told the miller's wife. "My husband is willing to buy it for fifty dollars—only so we can have a pair, you understand."

"I can't sell it," the miller's wife answered. "You will have to wait until my husband returns from work."

That evening when the miller came home from work his wife told him about the offer the jeweler had made for the piece of glass.

"But why would they offer fifty dollars for a worthless piece of glass?" the miller

wondered aloud. Before his wife could answer they were interrupted by the jeweler's wife.

"What do you say, neighbor, will you take fifty dollars for the glass?" she asked.

"No, that's not enough," the miller said cautiously. "Offer more."

"I'll give you fifty thousand!" the jeweler's wife blurted out.

"A little bit more," the miller replied.

"Impossible!" the jeweler's wife cried, "I can't offer any more without consulting my husband." She ran off to tell her husband how the bartering was going, and he told her he was prepared to pay a hundred thousand dollars to acquire the diamond.

He handed her seventy-five thousand dollars and said, "Take this and tell him that tomorrow, as soon as I open my shop, he'll have the rest."

When the miller heard the offer and saw the money he couldn't believe his eyes. He imagined the jeweler's wife was jesting with him, but it was a true offer and he received the hundred thousand dollars for the diamond. The miller had never seen so much money, but he still didn't quite trust the jeweler.

"I don't know about this money," he confided to his wife. "Maybe the jeweler plans to accuse us of robbing him and thus get it back."

"Oh no," his wife assured him, "the money is ours. We sold the diamond fair and square—we didn't rob anyone."

"I think I'll still go to work tomorrow," the miller said. "Who knows, something might happen and the money will disappear, then we would be without money and work. Then how would we live?"

So he went to work the next day, and all day he thought about how he could use the money. When he returned home that afternoon his wife asked him what he had decided to do with their new fortune.

"I think I will start my own mill," he answered, "like the one I operate for my master. Once I set up my business we'll see how our luck changes."

The next day he set about buying everything he needed to establish his mill and to build a new home. Soon he had everything going.

Six months had passed, more or less, since he had seen the two men who had given him the four hundred dollars and the piece of lead. He was eager to see them again and to tell them how the piece of lead had changed his luck and made him wealthy.

Time passed and the miller prospered. His business grew and he even built a summer cottage where he could take his family on vacation. He had many employees who worked for him. One day while he was at his store he saw his two benefactors riding by. He rushed out into the street to greet them and asked them to come in. He was overjoyed to see them, and he was happy to see that they admired his store.

"Tell us the truth," the man who had given him the four hundred dollars said. "You used that money to set up this business."

The miller swore he hadn't, and he told them how he had given the piece of lead to his neighbor and how the fisherman had in return given him a fish with a very large diamond in its stomach. And he told them how he had sold the diamond.

"And that's how I acquired this business and many other things I want to show you," he said. "But it's time to eat. Let's eat first and then I'll show you everything I have now."

The men agreed, but one of them still doubted the miller's story. So they ate and then the miller had three horses saddled and they rode out to see his summer home. The cabin was on the other side of the river where the mountains were cool and beautiful. When they arrived the men admired the place very much. It was such a peaceful place that they rode all afternoon through the forest. During their ride they came upon a tall pine tree.

"What is that on top of the tree?" one of them asked.

"That's the nest of a hawk," the miller replied.

"I have never seen one; I would like to take a closer look at it!"

"Of course," the miller said, and he ordered a servant to climb the tree and bring down the nest so his friend could see how it was built. When the hawk's nest was on the ground they examined it carefully.

They noticed that there was a cloth bag at the bottom of the nest. When the miller saw the bag he immediately knew that it was the very same bag he had lost to the hawk which fought him for the meat years ago.

"You won't believe me, friends, but this is the very same bag in which I put the first two hundred dollars you gave me," he told them.

"If it's the same bag," the man who had doubted him said, "then the money you said the hawk took should be there."

"No doubt about that," the miller said. "Let's see what we find."

The three of them examined the old weatherbeaten bag. Although it was full of holes and crumbling, when they tore it apart they found the money intact. The two men remembered what the miller had told them and they agreed he was an honest and honorable man. Still, the man who had given him the money wasn't satisfied. He wondered what had really happened to the second two hundred he had given the miller.

They spent the rest of the day riding in the mountains and returned very late to the house.

As he unsaddled their horses, the servant in charge of grooming and feeding the horses suddenly realized that he had no grain for them. He ran to the barn and checked, but there was no grain for the hungry horses. So he ran to the neighbor's granary and there he was able to buy a large clay jar of bran. He carried the jar home and emptied the bran into a bucket to wet it before he fed it to the horses. When he got to the bottom of the jar he noticed a large lump which turned out to be a rag covered package. He examined it and felt something inside. He immediately went to give it to his master who had been eating dinner.

"Master," he said, "look at this package which I found in an earthenware jar of grain which I just bought from our neighbor!"

The three men carefully unraveled the cloth and found the other one hundred and ninety dollars which the miller had told them he had lost. That is how the miller proved to his friends that he was truly an honest man.

And they had to decide for themselves whether it had been luck or money which had made the miller a wealthy man!

About the Author

Rudolfo A. Anaya (1937–) is known for his novels and short stories, which portray the experiences of Hispanic people in the American Southwest. Anaya was born in New Mexico, where he has lived all his life. He taught in public schools in Albuquerque before becoming a professor of English at the University of New Mexico. Anaya first received acclaim for his award-winning novel *Bless Me, Ultima,* which provides insights into Mexican American culture. Typical of Anaya's books, the work has a magical, mythical quality. Anaya has also written many articles about Spanish history and traditions in the state of New Mexico. He has long been fascinated by Spanish folktales such as "The Force of Luck."

THINK ABOUT THE STORY. The following questions help you check your reading comprehension. Put an *x* in the box next to the correct answer.

1. "The Force of Luck" is mainly about
   - ☐ a. how a hawk carries away a miller's money and puts it in its nest.
   - ☐ b. what happens when two men give money to a miller in the hope of resolving an argument.
   - ☐ c. how a miller manages to sell a beautiful diamond.

2. The miller lost the money the second time when
   - ☐ a. his wife traded the jar in which the money was hidden in return for some clay.
   - ☐ b. a jeweler's wife tricked him into giving her the money.
   - ☐ c. a bird attacked the miller and flew off with the money.

3. The miller's wife found the diamond
   - ☐ a. in the yard where the children were playing.
   - ☐ b. at the bottom of a fisherman's net.
   - ☐ c. in a fish she was cleaning.

4. How much did the jeweler end up paying for the diamond?
   - ☐ a. 50,000 dollars
   - ☐ b. 75,000 dollars
   - ☐ c. 100,000 dollars

HANDLE NEW VOCABULARY WORDS. The following questions check your vocabulary skills. Put an *x* in the box next to the correct answer. Each vocabulary word appears in the story.

1. Each of the two men believed strongly in his respective point of view. The word *respective* means
   - ☐ a. particular or individual.
   - ☐ b. absolutely correct.
   - ☐ c. respectful or polite.

2. "He contends that it is luck which elevates a man to high position, and I say it is money." As used in this sentence, the word *contends* means
   - ☐ a. is not certain.
   - ☐ b. desires or wishes.
   - ☐ c. declares to be true.

3. The miller was "afraid that they would think that he had squandered the money on worthless things." What is the meaning of the word *squandered*?
   - ☐ a. wasted
   - ☐ b. earned
   - ☐ c. given away

4. One day, the miller "saw his two benefactors riding by." Which of the following best defines the word *benefactors*?
   - ☐ a. friends or acquaintances
   - ☐ b. people who give money or help
   - ☐ c. people who cannot agree with each other

```
┌──────┐        ┌──────┐
│      │  × 5 = │      │
└──────┘        └──────┘
 NUMBER          YOUR
 CORRECT         SCORE
```

```
┌──────┐        ┌──────┐
│      │  × 5 = │      │
└──────┘        └──────┘
 NUMBER          YOUR
 CORRECT         SCORE
```

EXAMINE STORY ELEMENTS. The following questions check your knowledge of story elements. Put an *x* in the box next to each correct answer.

1. Who is the *main character* in "The Force of Luck"?
   - ☐ a. the miller
   - ☐ b. the miller's wife
   - ☐ c. the jeweler

2. Of these events, which happened first in the *plot* of the story?
   - ☐ a. The miller and the two friends rode out to see the miller's home.
   - ☐ b. A man gave the miller a piece of lead.
   - ☐ c. The miller was attacked by a hawk.

3. Which of the following statements best *characterizes* the miller?
   - ☐ a. He was lazy but lucky.
   - ☐ b. He was honest and hardworking.
   - ☐ c. He was a liar and a spendthrift.

4. The *climax* of the story occurred when
   - ☐ a. the miller obtained enough money to establish his own mill.
   - ☐ b. the miller explained, for the second time, how he had lost the money.
   - ☐ c. two wealthy friends got into an argument.

MASTER CRITICAL THINKING. The following questions check your critical thinking skills. Put an *x* in the box next to each correct answer.

1. Probably, one rich man found the miller's tales of how he had lost the money "hard to believe" because
   - ☐ a. the events seemed so unlikely.
   - ☐ b. the man learned that the miller had the reputation of being a liar.
   - ☐ c. the man believed all along that the miller was a thief.

2. Which statement is *not* true?
   - ☐ a. A servant climbed to the top of a tree and brought down a bird's nest.
   - ☐ b. Both friends believed that a diamond had been found in the stomach of a fish.
   - ☐ c. The miller supported a family of five.

3. We may conclude that the miller's life was changed greatly by
   - ☐ a. the clay that his wife obtained.
   - ☐ b. the fifty dollars that the jeweler's wife offered him.
   - ☐ c. a piece of lead.

4. In the last paragraph, the two friends
   - ☐ a. agreed that luck had made the miller a wealthy man.
   - ☐ b. decided that money had made the miller a wealthy man.
   - ☐ c. had not resolved what had made the miller a wealthy man.

☐ × 5 = ☐
NUMBER CORRECT   YOUR SCORE

☐ × 5 = ☐
NUMBER CORRECT   YOUR SCORE

190

EXPLORE THE WRITER'S CRAFT. The following questions check your knowledge of skills related to the craft of writing. Put an *x* in the box next to each correct answer. You may refer to pages 4 and 5.

1. "When [the miller] threw his jacket on a chair he heard a thump." This sentence contains
   ☐ a. onomatopoeia.
   ☐ b. a simile.
   ☐ c. a symbol.

2. When the children tried to take the diamond from the boy, "he raised a storm." This statement
   ☐ a. contains a simile.
   ☐ b. offers an example of irony.
   ☐ c. contains figurative language that indicates the boy argued loudly.

3. Since this story was originally passed from generation to generation by word of mouth, it is known as
   ☐ a. an autobiography.
   ☐ b. a biography.
   ☐ c. a folktale.

4. What is the likely moral to the story?
   ☐ a. One is fortunate to have generous friends.
   ☐ b. Luck and money can help one become successful, but it is important to be industrious and to make wise decisions.
   ☐ c. You never can tell when your luck will change.

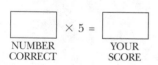

NUMBER CORRECT × 5 = YOUR SCORE

Questions for Writing and Discussion

- Explain how, on two occasions, the miller lost the money he was given.
- Suppose that you were one of the two wealthy friends. Would you have believed the miller the second time that he explained how he lost the money? Tell why.
- What eventually made the miller so successful? Was it luck or money—or a combination of both? Was it another quality that the miller possessed? Give reasons for your opinion.
- What lesson or lessons does "The Force of Luck" teach? Explain.

See additional questions for extended writing on pages 222 and 223.

Use the boxes below to total your scores for the exercises. Then record your scores on pages 224 and 225.

☐ **T**HINK ABOUT THE STORY
+
☐ **H**ANDLE NEW VOCABULARY WORDS
+
☐ **E**XAMINE STORY ELEMENTS
+
☐ **M**ASTER CRITICAL THINKING
+
☐ **E**XPLORE THE WRITER'S CRAFT
▼
☐ **Total Score:** Story 15

Old Mrs. Pan knew that a good deed was required. But she, alone, could perform . . .

The Good Deed

by Pearl S. Buck

Mr. Pan was worried about his mother. He had been worried about her when she was in China, and now he was worried about her in New York, although he had thought that once he got her out of his ancestral village, his anxieties would be ended. To this end he had risked his own life and paid out large sums of American money, and he felt that day when he saw her on the wharf, a tiny, dazed little old woman, in a lavender silk coat and black skirt, that now they would live happily together, he and his wife, their four small children and his beloved mother, in the huge safety of the American city.

It soon became clear, however, that safety was not enough for old Mrs. Pan. Her eyes, looking very large in her small withered face, were haunted with homesickness.

"There are many things worse than death, especially at my age," she replied at last, when again her son reminded her of her good fortune in being where she was.

He became impassioned when she said this.

Yet there was nothing that Mr. Pan and his wife did not try to do for his mother in order to made her happy. They prepared the food that she had once enjoyed, but she was now beyond the age of pleasure in food, and she had no appetite. She touched one dish and another with the ends of her ivory chopsticks,[1] which she had brought with her from her home, and she thanked them prettily. "It is all good," she said, "but the water is not the same as our village water; it tastes of metal and not of earth, and so the flavor is not the same. Please allow the children to eat it."

She was afraid of the children. They went to an American school and they spoke English very well and Chinese very badly, and since she could speak no English, it distressed her to hear her own language maltreated by their careless tongues. For a time she tried to coax them to a few lessons, or she told them stories, to which they were too busy to listen. Instead they preferred to look at the moving pictures in the box that stood on a table in

the living room. She gave them up finally and merely watched them contemplatively when they were in the same room with her and was glad when they were gone. She liked her son's wife. She did not understand how there could be a Chinese woman who had never been in China, but such her son's wife was. When her son was away, she could not say to her daughter-in-law, "Do you remember how the willows grew over the gate?" For her son's wife had no such memories. She had grown up here in the city and she did not even hear its noise. At the same time, though, she was so foreign, she was very kind to the old lady, and she spoke to her always in a gentle voice, however she might shout at the children, who were often disobedient.

The disobedience of the children was another grief to old Mrs. Pan. She did not understand how it was that four children could all be disobedient, for this meant that they had never been taught to obey their parents and revere their elders, which are the first lessons a child should learn.

"How is it," she once asked her son, "that the children do not know how to obey?"

---

1. **chopsticks:** thin pair of sticks used for eating

The Good Deed

Mr. Pan had laughed, though uncomfortably. "Here in America the children are not taught as we were in China," he explained.

"But my grandchildren are Chinese nevertheless," old Mrs. Pan said in some astonishment.

"They are always with Americans," Mr. Pan explained. "It is very difficult to teach them."

Old Mrs. Pan did not understand, for Chinese and Americans are different beings, one on the west side of the sea and one on the east, and the sea is always between. Therefore, why should they not continue to live apart even in the same city? She felt in her heart that the children should be kept at home and taught those things which must be learned, but she said nothing. She felt lonely and there was no one who understood the things she felt and she was quite useless. That was the most difficult thing: She was no use here. She could not even remember which spout the hot water came from and which brought the cold. Sometimes she turned on one and then the other, until her son's wife came in briskly and said, "Let me, Mother."

So she gave up and sat uselessly all day, not by the window, because the machines and the many people frightened her. She sat where she could not see out; she looked at a few books, and day by day she grew thinner and thinner until Mr. Pan was concerned beyond endurance.

One day he said to his wife, "Sophia, we must do something for my mother. Do you see how thin her hands are?"

"I have seen," his good young wife said. "But what can we do?"

"Is there no woman you know who can speak Chinese with her?" Mr. Pan asked. "She needs to have someone to whom she can talk about the village and all the things she knows. She cannot talk to you because you can only speak English, and I am too busy making our living to sit and listen to her."

Young Mrs. Pan considered. "I have a friend," she said at last, "a schoolmate whose family compelled her to speak Chinese. Now she is a social worker here in the city. She visits families in Chinatown and this is her work. I will call her up and ask her to spend some time here so that our old mother can be happy enough to eat again."

"Do so," Mr. Pan said.

That very morning, when Mr. Pan was gone, young Mrs. Pan made the call and found her friend, Lili Yang, and she explained everything to her.

"We are really in very much trouble," she said finally. "His mother is thinner every day. Please help us, Lili."

Lili Yang promised and within a few days she came to the apartment and young Mrs. Pan led her into the inner room, which was old Mrs. Pan's room and where she always sat, wrapped in her satin coat and holding a magazine at whose pictures she did not care to look. She took up that magazine when her daughter-in-law came in, because she did not want to hurt her feelings, but the pictures frightened her. The women looked bold and evil. She wondered that her son's wife would put such a magazine into her hands, but she did not ask questions. There would have been no end to them had she once begun, and the ways of foreigners did not interest her. Most of the time she sat silent and still, dreaming of the village, the big house there where she and her husband had lived together with his parents and where their children were born. She knew that the village had fallen into the hands of their enemies and that strangers lived in the house, but she hoped even so that the land was tilled. All that she remembered was the way it had been when she was a young woman and before the evil had come to pass.

She heard now her daughter-in-law's voice, "Mother, this is a friend. She is Miss Lili Yang. She has come to see you."

Old Mrs. Pan remembered her manners. She tried to rise but Lili took her hands and begged her to keep seated.

"You must not rise to one so much younger," she exclaimed.

Old Mrs. Pan lifted her head. "You speak such good Chinese!"

"I was taught by my parents," Lili said. She sat down on a chair near the old lady.

Mrs. Pan leaned forward and put her hand on Lili's knee. "Have you been in our own country?" she asked eagerly.

Lili shook her head. "That is my sorrow. I have not and I want to know about it. I have come here to listen to you tell me."

"Excuse me," young Mrs. Pan said, "I must prepare the dinner for the family."

She slipped away so that the two could be alone and old Mrs. Pan looked after her sadly. "She never wishes to hear; she is always busy."

"You must remember in this country we have no servants," Lili reminded her gently.

"Yes," old Mrs. Pan said, "and why not?"

Lili did not try to explain. "Everything is different here and let us not talk about it," she said. "Let us talk about your home and the village. I want to know how it looks and what goes on there."

Old Mrs. Pan was delighted. She smoothed the gray satin of her coat as it lay on her knees and she began.

"You must know that our village lies in a wide valley from which the mountains rise as sharply as tiger's teeth."

"Is it so?" Lili said, making a voice of wonder.

"It is, and the village is not a small one. On the contrary, the walls encircle more than one thousand souls, all of whom are relatives of our family."

"A large family," Lili said.

"It is," old Mrs. Pan said, "and my son's father was the head of it. We lived in a house with seventy rooms. It was in the midst of the village. We had gardens in the courtyards. My own garden contained also a pool wherein are aged goldfish, very fat. I fed them millet[2] and they knew me."

"How amusing." Lili saw with pleasure that the old lady's cheeks were faintly pink and that her large beautiful eyes were beginning to shine and glow. "And how many years did you live there, Ancient One?"

"I went there as a bride. I was seventeen." She looked at Lili, questioning, "How old are you?"

Lili smiled, somewhat ashamed, "I am twenty-seven."

Mrs. Pan was shocked. "Twenty-seven? But my son's wife called you Miss."

"I am not married," Lili confessed.

Mrs. Pan was instantly concerned. "How is this?" she asked. "Are your parents dead?"

"They are dead," Lili said, "but it is not their fault that I am not married."

Old Mrs. Pan would not agree to this. She shook her head with decision. "It is the duty of the parents to arrange the marriage of the children. When death approached, they should have attended to this for you.

---

2. **millet:** a type of grain

The Good Deed

Now who is left to perform the task? Have you brothers?"

"No," Lili said, "I am an only child. But please don't worry yourself, Madame Pan. I am earning my own living and there are many young women like me in this country."

Old Mrs. Pan was dignified about this. "I cannot be responsible for what other persons do, but I must be responsible for my own kind," she declared. "Allow me to know the names of the suitable persons who can arrange your marriage. I will stand in the place of your mother. We are all in a foreign country now and we must keep together and the old must help the young in these important matters."

Lili was kind and she knew that Mrs. Pan meant kindness. "Dear Madame Pan," she said. "Marriage in America is very different from marriage in China. Here the young people choose their own mates."

"Why do you not choose, then?" Mrs. Pan said with some spirit.

Lili Yang looked abashed.[3] "Perhaps it would be better for me to say that only the young men choose. It is they who must ask the young women."

"What do the young women do?" Mrs. Pan inquired.

"They wait," Lili confessed.

"And if they are not asked?"

"They continue to wait," Lili said gently.

"How long?" Mrs. Pan demanded.

"As long as they live."

Old Mrs. Pan was profoundly shocked. "Do you tell me that there is no person who arranges such matters when it is necessary?"

"Such an arrangement is not thought of here," Lili told her.

"And they allow their women to remain unmarried?" Mrs. Pan exclaimed. "Are there also sons who do not marry?"

"Here men do not marry unless they wish to do so."

Mrs. Pan was even more shocked. "How can this be?" she asked. "Of course, men will not marry unless they are compelled to do so to provide grandchildren for the family. It is necessary to make laws and create customs so that a man who will not marry is denounced as an unfilial[4] son and one who does not fulfill his duty to his ancestors."

"Here the ancestors are forgotten and parents are not important," Lili said unwillingly.

"What a country is this," Mrs. Pan exclaimed. "How can such a country endure?"

Lili did not reply. Old Mrs. Pan had unknowingly touched upon a wound in her heart. No man had ever asked her to marry him. Yet above all else she would like to be married and to have children. She was a good social worker, and the head of the Children's Bureau sometimes told her that he would not know what to do without her and she must never leave them, for then there would be no one to serve the people in Chinatown. She did not wish to leave except to be married, but how could she find a husband? She looked down at her hands, clasped in her lap, and thought that if she had been in her own country, if her father had not come here as a young man and married here, she would have been in China and by now the mother of many children. Instead what would become of

---

3. **abashed:** embarrassed and uncomfortable

4. **unfilial:** not showing respect for one's parents

her? She would grow older and older, and twenty-seven was already old, and at last hope must die. She knew several American girls quite well; they liked her, and she knew that they faced the same fate. They, too, were waiting. They tried very hard; they went in summer to hotels and in winter to ski lodges, where men gathered and were at leisure enough to think about them, and in confidence they told one another of their efforts. They compared their experiences and they asked anxious questions. "Do you think men like talkative women or quiet ones?" "Do you think men like lipstick or none?" Such questions they asked of one another and who could answer them? If a girl succeeded in winning a proposal from a man, then all the other girls envied her and asked her special questions and immediately she became someone above them all, a successful woman. The job which had once been so valuable then became worthless and it was given away easily and gladly. But how could she explain this to old Mrs. Pan?

Meanwhile Mrs. Pan had been studying Lili's face carefully and with thought. This was not a pretty girl. Her face was too flat, and her mouth was large. But she had nice skin, and her eyes, though small, were kind. She was the sort of girl, Mrs. Pan could see, who would make an excellent wife and a good mother, but certainly she was one for whom a marriage must be arranged. She was a decent, plain, good girl and, left to herself, Mrs. Pan could predict, nothing at all would happen. She would wither away like a dying flower.

Now as she looked at Lili's kind, ugly face it occurred to her that here there was something she could do. She could find a husband for this good girl. A good deed is a good deed, whether one is in China or in America.

She patted Lili's clasped hands. "Do not grieve anymore," she said tenderly. "I will arrange everything."

"I am not grieving," Lili said.

"Of course, you are," Mrs. Pan retorted. "I see you are a true woman, and women grieve when they are not wed so that they can have children. You are grieving for your children."

Lili could not deny it. She would have been ashamed to confess to any other person except this old Chinese lady who might have been her grandmother. She bent her head and bit her lip; she let a tear or two fall upon her hands. Then she nodded. Yes, she grieved in the secret places of her heart, in the darkness of the lonely nights, when she thought of the empty future of her life.

"Do not grieve," old Mrs. Pan was saying. "I will arrange it; I will do it."

It was so comforting a murmur that Lili could not bear it. She said, "I came to comfort you, but it is you who comfort me." The she got up and went out of the room quickly because she did not want to sob aloud. Lili went away telling herself that it was all absurd, that an old woman from the middle of China who could not speak a word of English would not be able to change this American world, even for her.

Old Mrs. Pan could scarcely wait for her son to come home at noon. She declined to join the family at the table, saying that she must speak to her son first.

When he came in, he saw at once that she was changed. She held up her head and she spoke to him sharply when he came into the room, as though it was her house and not his in which they now were.

"Let the children eat first," she commanded, "I shall need time to talk with you and I am not hungry."

He repressed his inclination to tell her that he was hungry and that he must get back to the office. Something in her look made it impossible for him to be disobedient to her. He went away and gave the children direction and then returned.

"Yes, my mother," he said, seating himself on a small and uncomfortable chair.

Then she related to him with much detail and repetition what had happened that morning; she declared with indignation that she had never before heard of a country where no marriages were arranged for the young, leaving to them the most important event of their lives and that at a time when their judgment was still unripe, and a mistake could bring disaster upon the whole family.

"Your own marriage," she reminded him, "was arranged by your father with great care, our two families knowing each other well. Even though you and my daughter-in-law were distant in this country, yet we met her parents through a suitable go-between, and her uncle here stood in her father's place, and your father's friend in place of your father, and so it was all done according to custom though so far away."

Mr. Pan did not have the heart to tell his mother that he and his wife Sophia had fallen in love first, and then, out of kindness to their elders, had allowed the marriage to be arranged for them as though they were not in love, and as though, indeed, they did not know each other. They were both young people of heart, and although it would have been much easier to be married in the

American fashion, they considered their elders.

"What has all this to do with us now, my mother?" he asked.

"This is what is to do," she replied with spirit. "A nice, ugly girl of our own people came here today to see me. She is twenty-seven years old and she is not married. What will become of her?"

"Do you mean Lili Yang?" her son asked.

"I do," she replied. "When I heard that she has no way of being married because, according to the custom of this country, she must wait for a man to ask her—"

Old Mrs. Pan broke off and gazed at her son with horrified eyes.

"What now," he asked.

"Suppose the only man who asks is one who is not at all suitable?"

"It is quite possible that it often happens thus," her son said, trying not to laugh.

"Then she has no choice," old Mrs. Pan said indignantly. "She can only remain unmarried or accept one who is unsuitable."

"Here she has no choice," Mr. Pan agreed, "unless she is very pretty, my mother, when several men may ask and then she has choice." It was on the tip of his tongue to tell how at least six young men had proposed to his Sophia, thereby distressing him continually until he was finally chosen, but he thought better of it. Would it not be very hard to explain so much to his old mother, and could she understand? He doubted it. Nevertheless, he felt it necessary at least to make one point.

"Something must be said for the man also, my mother. Sometimes he asks a girl who will not have him, because she chooses another, and then his sufferings are intense.

Unless he wishes to remain unmarried he must ask a second girl, who is not the first one. Here also is some injustice."

Old Mrs. Pan listened to this attentively and then declared, "It is all barbarous. Certainly it is very embarrassing to be compelled to speak of these matters, man and woman, face to face. They should be spared; others should speak for them."

She considered for a few seconds and then she said with fresh indignation, "And what woman can change the appearance her ancestors have given her? Because she is not pretty is she less a woman? Are not her feelings like any woman's; is it not her right to have husband and home and children?"

Mr. Pan allowed all this to be said and then he inquired, "What is on your mind, my mother?"

Old Mrs. Pan leaned toward him and lifted her forefinger. "This is what I command you to do for me, my son. I myself will find a husband for this good girl of our people. She is helpless and alone. But I know no one; I am a stranger and I must depend upon you. In your business there must be young men. Inquire of them and see who stands for them, so that we can arrange a meeting between them and me; I will stand for the girl's mother. I promised it."

Now Mr. Pan laughed heartily. "Oh, my mother!" he cried. "You are too kind but it cannot be done. They would laugh at me, and do you believe that Lili Yang herself would like such an arrangement? I think she would not. She has been in America too long."

Old Mrs. Pan would not yield, however, and in the end he was compelled to promise that he would see what he could do. Upon this promise she consented to eat her meal, and he led her out, her right hand resting upon his left wrist. The children were gone and they had a quiet meal together, and after it she said she felt that she would sleep. This was good news, for she had not slept well since she came, and young Mrs. Pan led her into the bedroom and helped her to lie down and placed a thin quilt over her.

When young Mrs. Pan went back to the small dining room where her husband waited to tell her what his mother had said, she listened thoughtfully.

"It is absurd," her husband said, "but what shall we do to satisfy my mother? She sees it as a good deed if she can find a husband for Lili Yang."

Here his wife surprised him. "I can see some good in it myself," she declared. "I have often felt for Lili. It is a problem, and our mother is right to see it as such. It is not only Lili—it is a problem here for all young women, especially if they are not pretty." She looked quizzically[5] at her husband for a moment and then said, "I too used to worry when I was very young, lest I should not find a husband for myself. It is a great burden for a young woman. It would be nice to have someone else arrange the matter."

"Remember," he told her, "how often in the old country the wrong men are arranged for and how often the young men leave home because they do not like the wives their parents choose for them."

"Well, so do they here," she said pertly. "Divorce, divorce, divorce!"

"Come, come," he told her. "It is not so bad."

---

5. **quizzically:** in a questioning or puzzled way

The Good Deed

"It is very bad for women," she insisted.

They did not know it but their voices roused old Mrs. Pan in the bedroom, and she opened her eyes. She could not understand what they said for they spoke in English, but she understood that there was an argument. She sat up on the bed to listen, then she heard the door slam and she knew her son was gone. She was about to lie down again when it occurred to her that it would be interesting to look out of the window to the street and see what young men there were coming to and fro. One did not choose men from the street, of course, but still she could see what their looks were.

She got up and tidied her hair and tottered on her small feet over to the window and opening the curtains a little she gazed into the street really for the first time since she came. She was pleased to see many Chinese men, some of them young. It was still not late, and they loitered in the sunshine before going back to work, talking and laughing and looking happy. It was interesting to her to watch them, keeping in mind Lili Yang and thinking to herself that it might be this one or that one, although still one did not choose men from the street. She stood so long that at last she became tired and she pulled a chair to the window and kept looking through the parted curtain.

Here her daughter-in-law saw her a little later, when she opened the door to see if her mother-in-law was awake, but she did not speak. She looked at the little satin-clad figure, and went away again, wondering why it was that the old lady found it pleasant today to look out of the window when every other day she had refused the same pleasure.

It became a pastime for old Mrs. Pan to look out of the window every day from then on. Gradually she came to know some of the young men, not by name but by their faces and by the way they walked by her window, never, of course looking up at her, until one day a certain young man did look up and smile. It was a warm day, and she had asked that the window be opened, which until now she had not allowed, for fear she might be assailed by the foreign winds and made ill. Today, however, was near to summer, she felt the room airless and she longed for freshness.

After this the young man habitually smiled when he passed or nodded his head. She was too old to have it mean anything but courtesy and so bit by bit she allowed herself to make a gesture of her hand in return. It was evident that he belonged in a china shop across the narrow street. She watched him go in and come out; she watched him stand at the door in his shirt sleeves on a fine day and talk and laugh, showing, as she observed, strong white teeth set off by two gold ones. Evidently he made money. She did not believe he was married, for she saw an old man who must be his father, and now and then an elderly woman, perhaps his mother, and a younger brother, but there was no young woman.

She began after some weeks of watching to fix upon this young man as a husband for Lili. But who could be the go-between except her own son?

She confided her plans one night to him, and, as always, he listened to her with courtesy and concealed amusement. "But the young man, my mother, is the son of Mr. Lim, who is the richest man on our street."

"That is nothing against him," she declared.

"No, but he will not submit to an arrangement, my mother. He is a college graduate. He is only spending the summer at home in the shop to help his father."

"Lili Yang has also been to school."

"I know, my mother, but, you see, the young man will want to choose his own wife, and it will not be someone who looks like Lili Yang. It will be someone who—"

He broke off. "You are like all these other men, though you are my son," she said and dismissed him sternly.

Nevertheless, she thought over what he had said when she went back to the window. The young man was standing on the street laughing at friends who passed, the sun shining on his glistening black hair. It was true he did not look at all obedient; it was perhaps true that he was no more wise than other men and so saw only what a girl's face was. She wished that she could speak to him, but that, of course, was impossible. Unless—

She drew in a long breath. Unless she went downstairs and out into that street and crossed it and entered the shop, pretending that she came to buy something! If she did this, she could speak to him. But what would she say, and who would help her cross the street? She did not want to tell her son or her son's wife, for they would suspect her and laugh. They teased her often even now about her purpose, and Lili was so embarrassed by their laughter that she did not want to come anymore.

Old Mrs. Pan reflected on the difficulty of her position as a lady in a strange country. Then she thought of her eldest grandson, Johnnie. On Saturday, when her son was at his office and her son's wife was at the market, she would coax Johnnie to lead her across the street to the china shop; she would pay him some money, and in the shop she would say she was looking for two bowls to match some that had been broken. It would be an expedition, but she might speak to the young man and tell him—what should she tell him? That must first be planned.

This was only Thursday and she had only two days to prepare. She was very restless during those two days, and she could not eat. But Saturday came at last and everything came about as she planned. Her son went away, and then her son's wife, and she crept downstairs with much effort to the sidewalk where her grandson was playing marbles and beckoned him to her. The child was terrified to see her there and came at once, and she pressed a coin into his palm and pointed across the street with her cane.

"Lead me there," she commanded and, shutting her eyes tightly, she put her hand on his shoulder and allowed him to lead her to the shop. Then to her dismay he left her and ran back to play and she stood wavering on the threshold, feeling dizzy, and the young man saw her and came hurrying toward her. To her joy he spoke good Chinese, and the words fell sweetly upon her old ears.

"Ancient One, Ancient One," he chided her kindly. "Come in and sit down. It is too much for you."

He led her inside the cool, dark shop and she sat down on a bamboo chair.

"I came to look for two bowls," she said faintly.

"Tell me the pattern and I will get them for you," he said. "Are they blue willow pattern or the thousand flowers?"

The Good Deed

"Thousand flowers," she said in the same faint voice, "but I do not wish to disturb you."

"I am here to be disturbed," he replied with the utmost courtesy.

He brought out some bowls and set them on a small table before her and she fell to talking with him. He was very pleasant; his rather large face was shining with kindness and he laughed easily. Now that she saw him close, she was glad to notice that he was not too handsome; his nose and mouth were big, and he had big hands and feet.

"You look like a countryman," she said. "Where is your ancestral home?"

"It is in the province of Shantung," he replied, "and there are not many of us here."

"That explains why you are so tall," she said. "These people from Canton are small. We of Szechuen are also big and our language is yours. I cannot understand the people of Canton."

From this they fell to talking of their own country, which he had never seen, and she told him about the village and how her son's father had left it many years ago to do business here in this foreign country and how he had sent for their son and then how she had been compelled to flee because the country was in fragments and torn between many leaders. When she had told this much, she found herself telling him how difficult it was to live here and how strange the city was to her and how she would never have looked out of the window had it not been for the sake of Lili Yang.

"Who is Lili Yang?" he asked.

Old Mrs. Pan did not answer him directly. That would not have been suitable. One does not speak of a reputable young woman to any man, not even one as good as this one. Instead she began a long speech about the virtues of young women who were not pretty.

To all this the young man listened, his small eyes twinkling with laughter.

"I take it that this Lili Yang is not beautiful," he said.

Old Mrs. Pan looked astonished. "I did not say so," she replied with spirit. "I will not say she is beautiful and I will not say she is ugly. What is beautiful to one is not so to another. Suppose you see her sometime for yourself, and then we will discuss it."

"Discuss what?" he demanded.

"Whether she is beautiful."

Suddenly she felt that she had come to a point and that she had better go home. It was enough for the first visit. She chose two bowls and paid for them and while he wrapped them up she waited in silence, for to say too much is worse than to say too little.

When the bowls were wrapped, the young man said courteously, "Let me lead you across the street, Ancient One."

So, putting her right hand on his left wrist, she let him lead her across and this time she did not shut her eyes, and she came home again feeling that she had been a long way and had accomplished much. When her daughter-in-law came home she said quite easily, "I went across the street and bought these two bowls."

Young Mrs. Pan opened her eyes wide. "My mother, how could you go alone?"

"I did not go alone," old Mrs. Pan said tranquilly. "My grandson led me across and young Mr. Lim brought me back."

Each had spoken in her own language with helpful gestures.

Young Mrs. Pan was astonished and she said no more until her husband came home, when she told him. He laughed a great deal and said, "Do not interfere with our old one. She is enjoying herself. It is good for her."

But all the time he knew what his mother was doing and he joined in it without her knowledge. That is to say, he telephoned the same afternoon from his office to Miss Lili Yang, and when she answered, he said, "Please come and see my old mother again. She asks after you every day. Your visit did her much good."

Lili Yang promised, not for today but for a week hence, and when Mr. Pan went home he told his mother carelessly, as though it were nothing, that Lili Yang had called him up to say she was coming again next week.

Old Mrs. Pan heard this with secret excitement. She had not gone out again, but every day young Mr. Lim nodded to her and smiled, and once he sent her a small gift of fresh ginger root. She made up her mind slowly but she made it up well. When Lili Yang came again, she would ask her to take her to the china shop, pretending that she wanted to buy something, and she would introduce the two to each other; that much she would do. It was too much, but, after all, these were modern times, and this was a country where it did not matter greatly whether the old customs were kept or not. The important thing was to find a husband for Lili, who was already twenty-seven years old.

So it all came about, and when Lili walked into her room the next week, while the fine weather still held, old Mrs. Pan greeted her with smiles. She seized Lili's small hand and noticed that the hand was very soft and pretty.

"Do not take off your foreign hat," she told Lili. "I wish to go across the street to

that shop and buy some dishes as a gift for my son's wife. She is very kind to me."

Lili Yang was pleased to see the old lady so changed and cheerful and in all innocence she agreed and they went across the street and into the shop. Today there were customers, and old Mr. Lim was there too, as well as his son. He was a tall, withered man, and he wore a small beard under his chin. When he saw old Mrs. Pan he stopped what he was doing and brought her a chair to sit upon while she waited. As soon as his customer was gone, he introduced himself, saying that he knew her son.

"My son had told me of your honored visit last week," he said. "Please come inside and have some tea. I will have my son bring the dishes, and you can look at them in quiet. It is too noisy here."

She accepted his courtesy, and in a few minutes young Mr. Lim came back to the inner room with the dishes while a servant brought tea.

Old Mrs. Pan did not introduce Lili Yang, for it was not well to embarrass a woman, but young Mr. Lim boldly introduced himself, in English.

"Are you Miss Lili Yang?" he asked. "I am James Lim."

"How did you know my name?" Lili asked, astonished.

"I have met you before, not face to face, but through Mrs. Pan," he said, his small eyes twinkling. "She has told me more about you than she knows."

Lili blushed. "Mrs. Pan is so old-fashioned," she murmured. "You must not believe her."

"I shall only believe what I see for myself," he said gallantly. He looked at her frankly and Lili kept blushing. Old Mrs. Pan had not done her justice, he thought. The young woman had a nice round face, the sort of face he liked. She was shy, and he liked that also. It was something new.

Meanwhile old Mrs. Pan watched all this with amazement. So this was the way it was: The young man began speaking immediately, and the young woman blushed. She wished that she knew what they were saying but perhaps it was better that she did not know.

She turned to old Mr. Lim, who was sitting across the square table sipping tea. At least here she could do her duty. "I hear your son is not married," she said in a tentative way.

"Not yet," Mr. Lim said. "He wants first to finish learning how to be a Western doctor."

"How old is he?" Mrs. Pan inquired.

"He is twenty-eight. It is very old but he did not make up his mind for some years, and the learning is long."

"Miss Lili Yang is twenty-seven," Mrs. Pan said in the same tentative voice.

The young people were still talking in English and not listening to them. Lili was telling James Lim about her work and about old Mrs. Pan. She was not blushing anymore; she had forgotten, it seemed, that he was a young man and she a young woman. Suddenly she stopped and blushed again. A woman was supposed to let a man talk about himself, not about her.

"Tell me about your work," she said. "I wanted to be a doctor, too, but it cost too much."

"I can't tell you here," he said. "There are customers waiting in the shop and it will take a long time. Let me come to see you, may I? I could come on Sunday when the shop is closed. Or we could take a ride on

one of the riverboats. Will you? The weather is so fine."

"I have never been on a riverboat," she said. "It would be delightful."

She forgot her work and remembered that he was a young man and that she was a young woman. She liked his big face and the way his black hair fell back from his forehead and she knew that a day on the river could be a day in heaven.

The customers were getting impatient. They began to call out and he got up. "Next Sunday," he said in a low voice. "Let's start early. I'll be at the wharf at nine o'clock."

"We do not know each other," she said, reluctant and yet eager. Would he think she was too eager?

He laughed. "You see my respectable father, and I know old Mrs. Pan very well. Let them guarantee us."

He hurried away, and old Mrs. Pan said immediately to Lili, "I have chosen these four dishes. Please take them and have them wrapped. Then we will go home."

Lili obeyed, and when she was gone, old Mrs. Pan leaned toward old Mr. Lim.

"I wanted to get her out of the way," she said in a low and important voice. "Now, while she is gone, what do you say? Shall we arrange a match? We do not need a go-between. I stand as her mother, let us say, and you are his father. But just between us, it looks as though it is suitable, does it not?"

Mr. Lim wagged his head. "If you recommend her, Honorable Old Lady, why not?"

Why not, indeed? After all, things were not so different here, after all.

"What day is convenient for you?" she asked.

"Shall we say Sunday?" old Mr. Lim suggested.

"Why not?" she replied. "All days are good, when one performs a good deed, and what is better than to arrange a marriage?"

"Nothing is better," old Mr. Lim agreed. "Of all good deeds under heaven, it is the best."

They fell silent, both pleased with themselves, while they waited.

About the Author

Pearl S. Buck (1892–1973) enjoyed phenomenal success as an author throughout her life. She is best known for *The Good Earth,* a novel about a Chinese family. This best-seller won the Pulitzer Prize for fiction in 1932, and movie rights for the book were sold for $50,000, then a record sum. Buck was born in West Virginia. With her parents, who were missionaries, she moved to China when she was only a few months old. She lived in China until the age of 17 and spoke Chinese before she learned English. Buck received her college education in the United States and returned to China, where she taught for 10 years. Among Buck's other popular novels are *Dragon Seed* and *Imperial Woman.* Buck won the Nobel Prize for literature in 1938. "The Good Deed," which deals with a clash of cultures, is a good example of the themes Buck explored.

THINK ABOUT THE STORY. The following questions help you check your reading comprehension. Put an *x* in the box next to the correct answer.

1. This story is mainly about
   - ☐ a. how and why Mr. Pan arranged for his mother to come to the United States from China.
   - ☐ b. the life of Lili Yang, a twenty-seven-year-old woman.
   - ☐ c. old Mrs. Pan's plan to do "a good deed" by arranging a marriage.

2. Mr. Pan wanted Lili to visit his mother because
   - ☐ a. he thought his mother needed someone to talk to.
   - ☐ b. he thought his mother could help Lili Yang.
   - ☐ c. Lili had often expressed a desire to speak to old Mrs. Pan.

3. Old Mrs. Pan first saw James Lim
   - ☐ a. at his father's shop.
   - ☐ b. in the street from her window.
   - ☐ c. when he was introduced to her by Mr. Pan.

4. At the end of the story, Lili and James Lim agreed
   - ☐ a. to get married.
   - ☐ b. to have dinner on Sunday at Mr. Pan's house.
   - ☐ c. to go for a ride on a boat.

HANDLE NEW VOCABULARY WORDS. The following questions check your vocabulary skills. Put an *x* in the box next to the correct answer. Each vocabulary word appears in the story.

1. "It distressed [old Mrs. Pan] to hear her own language maltreated by their careless tongues." Since the prefix *mal-* means "bad," the word *maltreated* means
   - ☐ a. spoken by evil people.
   - ☐ b. filled with foolish ideas.
   - ☐ c. abused or treated roughly.

2. Old Mrs. Pan believed that children should be taught "to obey their parents and revere their elders." Which best defines the word *revere*?
   - ☐ a. love and respect
   - ☐ b. make demands upon
   - ☐ c. argue with or question

3. Mr. Pan repressed his wish to go back to the office and decided, instead, to stay and listen. The word *repressed* means
   - ☐ a. expressed clearly.
   - ☐ b. held back.
   - ☐ c. acted upon.

4. Usually old Mrs. Pan did not keep the window open "for fear she might be assailed by the foreign winds and made ill." As used here, the word *assailed* means
   - ☐ a. attacked.
   - ☐ b. encouraged.
   - ☐ c. persuaded.

☐ × 5 = ☐

NUMBER
CORRECT

YOUR
SCORE

☐ × 5 = ☐

NUMBER
CORRECT

YOUR
SCORE

EXAMINE STORY ELEMENTS. The following questions check your knowledge of story elements. Put an *x* in the box next to each correct answer.

1. Which of the following best *characterizes* old Mrs. Pan?
   - ☐ a. She adjusted quickly to life in her new country.
   - ☐ b. She felt responsible for doing what she thought was appropriate.
   - ☐ c. She liked Lili Yang and enjoyed talking to her.

2. Of these events, which happened last in the *plot* of the story?
   - ☐ a. Old Mrs. Pan bought two bowls.
   - ☐ b. James Lim told Lili that his father and old Mrs. Pan would "guarantee" them.
   - ☐ c. Lili listened as old Mrs. Pan described her life in China.

3. What was old Mrs. Pan's *motive* for coaxing her grandson to take her to the china shop?
   - ☐ a. She wanted to leave the house to vary her schedule.
   - ☐ b. She wanted to buy some dishes for her son's wife.
   - ☐ c. She wanted to meet the young Mr. Lim.

4. "The Good Deed" is *set* in
   - ☐ a. New York City.
   - ☐ b. San Francisco.
   - ☐ c. a city in China.

☐ × 5 = ☐

NUMBER
CORRECT

YOUR
SCORE

MASTER CRITICAL THINKING. The following questions check your critical thinking skills. Put an *x* in the box next to each correct answer.

1. We may infer from old Mrs. Pan's actions at the beginning of the story that she
   - ☐ a. was thrilled to be living in a safe place.
   - ☐ b. had many friends with whom she could do interesting things.
   - ☐ c. was lonely and sad.

2. The way Lili Yang treated old Mrs. Pan suggests that Lili
   - ☐ a. did not have much patience with older people.
   - ☐ b. was sensitive and kind.
   - ☐ c. was annoyed that Mr. Pan had asked her to visit his mother.

3. Evidence in the story suggests that James Lim and Lili Yang
   - ☐ a. were each disappointed in the other's looks.
   - ☐ b. were attracted to each other.
   - ☐ c. had few things in common and little to discuss.

4. It is fair to say that "The Good Deed"
   - ☐ a. deals with a clash of cultures.
   - ☐ b. is not concerned with cultures or traditions.
   - ☐ c. has an unhappy ending.

☐ × 5 = ☐

NUMBER
CORRECT

YOUR
SCORE

EXPLORE THE WRITER'S CRAFT. The following questions check your knowledge of skills related to the craft of writing. Put an *x* in the box next to each correct answer. You may refer to pages 4 and 5.

1. Old Mrs. Pan's eyes "were haunted with homesickness." This statement provides an example of
   ☐ a. alliteration.
   ☐ b. symbolism.
   ☐ c. onomatopoeia.

2. Lili "would wither away like a dying flower." This sentence contains
   ☐ a. a metaphor.
   ☐ b. a simile.
   ☐ c. an allusion.

3. Which sentence best illustrates irony?
   ☐ a. "It became a pastime for old Mrs. Pan to look out of the window."
   ☐ b. "A good deed is a good deed, whether one is in China or in America."
   ☐ c. "An old woman from the middle of China who could not speak a word of English" sets out to change the American world for Lili.

4. "Our village lies in a wide valley from which the mountains rise as sharply as tiger's teeth." This sentence contains
   ☐ a. an example of personification.
   ☐ b. a flashback.
   ☐ c. a simile and alliteration.

$$\boxed{} \times 5 = \boxed{}$$

NUMBER   YOUR
CORRECT   SCORE

Questions for Writing and Discussion

- What is old Mrs. Pan's state of mind at the beginning of the story? At the conclusion? Support your opinions.
- What does old Mrs. Pan decide to do after she meets Lili Yang? Explain Mrs. Pan's reasoning.
- At one point, old Mrs. Pan waits in silence, "for to say too much is worse than to say too little." What is the meaning of the words in quotation marks? Is this always true? Explain.
- Do you think Lili Yang and James Lim will go their separate ways, or will they eventually get married? Why do you think so?

See additional questions for extended writing on pages 222 and 223.

Use the boxes below to total your scores for the exercises. Then record your scores on pages 224 and 225.

☐ **T**HINK ABOUT THE STORY
+
☐ **H**ANDLE NEW VOCABULARY WORDS
+
☐ **E**XAMINE STORY ELEMENTS
+
☐ **M**ASTER CRITICAL THINKING
+
☐ **E**XPLORE THE WRITER'S CRAFT
▼
☐ **Total Score:** Story 16

BY THE WATERS OF BABYLON

by Stephen Vincent Benét

The north and the west and the south are good hunting ground, but it is forbidden to go east. It is forbidden to go to any of the Dead Places except to search for metal and then he who touches the metal must be a priest or the son of a priest. Afterward, both the man and the metal must be purified. These are the rules and the laws; they are well made. It is forbidden to cross the great river and look upon the place that was the Place of the Gods—this is most strictly forbidden. We do not even say its name though we know its name. It is there that spirits live, and demons—it is there that there are the ashes of the Great Burning. These things are forbidden—they have been forbidden since the beginning of time.

By the Waters of Babylon

My father is a priest; I am the son of a priest. I have been in the Dead Places near us, with my father—at first, I was afraid. When my father went into the house to search for the metal, I stood by the door and my heart felt small and weak. It was a dead man's house, a spirit house. It did not have the smell of man, though there were old bones in a corner. But it is not fitting that a priest's son should show fear. I looked at the bones in the shadow and kept my voice still.

Then my father came out with the metal—a good, strong piece. He looked at me with both eyes but I had not run away. He gave me the metal to hold—I took it and did not die. So he knew that I was truly his son and would be a priest in my time. That was when I was very young—nevertheless, my brothers would not have done it, though they are good hunters. After that, they gave me the good piece of meat and the warm corner by the fire. My father watched over me—he was glad that I should be a priest. But when I boasted or wept without a reason, he punished me more strictly than my brothers. That was right.

After a time, I myself was allowed to go into the dead-houses and search for metal. So I learned the ways of those houses—and if I saw bones, I was no longer afraid. The bones are light and old—sometimes they will fall into dust if you touch them. But that is a great sin.

I was taught the chants and the spells—I was taught how to stop the running of blood from a wound and many secrets. A priest must know many secrets—that was what my father said. If the hunters think we do all things by chants and spells, they may believe so—it does not hurt them. I was taught how to read in the old books and how to make the old writings—that was hard and took a long time. My knowledge made me happy—it was like a fire in my heart. Most of all, I liked to hear of the Old Days and the stories of the gods. I asked myself many questions that I could not answer, but it was good to ask them. At night, I would lie awake and listen to the wind—it seemed to me that it was the voice of the gods as they flew through the air.

We are not ignorant like the Forest People—our women spin wool on the wheel, our priests wear a white robe. We do not eat grubs from the tree, we have not forgotten the old writings, although they are hard to understand. Nevertheless, my knowledge and my lack of knowledge burned in me—I wished to know more. When I was a man at last, I came to my father and said, "It is time for me to go on my journey. Give me your leave."

He looked at me for long time, stroking his beard; then he said at last, "Yes. It is time." That night, in the house of the priesthood, I asked for and received purification. My body hurt but my spirit was a cool stone. It was my father himself who questioned me about my dreams.

He bade me look into the smoke of the fire and see—I saw and told what I saw. It was what I have always seen—a river, and, beyond it, a great Dead Place and in it the gods walking. I have always thought about that. His eyes were stern when I told him— he was no longer my father but a priest. He said, "This is a strong dream."

"It is mine," I said, while the smoke waved and my head felt light. They were singing the Star song in the outer chamber and it was like the buzzing of bees in my head.

He asked me how the gods were dressed and I told him how they were dressed. We know how they were dressed from the book, but I saw them as if they were before me. When I had finished, he threw the sticks three times and studied them as they fell.

"This is a very strong dream," he said. "It may eat you up."

"I am not afraid," I said and looked at him with both eyes. My voice sounded thin in my ears but that was because of the smoke.

He touched me on the breast and the forehead. He gave me the bow and the three arrows.

"Take them," he said. "It is forbidden to travel east. It is forbidden to cross the river. It is forbidden to go to the Place of the Gods. All these things are forbidden."

"All these things are forbidden," I said, but it was my voice that spoke and not my spirit. He looked at me again.

"My son," he said. "Once I had young dreams. If your dreams do not eat you up, you may be a great priest. If they eat you, you are still my son. Now go on your journey."

I went fasting, as is the law. My body hurt but not my heart. When the dawn came, I was out of sight of the village. I prayed and purified myself, waiting for a sign. The sign was an eagle. It flew east.

Sometimes signs are sent by bad spirits. I waited again on the flat rock, fasting, taking no food. I was very still—I could feel the sky above me and the earth beneath. I waited till the sun was beginning to sink. Then three deer passed in the valley, going east— they did not wind me or see me. There was a white fawn with them—a very great sign.

I followed them, at a distance, waiting for what would happen. My heart was troubled about going east, yet I knew that I must go. My head hummed with my fasting—I did not even see the panther spring upon the white fawn. But, before I knew it, the bow was in my hand. I shouted and the panther lifted his head from the fawn. It is not easy to kill a panther with one arrow but the arrow went though his eye and into his brain. He died as he tried to spring—he rolled over, tearing at the ground. Then I knew I was meant to go east—I knew that was my journey. When the night came, I made my fire and roasted meat.

It is eight suns' journey to the east and a man passes by many Dead Places. The Forest People are afraid of them but I am not. Once I made my fire on the edge of a Dead Place at night and, next morning, in the dead-house, I found a good knife, little rusted. That was small to what came afterward but it made my heart feel big. Always when I looked for game, it was in front of my arrow, and twice I passed hunting parties of the Forest People without their knowing. So I knew my magic was strong and my journey clean, in spite of the law.

Toward the setting of the eighth sun, I came to the banks of the great river. It was half a day's journey after I had left the god-road—we do not use the god-roads now, for they are falling apart into great blocks of stone, and the forest is safer going. A long way off, I had seen the water through the trees but the trees were thick. At last, I came out upon an open place at the top of a cliff. There was the great river below, like a giant in the sun. It is very long, very wide. It could eat all the streams we know and still be thirsty. Its name is Ou-dis-sun, the Sacred, the Long. No man of my tribe had seen it, not even my father, the priest. It was magic and I prayed.

Then I raised my eyes and looked south. It was there, the Place of the Gods.

How can I tell what it was like—you do not know. It was there, in the red light, and they were too big to be houses. It was there with the red light upon it, mighty and ruined. I knew that in another moment the gods would see me. I covered my eyes with my hands and crept back into the forest.

Surely, that was enough to do, and live. Surely it was enough to spend the night upon the cliff. The Forest People themselves do not come near. Yet, all through the night, I knew that I should have to cross the river and walk in the places of the gods, although the gods ate me up. My magic did not help me at all and yet there was a fire in my bowels, a fire in my mind. When the sun rose, I thought, "My journey has been clean. Now I will go home from my journey." But, even as I thought so, I knew I could not. If I went to the Place of the Gods, I would surely die, but, if I did not go, I could never be at peace with my spirit again. It is better to lose one's life than one's spirit, if one is a priest and the son of a priest.

Nevertheless, as I made the raft, the tears ran out of my eyes. The Forest People could have killed me without a fight, if they had come upon me then, but they did not come. When the raft was made, I said the sayings for the dead and painted myself for death. My heart was cold as a frog and my knees like water, but

the burning in my mind would not let me have peace. As I pushed the raft from the shore, I began my death song—I had the right. It was a fine song.

"I am John, son of John," I sang. "My people
    are the Hill People. They are the men.
I go into the Dead Places but I am not slain.
I take the metal from the Dead Places but I
    am not blasted.
I travel upon the god-roads and am not
    afraid. E-yah! I have killed the panther, I
    have killed the fawn!
E-yah! I have come to the great river. No
    man has come there before.
It is forbidden to go east, but I have gone,
    forbidden to go on the great river, but I
    am there.
Open your hearts, you spirits, and hear my
    song.
Now I go to the Place of the Gods, I shall
    not return.
My body is painted for death and my limbs
    weak, but my heart is big as I go to the
    Place of the Gods!"

All the same, when I came to the Place of the Gods, I was afraid, afraid. The current of the great river is very strong—it gripped my raft with its hands. That was magic, for the river itself is wide and calm. I could feel evil spirits about me, in the bright morning; I could feel their breath on my neck as I was swept down the stream. Never have I been so much alone—I tried to think of my knowledge, but it was a squirrel's heap of winter nuts. There was no strength in my knowledge any more and I felt small and naked as a new-hatched bird—alone upon the great river, the servant of the gods.

Yet, after a while, my eyes were opened and I saw. I saw both banks of the river—I saw that once there had been god-roads across it, though now they were broken and fallen like broken vines. Very great they were, and wonderful and broken—broken in the time of the Great Burning, when the fire fell out of the sky. And always the current took me nearer to the Place of the Gods, and the huge ruins rose before my eyes.

I do not know the customs of rivers—we are the People of the Hills. I tried to guide my raft with the pole but it spun around. I thought the river meant to take me past the Place of the Gods and out into the Bitter Water of the legends. I grew angry then— my heart felt strong. I said aloud, "I am a priest and the son of a priest!" The gods heard me—they showed me how to paddle the pole on one side of the raft. The current changed itself—I drew near to the Place of the Gods.

When I was very near, my raft struck and turned over. I can swim in our lakes—I swam to the shore. There was a great spike of rusted metal sticking out into the river—I hauled myself up upon it and sat there, panting. I had saved my bow and two arrows and the knife I found in the Dead Place but that was all. My raft went whirling down-stream toward the Bitter Water. I looked after it, and thought if it had trod me under, at least I would be safely dead. Nevertheless, when I had dried my bowstring and restrung it, I walked forward to the Place of the Gods.

It felt like ground underfoot; it did not burn me. It is not true what some of the tales say, that the ground there burns forever, for I have been there. Here and there were the marks and stains of the

Great Burning, on the ruins, that is true. But they were old marks and old stains. It is not true either, what some of our priests say, that it is an island covered with fogs and enchantments. It is not. It is a great Dead Place—greater than any Dead Place we know. Everywhere in it there are god-roads, though most are cracked and broken. Everywhere there are the ruins of the high towers of the gods.

How shall I tell what I saw? I went care-fully, my strung bow in my hand, my skin ready for danger. There should have been the wailings of spirits and the shrieks of demons, but there were not. It was very silent and sunny where I had landed—the wind and the rain and the birds that drop seeds had done their work—the grass grew in the cracks of the broken stone. It is a fair island—no wonder the gods built there. If I had come there, a god, I also would have built.

How shall I tell what I saw? The towers are not all broken—here and there one still stands, like a great tree in a forest, and the birds nest high. But the towers themselves look blind, for the gods are gone. I saw a fish-hawk, catching fish in the river. I saw a little dance of white butterflies over a heap of broken stones and columns. I went there and looked about me—there was a carved stone with cut letters, broken in half. I can read letters but I could not understand these. They said UBTREAS. There was also the shattered image of a man or a god. It had been made of white stone and he wore his hair tied back like a woman's. His name was ASHING, as I read on the cracked half of the stone. I thought it wise to pray to ASHING, though I do not know that god.

How shall I tell what I saw? There was no smell of man left, on stone or metal. Nor were there many trees in that wilderness of stone. There are many pigeons, nesting and dropping in the towers—the gods must have loved them, or, perhaps, they used them for sacrifices. There are wild cats that roam the god-roads, green-eyed, unafraid of man. At night they wail like demons but they are not demons. The wild dogs are more dangerous, for they hunt in a pack, but them I did not meet till later. Everywhere there are the carved stones, carved with magical numbers or words.

I went north—I did not try to hide myself. When a god or a demon saw me, then I would die, but meanwhile I was no longer afraid. My hunger for knowledge burned in me—there was so much that I could not understand. After a while, I knew that my belly was hungry. I could have hunted for my meat, but I did not hunt. It is known that the gods did not hunt as we do—they got their food from enchanted boxes and jars. Sometimes these are still found in the Dead Places—once, when I was a child and foolish, I opened such a jar and tasted it and found the food sweet. But my father found out and punished me for it strictly, for, often, that food is death. Now, though, I had long gone past what was forbidden, and I entered the likeliest towers, looking for the food of the gods.

I found it at last in the ruins of a great temple in the mid-city. A mighty temple it must have been, for the roof was painted like the sky at night with its stars—that much I could see, though the colors were faint and dim. It went down into the great caves and tunnels—perhaps they kept their slaves there. But when I started to climb down, I heard the squeaking of rats, so I did not go—rats are unclean, and there must have been many tribes of them, from the squeaking. But near there, I found food, in the heart of a ruin, behind a door that still opened. I ate only the fruits from the jars—they had a very sweet taste. There was drink, too, in bottles of glass—the drink of the gods was strong and made my head swim. After I had eaten and drunk, I slept on the top of a stone, my bow at my side.

When I woke, the sun was low. Looking down from where I lay, I saw a dog sitting on his haunches. His tongue was hanging out of his mouth; he looked as if he were laughing. He was a big dog, with a gray-brown coat, as big as a wolf. I sprang up and shouted at him but he did not move—he just sat there as if he were laughing. I did not like that. When I reached for a stone to throw, he moved swiftly out of the way of the stone. He was not afraid of me; he looked at me as if I were meat. No doubt I could have killed him with an arrow, but I did not know if there were others. Moreover, night was falling.

I looked about me—not far away was a great, broken god-road, leading north. The towers were high enough, but not so high, and while many of the dead-houses were wrecked, there were some that stood. I went toward this god-road, keeping to the heights of the ruins, while the dog followed. When I had reached the god-road, I saw that there were others behind him. If I had slept later, they would have come upon me asleep and torn out my throat. As it was, they were sure enough of me; they did not hurry. When I went into the dead-house, they kept watch at the entrance—doubtless they thought they would have a fine hunt. But a dog cannot open a door and I knew, from the books, that the gods did not like to live on the ground but on high.

I had just found a door I could open when the dogs decided to rush. Ha! They were surprised when I shut the door in their faces—it was a good door, of strong metal. I could hear their foolish baying beyond it but I did not stop to answer them. I was in darkness—I found stairs and climbed. There were many stairs, turning around till my head was dizzy. At the top was another door—I found the knob and opened it. I was in a long small chamber—on one side of it was a bronze door that could not be opened, for it had no handle. Perhaps there was a magic word to open it but I did not have the word. I turned to the door in the opposite side of the wall. The lock of it was broken and I opened it and went in.

Within, there was a place of great riches. The god who lived there must have been a powerful god. The first room was a small anteroom—I waited there for some time, telling the spirits of the place that I came in peace and not as a robber. When it seemed to me that they had had time to hear me, I went on. Ah, what riches! Few, even, of the windows had been broken—it was all as it had been. The great windows that looked over the city had not been broken at all though they were dusty and streaked with many years. There were coverings on the floors, the colors not greatly faded, and the chairs were soft and deep. There were pictures upon the walls, very strange, very wonderful—I remember one of a bunch of flowers in a jar—if you came close to it, you could see nothing but bits of color, but if you stood away from it, the flowers might have been picked yesterday. It made my heart feel strange to look at this picture—and to look at the figure of a bird, in some hard clay, on a table and see it so like our birds.

Everywhere there were books and writings, many in tongues that I could not read. The god who lived there must have been a wise god and full of knowledge. I felt I had right there, as I sought knowledge also.

Nevertheless, it was strange. There was a washing place but no water—perhaps the gods washed in air. There was a cooking place but no wood, and though there was a machine to cook food, there was no place to put fire in it. Nor were there candles or lamps—there were things that looked like lamps but they had neither oil nor wick. All these things were magic, but I touched them and lived—the magic had gone out of them. Let me tell one thing to show. In the washing place, a thing said "Hot" but it was not hot to the touch—another thing said "Cold" but it was not cold. This must have been a strong magic but the magic was gone. I do not understand—they had ways—I wish that I knew.

It was close and dry and dusty in their house of the gods. I have said the magic was gone but that is not true—it had gone from the magic things but it had not gone from the place. I felt the spirits about me, weighing upon me. Nor had I ever slept in a Dead Place before—and yet, tonight, I must sleep there. When I thought of it, my tongue felt dry in my throat, in spite of my wish for knowledge. Almost I could have gone down again and faced the dogs, but I did not.

I had not gone through all the rooms when darkness fell. When it fell, I went back to the big room looking over the city and made fire. There was a place to make fire and a box with wood in it, though I do not think they cooked there. I wrapped myself in a floor covering and slept in front of the fire—I was very tired.

By the Waters of Babylon

Now I tell what is very strong magic. I woke in the midst of the night. When I woke, the fire had gone out and I was cold. It seemed to me that all around me there were whisperings and voices. I closed my eyes to shut them out. Some will say that I slept again, but I do not think that I slept. I could feel the spirits drawing my spirit out of my body as a fish is drawn on a line.

Why should I lie about it? I am a priest and the son of a priest. If there are spirits, as they say, in the small Dead Places near us, what spirits must there not be in that great Place of the Gods? And would not they wish to speak? After such long years? I know that I felt myself drawn as a fish is drawn on a line. I had stepped out of my body—I could see my body asleep in front of the cold fire, but it was not I. I was drawn to look out upon the city of the gods.

It should have been dark, for it was night, but it was not dark. Everywhere there were lights—lines of light—circles and blurs of light—ten thousand torches would not have been the same. The sky itself was alight—you could barely see the stars for the glow in the sky. I thought to myself, "This is strong magic," and trembled. There was a roaring in my ears like the rushing of rivers. Then my eyes grew used to the light and my ears to the sound. I knew that I was seeing the city as it had been when the gods were alive.

That was a sight indeed—yes, that was a sight: I could not have seen it in the body— my body would have died. Everywhere went the gods, on foot and in chariots—there were gods beyond number and counting and their chariots blocked the streets. They had turned night to day for their pleasure— they did not sleep with the sun. The noise of their coming and going was the noise of many waters. It was magic what they could do—it was magic what they did.

I looked out of another window—the great vines of their bridges were mended and the god-roads went east and west. Restless, restless, were the gods and always in motion! They burrowed tunnels under rivers—they flew in the air. With unbelievable tools they did giant works—no part of the earth was safe from them, for, if they wished for a thing, they summoned it from the other side of the world. And always, as they labored and rested, as they feasted and made love, there was a drum in their ears— the pulse of the giant city, beating and beating like a man's heart.

Were they happy? What is happiness to the gods? They were great, they were mighty, they were wonderful and terrible. As I looked upon them and their magic, I felt like a child—but a little more, it seemed to me, and they would pull down the moon from the sky. I saw them with wisdom beyond wisdom and knowledge beyond knowledge. And yet not all they did was well done—even I could see that—and yet their wisdom could not but grow until all was peace.

Then I saw their fate come upon them and that was terrible past speech. It came upon them as they walked the streets of their city. I have been in the fights with the Forest People—I have seen men die. But this was not like that. When gods war with gods, they use weapons we do not know. It was fire falling out of the sky and a mist that poisoned. It was the time of the Great Burning and Destruction. They ran about like ants in the streets of their city—poor gods, poor gods! Then the towers began to fall. A few escaped—yes, a few. The legends tell it. But, even after the city had become a Dead Place, for many years the poison was still in the ground. I saw it happen, I saw the last of them die. It was darkness over the broken city and I wept.

All this, I saw. I saw it as I have told it, though not in the body. When I woke in the morning, I was hungry, but I did not think first of my hunger for my heart was perplexed and confused. I knew the reason for the Dead Places but I did not see why it had happened. It seemed to me it should not have happened, with all the magic they had. I went through the house looking for an answer. There was so much in the house I could not understand—and yet I am a priest and the son of a priest. It was like being on one side of the great river, at night, with no light to show the way.

Then I saw the dead god. He was sitting in his chair, by the window, in a room I had not entered before and, for the first moment, I thought that he was alive. Then I saw the skin on the back of his hand—it was like dry leather. The room was shut, hot and dry—no doubt that had kept him as he was. At first I was afraid to approach him—then the fear left me. He was sitting looking out over the city—he was dressed in the clothes of the gods. His age was neither young nor old—I could not tell his age. But there was wisdom in his face and great sadness. You could see that he would not have run away. He had sat at his window, watching his city die—then he himself had died. But it is better to lose one's life than one's spirit— and you could see from the face that his spirit had not been lost. I knew that, if I touched him, he would fall into dust—and yet, there was something unconquered in the face.

That is all of my story, for then I knew he was a man—I knew then that they had all been men, neither gods nor demons. It is a great knowledge, hard to tell and believe. They were men—they went a dark road, but they were men. I had no fear after that—I had no fear going home, though twice I fought off the dogs and once I was hunted for two days by the Forest People. When I saw my father again, I prayed and was purified. He touched my lips and my breast, he said, "You went away a boy. You come back a man and a priest." I said, "Father, they were men! I have been in the Place of the Gods and seen it! Now slay me, if it is the law—but still I know they were men."

He looked at me out of both eyes. He said, "The law is not always the same shape—you have done what you have done. I could not have done it in my time, but you have come after me. Tell!"

I told and he listened. After that, I wished to tell all the people but he showed me otherwise. He said, "Truth is a hard deer to hunt. If you eat too much truth at once, you may die of the truth. It was not idly that our fathers forbade the Dead Places." He was right—it is better the truth should come little by little. I have learned that, being a priest. Perhaps, in the old days, they ate knowledge too fast.

Nevertheless, we make a beginning. It is not for the metal alone we go to the Dead Places now—there are the books and the writings. They are hard to learn. And the magic tools are broken—but we can look at them and wonder. At least, we make a beginning. And when I am chief priest we shall go beyond the great river. We shall go to the Place of the Gods—the place newyork—not one man but a company.

By the Waters of Babylon

We shall look for the images of the gods and find the god ASHING and the others—the gods Lincoln and Biltmore[1] and Moses.[2] But they were men who built the city, not gods or demons. They were men. I remember the dead man's face. They were men who were here before us. We must build again.

---

1. **Biltmore:** a hotel in New York City

2. **Moses:** Robert Moses (1888–1981), an important New York City and New York state official whose name appears on many buildings

About the Author

Stephen Vincent Benét (1898–1943) was born in Bethlehem, Pennsylvania, the son and grandson of high-ranking army officers. A gifted writer, Benét had already published a volume of poetry before he entered Yale University. Benét wrote five novels and numerous short stories, but he considered himself to be primarily a poet. His interest in American history led him to write *John Brown's Body,* a long poem with a Civil War background, for which he won a Pulitzer Prize for literature. Benét's most popular story is "The Devil and Daniel Webster," which was made into a motion picture, an opera, and a play. "By the Waters of Babylon" was originally begun as a poem and was later transformed by Benét into a short story.

THINK ABOUT THE STORY. The following questions help you check your reading comprehension. Put an *x* in the box next to the correct answer.

1. This story is mainly about
   - ☐ a. a young man's perilous—and remarkable—journey in search of knowledge.
   - ☐ b. the way people lived many years ago.
   - ☐ c. how a great city and its inhabitants were destroyed.

2. The narrator, John, crossed the great river by
   - ☐ a. swimming with the current.
   - ☐ b. making his way over the scraps of a shattered bridge.
   - ☐ c. using a raft he had built.

3. John escaped from the dogs by
   - ☐ a. hiding in a cave.
   - ☐ b. entering a "dead-house" and slamming the door shut.
   - ☐ c. scaring the pack away with his knife and his bow and arrows.

4. At the end of the story, John stated that it was necessary to
   - ☐ a. disobey his father and tell the people everything he had learned.
   - ☐ b. stay away from the Dead Places.
   - ☐ c. build again.

HANDLE NEW VOCABULARY WORDS. The following questions check your vocabulary skills. Put an *x* in the box next to the correct answer. Each vocabulary word appears in the story.

1. Before setting out, John went to "the house of the priesthood" and "asked for and received purification." Which of the following best defines *purification*?
   - ☐ a. obtaining a purpose
   - ☐ b. receiving permission
   - ☐ c. making clean or free from impurity

2. If his raft had trod him under the water, he would have died. As used here, the word *trod* means
   - ☐ a. thrown up in the air.
   - ☐ b. pushed down sharply.
   - ☐ c. slipped away from.

3. After John closed the door, he could hear the "foolish baying" of the pack. What is the meaning of the word *baying*?
   - ☐ a. a long, deep barking
   - ☐ b. a heavy banging
   - ☐ c. the sound of animals sniffing

4. John came to an anteroom; he waited there before he went on. What is an *anteroom*?
   - ☐ a. a staircase
   - ☐ b. a small room that leads to a larger one
   - ☐ c. a closet

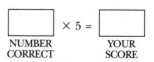

⬜ × 5 = ⬜
NUMBER   YOUR
CORRECT   SCORE

⬜ × 5 = ⬜
NUMBER   YOUR
CORRECT   SCORE

EXAMINE STORY ELEMENTS. The following questions check your knowledge of story elements. Put an *x* in the box next to each correct answer.

1. The quality that best *characterizes* John is
   - ☐ a. his great physical strength.
   - ☐ b. the caution with which he proceeded.
   - ☐ c. his hunger for knowledge.

2. John's *inner conflict* concerning whether to travel east, which was forbidden, was resolved when
   - ☐ a. some priests gave him permission to go.
   - ☐ b. he received powerful signs to proceed.
   - ☐ c. the Forest People chased him in that direction.

3. The *climax* of the story occurred when
   - ☐ a. John was allowed to go into the "dead-houses" to search for metal.
   - ☐ b. John realized that the figure in a chair was a man—and that it was *people,* not gods, who had destroyed the great civilization.
   - ☐ c. John entered "the ruins of a great temple" and ate and drank from jars and bottles there.

4. The *theme* of the story deals with
   - ☐ a. superstition and taboos.
   - ☐ b. knowledge and destruction and the survival of human beings.
   - ☐ c. the need to consult with and to respect one's elders and leaders.

$$\boxed{} \times 5 = \boxed{}$$

NUMBER   YOUR
CORRECT   SCORE

MASTER CRITICAL THINKING. The following questions check your critical thinking skills. Put an *x* in the box next to each correct answer.

1. We may infer that John is
   - ☐ a. a character from another planet.
   - ☐ b. a member of a primitive hunting society, the Hill People.
   - ☐ c. a hot-tempered young man who is interested in attaining glory.

2. Evidence in the story indicates that the Ou-dis-sun is the Hudson River, that the broken statue marked ASHING is of Washington, and that the letters UBTREAS were part of a sign that said
   - ☐ a. SUBWAY STATION.
   - ☐ b. ANTIQUE TREASURES.
   - ☐ c. SUBTREASURY BUILDING.

3. John notes, "Everywhere there are the ruins of the high towers of the gods." We may conclude that John is referring to
   - ☐ a. skyscrapers and apartment houses.
   - ☐ b. cliffs where the mighty and powerful lived.
   - ☐ c. the mountain homes of the wealthy.

4. The author seems to be warning that
   - ☐ a. one should never venture alone into dangerous territory.
   - ☐ b. occasionally foolish rules and laws must be broken.
   - ☐ c. technology may advance beyond human control with disastrous results.

$$\boxed{} \times 5 = \boxed{}$$

NUMBER   YOUR
CORRECT   SCORE

EXPLORE THE WRITER'S CRAFT. The following questions check your knowledge of skills related to the craft of writing. Put an *x* in the box next to each correct answer. You may refer to pages 4 and 5.

1. "Everywhere there were lights—lines of light—circles and blurs of light—ten thousand torches would not have been the same." Since this passage appeals strongly to the sense of sight, it is an example of
   ☐ a. irony.
   ☐ b. connotation.
   ☐ c. imagery.

2. "The great river . . . gripped my raft with its hands." This sentence illustrates
   ☐ a. personification.
   ☐ b. onomatopoeia.
   ☐ c. a flashback.

3. The statements "My heart was cold as a frog" and "One [tower] still stands, like a great tree in a forest" are
   ☐ a. metaphors.
   ☐ b. similes.
   ☐ c. symbols.

4. The statements "My spirit was a cool stone" and "My knowledge . . . was a squirrel's heap of winter nuts" are
   ☐ a. similes.
   ☐ b. metaphors.
   ☐ c. examples of alliteration.

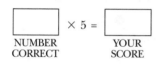

NUMBER CORRECT × 5 = YOUR SCORE

Questions for Writing and Discussion

- Offer several reasons why John set out for the Place of the Gods.
- John spoke of "the time of the Great Burning, when the fire fell out of the sky." He said, "It seemed to me it should not have happened, with all the magic they had," and "Perhaps, in the old days, they ate knowledge too fast." What did John mean?
- Reread the last paragraph. Tell why it offers an optimistic view.
- In the ancient world, Babylon, a great city by a great river, was eventually destroyed in a war. Why do you think the author called the story "By the Waters of Babylon"?

See additional questions for extended writing on pages 222 and 223.

Use the boxes below to total your scores for the exercises. Then record your scores on pages 224 and 225.

☐ **T**HINK ABOUT THE STORY
+
☐ **H**ANDLE NEW VOCABULARY WORDS
+
☐ **E**XAMINE STORY ELEMENTS
+
☐ **M**ASTER CRITICAL THINKING
+
☐ **E**XPLORE THE WRITER'S CRAFT
▼
☐ **Total Score:** Story 17

Searching for Answers

Questions for Discussion and Extended Writing

The following questions provide you with opportunities to express your thoughts and feelings about the selections in this unit. Your teacher may assign selected questions. When you write your responses, remember to state your point of view clearly and to support your position by presenting specific details—examples, illustrations, and references drawn from the story and, in some cases, from your life. Organize your writing carefully and check your work for correct spelling, capitalization, punctuation, and grammar.

1. The theme of this unit is "Searching for Answers." Show how each story in the unit is related to the theme.

2. Consider the two quotations below:

   "The beginning of knowledge is the discovery of something we do not understand."
   —Frank Herbert

   "Be not afraid of growing slowly; be afraid only of standing still."
   —a Chinese proverb

   Write an essay in which you apply *one* of the quotations to old Mrs. Pan in "The Good Deed" and to John in "By the Waters of Babylon."

3. In many ways, "The Force of Luck" is very different from the other stories in the unit. Support this statement in a clearly organized essay that has an introduction, a body, and a conclusion.

4. Draw upon material found in "By the Waters of Babylon" to write a descriptive essay. Give your essay a title that clearly identifies the focus of your writing.

5. Compare and contrast old Mrs. Pan and Lili Yang. In what ways are they similar? How are they different?

6. In which two selections in the unit does the setting of the story play the most significant role? Give titles and authors and present reasons for your answer.

7. Select two stories in the unit and demonstrate how one or more characters in each story overcame an obstacle. Give titles and authors.

8. Each selection teaches one or more lessons. Choose two of the stories and indicate what lessons these stories teach.

9. More than 80 years ago, the renowned English author H. G. Wells wrote, "Human history becomes more and more a race between education and catastrophe." Use specific references to show that one theme of "By the Waters of Babylon" is that civilization is "a race between education and catastrophe."

10. Some philosophers have suggested that there will always be more questions than answers. In fact, the search for answers may very well be an ongoing pursuit. What are some of the issues *you* will confront in the future? What major decisions lie ahead? What are some of the challenges you know you will be facing? Write an essay entitled "Searching for Answers." Your essay should have an introduction, a body, and a conclusion.

Progress Chart

1. Write in your score for each exercise.
2. Write in your Total Score.

Story	T	H	E	M	E	Total Score
1						
2						
3						
4						
5						
6						
7						
8						
9						
10						
11						
12						
13						
14						
15						
16						
17						

Progress Graph

1. Write your Total Score in the box under the number for each story.
2. Put an *x* along the line above each box to show your Total Score for that story.
3. Make a graph of your progress by drawing a line to connect the *x*'s.

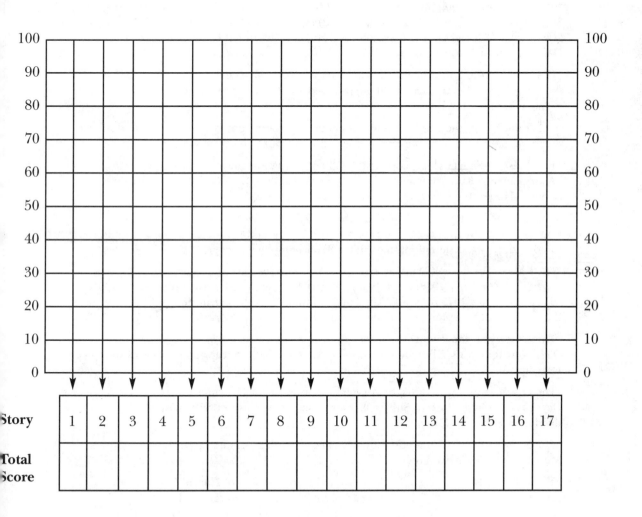

Acknowledgments

Acknowledgment is gratefully made to the following publishers, authors, and agents for permission to reprint these works. Every effort has been made to determine copyright owners. In case of any omissions, the Publisher will be pleased to make suitable acknowledgments in future editions. Adaptations and abridgments are by Burton Goodman. All rights reserved.

"The Smuggler," reproduced with permission of Curtis Brown Group, Ltd., London on behalf of the Estate of Victor Canning. Copyright Victor Canning.

"Initiation" from *Johnny Panic and the Bible of Dreams: Short Stories, Prose and Diary Excerpts* by Sylvia Plath. Copyright © 1952, 1953, 1954, 1955, 1956, 1957, 1960, 1961, 1962, 1963 by Sylvia Plath. Copyright © 1977, 1979 by Ted Hughes. Reprinted by permission of HarperCollins Publishers, Inc.

"The Street of the Cañon" from *Mexican Village* by Josefina Niggli. Copyright © 1945 by the University of North Carolina Press, renewed 1972 by Josefina Niggli. Used by permission of the publisher.

"Geraldine Moore the Poet" by Toni Cade Bambara. Copyright © 1972 by Toni Cade Bambara. Reprinted by permission of the Estate of Toni Cade Bambara.

"Tom Edison's Shaggy Dog," copyright 1953 by Kurt Vonnegut Jr., from *Welcome to the Monkey House* by Kurt Vonnegut Jr. Used by permisssion of Dell Publishing, a division of Random House, Inc.

"The Inspiration of Mr. Budd" from *In the Teeth of the Evidence* by Dorothy L. Sayers. Copyright 1940 by Dorothy Leigh Sayers Fleming, renewed © 1968 by Anthony Fleming. Reprinted by permission of HarperCollins Publishers, Inc.

"The Case of the Perfect Maid" from *Three Blind Mice and Other Stories* by Agatha Christie; copyright 1925, 1926, 1928, 1940, 1941, 1942, 1948, by Agatha Christie; renewed © 1954, 1956, 1968, 1969, 1975 by Agatha Christie Mallowan. Used by permission of G. P. Putnam's Sons, a division of Penguin Putnam Inc.

"The Widow and the Parrot" from *The Complete Shorter Fiction of Virginia Woolf* by Susan Dick, copyright © 1985 by Quentin Bell and Angelica Garnett, reprinted by permission of Harcourt, Inc.

"The Possibility of Evil" copyright © 1965 by Stanley Edgar Hyman, from *Just an Ordinary Day: The Uncollected Stories* by Shirley Jackson. Used by permission of Bantam Books, a division of Random House, Inc.

"The Force of Luck" by Rudolfo A. Anaya, adapted and reprinted by permission of the Museum of New Mexico Press.

"The Good Deed" by Pearl S. Buck. Reprinted by permission of Harold Ober Associates, Incorporated. Copyright © 1953 by Pearl S. Buck. Copyright © renewed 1981.

"By the Waters of Babylon" by Stephen Vincent Benét from *The Selected Works of Stephen Vincent Benét*. Copyright © 1937 by Stephen Vincent Benét. Copyright © renewed 1965 by Thomas C. Benét, Stephanie B. Mahin, and Rachel Benét Lewis. Reprinted by permission of Brandt & Hochman Literary Agents, Inc.